Literary Analysis for
English Literature

Skills for Success

Carolyn P. Henly
Angela Stancar Johnson

Carrie: With many thanks to my husband for his unending patience with my many projects.

Angela: I would like to dedicate this book to Adrian, Ella, Freya and Oskar – my in-house support team.

Acknowledgements

Every effort has been made to trace all copyright holders, but if any have been inadvertently overlooked, the Publishers will be pleased to make the necessary arrangements at the first opportunity.

Although every effort has been made to ensure that website addresses are correct at time of going to press, Hodder Education cannot be held responsible for the content of any website mentioned in this book. It is sometimes possible to find a relocated web page by typing in the address of the home page for a website in the URL window of your browser.

Hachette UK's policy is to use papers that are natural, renewable and recyclable products and made from wood grown in well-managed forests and other controlled sources. The logging and manufacturing processes are expected to conform to the environmental regulations of the country of origin.

Orders: please contact Bookpoint Ltd, 130 Park Drive, Milton Park, Abingdon, Oxon OX14 4SE. Telephone: +44 (0)1235 827827. Fax: +44 (0)1235 400401. Email education@bookpoint.co.uk Lines are open from 9 a.m. to 5 p.m., Monday to Saturday, with a 24-hour message answering service. You can also order through our website: www.hoddereducation.com

ISBN: 9781510467149

© Carolyn P. Henly and Angela Stancar Johnson 2019

First published in 2019 by
Hodder Education,
An Hachette UK Company
Carmelite House
50 Victoria Embankment
London EC4Y 0DZ

www.hoddereducation.co.uk

Impression number 10 9 8 7 6 5 4 3 2 1

Year   2023 2022 2021 2020 2019

Cover photo © sveta - stock.adobe.com

Typeset in Integra Software Services Pvt. Ltd., Pondicherry, India

Printed in Spain

A catalogue record for this title is available from the British Library.

Contents

How to use this book

This book is focused on helping you build and develop your skills in literary analysis. Each of the main forms will be covered, and you will have the opportunity to examine works or extracts of works that focus on certain features of the form. Many of the extracts that are included have appeared on past exam papers, so the book also serves as a sort of anthology of the types of texts that you may encounter in your final examination.

The main focus of this book is on developing your skills in unseen literary analysis, which is the basis of Paper 1; however, many of the exercises are also applicable to the works that you will be studying within the classroom. Therefore, the skills targeted here can be applied in a variety of contexts. The book is designed to be used independently by students or in a more guided teacher-led approach.

Features of this book

There are some features you should look for throughout the book to help with your understanding of literary analysis.

KEY TERMS

These are highlighted to give you access to vocabulary you need for each topic. These terms are also included in the glossary.

TECHNIQUES, FEATURES AND TIPS

These boxes provide handy tips and guidance on how to identify features of a text and apply them to your own writing.

ACTIVITY

Activities are designed to test your understanding of each topic and provide practice to develop your skills for the exam. After the activity go to the end of this book for the explanatory notes.

■ Using QR codes

Look out for the QR codes throughout the book. They are placed in the margin alongside weblinks for quick scanning. They look like the one on the left.

To use the QR codes to access the web links you will need a QR code reader for your smartphone/tablet. There are many free readers available, depending on the device that you use. We have supplied some suggestions below, but this is not an exhaustive list and you should only download software compatible with your device and operating system. We do not endorse any of the third-party products listed below and downloading them is done at your own risk.

- For iPhone/iPad, Qrafter – **https://itunes.apple.com/us/app/qrafter-qr-code/id416098700?mt=8**

- For Android, QR Droid – **https://play.google.com/store/apps/details?id=la.droid.qr&hl=en**

- For Blackberry, QR Code Scanner – **https://appworld.blackberry.com/webstore/content/19908464/?lang=en**
- For Windows/Symbian, Upcode – **https://www.microsoft.com/en-gb/p/upcode/9nblggh081ps?rtc=1&activetab=pivot:overviewtab**

Notes on the activities

Literary analysis is not a science. Interpretation is largely about developing a personal response to the text rather than arriving at a definitive answer, and therefore each interpretation may be slightly different. The notes on the activities at the back of the book are not intended to be comprehensive. You may have discovered some things that are not mentioned, and missed some things that are. That's nothing to worry about, so long as you made an effort to notice what was in the passage and to consider what it might mean. If you feel that you missed more than you should have, don't worry! As with developing any other skill, your skill as an astute reader of literature will improve with practice.

About the authors

Carolyn P. Henly (A.B. M.Ed, National Board Certification 2001, 2011) has recently retired after 33 years of teaching, 20 of those in the International Baccalaureate Programme. She has taught English HL, Theory of Knowledge, and IB Philosophy. She has served in a number of roles in the IB, including coordinator, examiner (both TOK and English), workshop leader, President of the Mid-Atlantic subregional organization, and member of two TOK curriculum review committees. She co-authored the third edition of the *Theory of Knowledge* textbook (Hodder Education), and series edited both *Language and Literature for the IB Diploma* and *English Literature for the IB Diploma* (Hodder Education) as well as contributing as author in the latter.

Angela Stancar Johnson (B.A., M.A., M.Ed.) is Head of English at Southbank International School in London, where she has taught all grades and levels of MYP English Language & Literature, DP English A, and Theory of Knowledge since 2009. Prior to that, she taught English and journalism in US public schools. Angela has served as an examiner for DP English and currently examines the MYP Interdisciplinary eAssessment and Personal Project. She co-authored the *Personal Project for the IB MYP 4 & 5: Skills for Success* and *Community Project for the IB MYP 3 & 4: Skills for Success* textbooks and contributed to *English Literature for the IB Diploma*, all published by Hodder Education.

Carolyn and Angela also authored *Textual Analysis for English Language & Literature for the IB Diploma: Skills for Success* (Hodder Education, 2019).

1 What is literary analysis?

Literary analysis

Analyse is one of the 18 International Baccalaureate (IB) Diploma Programme (DP) command terms, and it means 'to break down in order to bring out the essential elements or structure; to identify parts and relationships, and to interpret information to reach conclusions' (International Baccalaureate, 2019).

Literary analysis is the systematic examination of a literary work or aspect(s) of a work – a consideration of how the individual parts contribute to the whole. Literary analysis is not just about identifying what literary devices a writer uses; it is about exploring the effects of those devices. For example, does the choice of a particular word evoke a certain mood or reflect the writer's or speaker's attitude? Does the use of a particular image relate to an overarching theme? Literary analysis is about moving beyond the surface level of a work and exploring different layers of meaning that are created through language.

Literary analysis is a skill that can be learned and developed. Students who are intimidated by the process often view a literary work as a puzzle that needs to be solved. Literary analysis is not about guessing what an author might have meant. Instead, it is about developing an appreciation for the thought and feeling expressed in the piece, and this can be achieved through an understanding and appreciation of the language of the work itself.

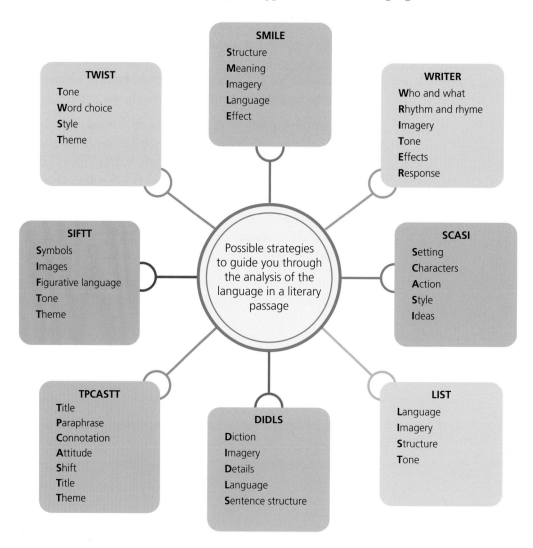

SMILE
Structure
Meaning
Imagery
Language
Effect

TWIST
Tone
Word choice
Style
Theme

WRITER
Who and what
Rhythm and rhyme
Imagery
Tone
Effects
Response

SIFTT
Symbols
Images
Figurative language
Tone
Theme

Possible strategies to guide you through the analysis of the language in a literary passage

SCASI
Setting
Characters
Action
Style
Ideas

TPCASTT
Title
Paraphrase
Connotation
Attitude
Shift
Title
Theme

DIDLS
Diction
Imagery
Details
Language
Sentence structure

LIST
Language
Imagery
Structure
Tone

■ Strategies for literary analysis

There are a number of different strategies that you can employ to guide you through the analysis of the language of a literary passage. The key thing to remember is that there is no right or wrong way to approach a passage, and you will need to find a strategy that works best for you. The diagram on the previous page shows some of the strategies that you could use; this list is not exhaustive.

Critical theory

Literary scholars often focus their analysis of a work through a particular theory or lens. There are many theories, but the following are the most notable within the field of literary criticism – and these are the ones that you will most commonly encounter in literary journals. A basic definition is provided for each theory here.

■ Moral criticism

Moral criticism centres around the moral lessons that a work conveys; a moral critic is concerned with the didactic nature of literature (that is, whether it teaches, offers meaning or improves the reader in any way).

■ Formalism

A formalist critic would consider style over substance. Formalism is more concerned with the aesthetic qualities of literature and the specific techniques an author has used and their effects on the reader.

■ Psychoanalytic criticism

Rooted in the theories of Sigmund Freud, psychoanalytic criticism considers a work as the product of an author's unconscious desires.

■ Marxist criticism

Marxist criticism, based on the theories of Karl Marx, examines literature through a social and economic context. Marxist critics consider the work as a product of the time and place in which the narrative was set and/or composed.

■ Post-colonial criticism

Post-colonial criticism considers the impact of colonisation and the role race plays in a work of literature.

■ Feminist criticism

Feminist criticism is concerned with the way that men and women are represented in literature by both male and female writers. It considers gender roles and societal conventions and how characters conform to, or deviate from, the cultural norm.

When approaching unseen texts, you would probably not focus your analysis through one of these critical lenses as many of them require a certain level of contextual knowledge, which you most likely will not have for an unseen text. However, as you work through the various works on the syllabus you may wish to consider them in light of one or more of these theories as a way of deepening your engagement.

Engaging with literature

In order to write convincingly about literature, you need to fully engage with the works. This means actively reading, making notes, asking questions and developing a personal response to the work.

One of the best ways to engage with literature is to annotate as you read. Effective annotation is like having a dialogue with the work. You are noting down first impressions, posing questions and suggesting possible interpretations (which may or may not change as you read further – and as you read again).

KEY TERMS

Semantic fields – a collection of words or phrases that are related to each other in meaning and connotation, for example: safety, welcome, support, shelter, structure and warmth would all be part of the same semantic field in relation to the word 'home'.

Lexical sets – a group of words that are related to each other in meaning, for example: leaf, green, trunk, bark and branch would all be part of the same lexical set in relation to the word 'tree'.

Diction – the words chosen in a text.

Figurative language – language that uses figures of speech, such as metaphors or symbols, to embellish meaning beyond the literal.

ANNOTATION TIPS

✔ Do not try to underline or highlight everything. Focus on key words and phrases, especially those that seem to form a pattern. Look for **semantic fields** and **lexical sets**.

✔ Focus on **diction**. Colour code your markings according to word type. For example, you could highlight verbs in blue, words that reflect tone in pink, words associated with a particular theme in green and examples of **figurative language** in orange.

✔ Underline or highlight unfamiliar words or phrases. You will not have the benefit of a dictionary in the exam, but you can try to rely on context to help you work out meaning. Defining and learning the words in the works you study in class will help you be better prepared for dealing with an unseen extract; the bigger and more varied your vocabulary, the better a reader you will be.

✔ Try to sum up a section of the extract or work in one or two sentences in the margin. Summarizing in your own words can help you reach a deeper understanding of the work.

✔ Ask questions! If something confuses you, write it down in the margin. Often the act of posing a question can help you work towards an understanding of the work; this is called 'interrogating' the text. If you can't work out the answer for yourself, having noted it in the margin means that it will be there for you to raise in a discussion with others.

✔ Ultimately, there is no right or wrong way to annotate. Annotation is about engagement, and everyone engages differently. This engagement will guide you towards a personal connection with, and interpretation of, a work of literature.

Look at the following poem that a student has annotated. This is an example of an unseen poem. If the student were studying this poem in class as part of the course, he or she could add to the annotations as class discussions unfolded; this might be done using a different coloured pen. Consider the student's thinking process or the strategies that have been used. What seems to be the focus? As you read the poem yourself, you may pick up on things that the student has seemingly missed. The point of annotation is not to cover everything but to make initial observations, which could lead to further insights.

Nighttime Fires

Campfire? Theme: nostalgia, remembrance?
Contrast between dark and light: possible recurring symbol/motif?

by Regina Barreca

When I was five in Louisville   Time and place, reminiscent speaker.
we drove to see nighttime fires. Piled seven of us,
all pajamas and running noses, into the Olds,   Suggests vulnerability.
drove fast toward smoke. It was after my father   Why is the father driving towards
5   lost his job, so not getting up in the morning   the smoke? Most people would run/
gave him time: awake past midnight, he read old newspapers   drive away. Perhaps this is a hint
with no news, tried crosswords until he split the pencil   that he is reckless.
between his teeth, mad. When he heard   Angry or deranged?
the wolf whine of the siren, he woke my mother,   Aggressive   Double meaning: allusion to Greek
10   and she pushed and shoved   language.   sirens; the fire is luring him to
us all into waking. Once roused we longed for burnt wood   it and each time he succumbs he
and a smell of flames high into the pines. My old man liked   moves further away from sanity.
driving to rich neighborhoods best, swearing in a good mood   Contrast reflects mood.
as he followed the fire engines that snaked like dragons   Alliteration/sibilance:
15   and split the silent streets. It was festival, carnival.   sounds snake-like.

If there were a Cadillac or any car
in a curved driveway, my father smiled a smile
from a secret, brittle heart.   The tone shifts in this line from a
His face lit up in the heat given off by destruction   Juxtaposition.   child-like sense of excitement and
20   like something was being made, or was being set right.   fascination (festival, carnival) to
I bent my head back to see where sparks   more adult wistfulness.
ate up the sky. My father who never held us   The relationship between the father and
would take my hand and point to falling cinders that   children is further explored here.
covered the ground like snow, or, excited, show us
25   the swollen collapse of a staircase. My mother   The mother has quite a passive role
watched my father, not the house. She was happy   in this experience – and perhaps in
only when we were ready to go, when it was finally over   her relationship with the father?
and nothing else could burn.
Driving home, she would sleep in the front seat
30   as we huddled behind. I could see his quiet face in the   Like the houses that he has watched burn,
rearview mirror, eyes like hallways filled with smoke.   the father, too, is an empty shell of a man.

Another way of engaging with literature is through note-taking. One method of organizing your notes is by using the Cornell Note-taking System, originally developed in the 1940s by Walter Pauk of Cornell University. A very basic template for Cornell Notes is on the next page.

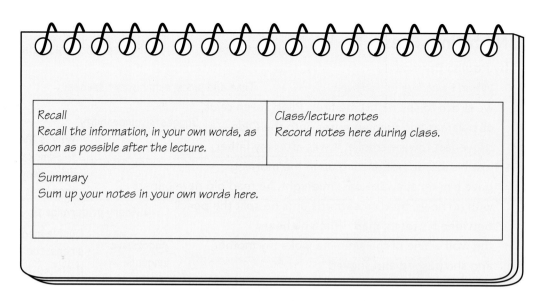

While this method may work best for more content-based subjects (for example, history or biology), it can easily be adapted to work for English literature. Consider the following as an example of how to format your notes on a literary work:

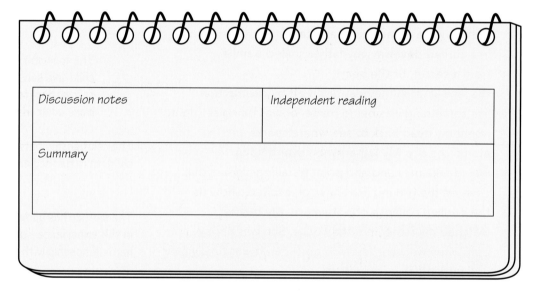

Instead of focusing the largest column on class notes, you could jot down your ideas while reading the work independently. What features do you notice? What questions arise? The left-hand column could be devoted to notes you take during class discussions on the work. Perhaps a classmate makes an interesting observation or inspires you to consider a work from a different point of view. Finally, the summary section could be a place for you to synthesize your independent notes with those you have taken during class.

Alternatively, you could format your notes using a three-column approach, as in the example on the next page.

It is worth noting that there are many apps available which make electronic note-taking simple and straightforward. Research supports handwritten notes as the most effective way of remembering information, but you will need to find a method that works for you. As with annotation, there is no right or wrong way to take notes, but you will gain much more from note-taking if you establish some sort of structure to your notes rather than randomly listing your observations as you read.

Quotes	Notes	Questions

Assessment overview

Literary analysis is a key element of the Language A: Literature course and features in each of the assessments, some more explicitly than others.

■ Paper 1

Paper 1 assesses your ability to independently analyse unseen literary texts under timed conditions. You will have 1 hour and 15 minutes at Standard Level or 2 hours and 15 minutes at Higher Level to write a guided literary analysis on one (SL) or two (HL) unseen literary texts. The texts will include guiding questions which will suggest a stylistic point of entry into each text. You are not expected to produce a fully-fledged commentary on all aspects of the text, but a focused reading of the text.

You will develop your skills in literary analysis throughout the Language A: Literature course. Paper 1 is not connected to any one particular area of study, but is a holistic assessment of your ability to demonstrate an appreciation of the aesthetic qualities of literature, which is one of the main aims of the course.

■ Paper 2

In Paper 2, you are required to choose one out of four questions to compare and contrast two works you have studied. Because you will not have access to the works that you choose to write about during the exam, you will not be expected to demonstrate the same level of close reading that you will for Paper 1. Your analysis may be broader in nature, as opposed to being focused on the specific language of the work, but you will still have to analyse certain aspects of the works in relation to your chosen question. The IBO guide recommends preparing three works for the paper in conjunction and consultation with your teacher.

■ Higher Level essay

The HL essay is a 1 200–1 500-word formal essay, following a line of inquiry of your own choice into one of the works studied. You are recommended to begin your inquiry from one of the seven course concepts; however, you may choose to focus your inquiry through one of the critical lenses, or you may choose a specific literary feature such as characterization, narrative structure or symbol.

■ Individual oral

The internal assessment component of the course consists of a 15-minute individual oral (IO) exploring two of the works in relation to a global issue of your choice. The first ten minutes consists of your analysis of a chosen extract or extracts and the overall works in connection with the chosen global issue. In the remaining five minutes, your teacher will ask you questions that will encourage further development, exploration or discussion. Many of the close-reading skills that you will have to demonstrate for Paper 1 will also be demonstrated here in the IO.

■ Learner portfolio

Although the learner portfolio (LP) is not formally assessed by the IB, it is a central element of the course and is instrumental in the preparation of all assessment components. The LP is a collection of tasks you might develop in your interaction with the works and in your preparation of all assessment components. It consists not only of entries where you reflect on the works studied, but also of all kinds of activities which you might engage in as you respond critically or creatively to the works you read. This could include annotations, notes or other activities which show your active engagement with the works. The LP can be either an electronic portfolio or a paper one, or it can be multi-modal.

Literary analysis and the approaches to learning (ATL)

Throughout your Language A: Literature course of study, you will have the opportunity to develop many of the approaches to learning (ATL) skills – both in and outside the classroom, in group and individual settings. Through the process of literary analysis, you will specifically develop your critical-thinking and creative-thinking skills, as outlined here.

	How can students think critically?
	Gather and organize relevant information to formulate an argument
Critical-thinking skills	Evaluate evidence and arguments
	Draw reasonable conclusions and generalizations
	Consider ideas from multiple perspectives
	Develop contrary or opposing arguments
	How can students be creative?
	Generate novel ideas and consider new perspectives
	Make unexpected or unusual connections between objects and/ or ideas
Creative-thinking skills	Create original works and ideas; use existing works and ideas in new ways
	Generate metaphors and analogies
	Consider multiple alternatives, including those that might be unlikely or impossible
	Practise flexible thinking – develop multiple opposing, contradictory and complementary arguments

Conclusion

You may think that this book is only useful within the context of your English studies. However, the practice of literary analysis can have many wider-reaching benefits. Developing your analytical skills can increase your vocabulary; improve your verbal skills, critical thinking and memory function; encourage you to develop empathy and engagement with other art forms; and help you become a better writer yourself.

The remaining chapters in this book will help you develop specific skills for interpreting poetry, prose and drama, as well as for writing about those forms for your IB assessments.

Resources for additional study

For more detailed information on critical theory, Purdue University's Online Writing Lab (known as Purdue OWL) is a good resource. Jonathan Culler's *Literary Theory: A Very Short Introduction* (part of the *Very Short Introduction* series) is another useful point of reference. For more information on the Cornell Note-Taking system, you can visit Cornell University's Learning Strategies Center **http://lsc.cornell.edu/notes.html**.

Works cited

Barreca, Regina, 'Nighttime Fires', *Minnesota Review*, vol.27, 1986, p.5. *Project MUSE, muse.*
International Baccalaureate Organization, *Language A: Language and Literature guide*, Cardiff, 2019.

2 Approaches to poetry

Introduction to Poetry
by Billy Collins

I ask them to take a poem
and hold it up to the light
like a color slide

or press an ear against its hive.

5   I say drop a mouse into a poem
and watch him probe his way out,

or walk inside the poem's room
and feel the walls for a light switch.

I want them to waterski
10 across the surface of a poem
waving at the author's name on the shore.

But all they want to do
is tie the poem to a chair with rope
and torture a confession out of it.

15 They begin beating it with a hose
to find out what it really means.

The above poem by Billy Collins, former US Poet Laureate (2001–03), is a good place to start when considering how to approach poetry. Here, the speaker talks about the *experience* of poetry. He wants his students to appreciate the look, sound and feel of a poem, but, inevitably, all they want to do is come up with an answer; the students in the poem want to be *told* what a poem is about rather than putting in the effort to explore the many possible layers to a poem.

The analysis of poetry is much like Collins describes in the first few stanzas: it is about puzzling your way through possibilities rather than reaching a definitive conclusion. This chapter will guide you through some of the key aspects of poetry, with the aim of making you feel more comfortable approaching unseen poems in preparation for the Paper 1 examination, or for writing about poetry in any of your other IB assessments.

What is poetry?

What is poetry? This is a question without a straightforward answer. The *Oxford English Dictionary* defines poetry as the 'composition in verse or some comparable patterned arrangement of language in which the expression of feelings and ideas is given intensity by the use of distinctive style and rhythm'. While this may give us some idea of a technical definition of poetry as a form of literature, for many readers and poets themselves it is difficult to express the emotional impact that poetry has. Mark Strand comes close to expressing the transformative power of poetry in his poem 'Eating Poetry'.

Eating Poetry

by Mark Strand

Ink runs from the corners of my mouth.
There is no happiness like mine.
I have been eating poetry.

The librarian does not believe what she sees.
5 Her eyes are sad
and she walks with her hands in her dress.

The poems are gone.
The light is dim.
The dogs are on the basement stairs and coming up.

10 Their eyeballs roll,
their blond legs burn like brush.
The poor librarian begins to stamp her feet and weep.

She does not understand.
When I get on my knees and lick her hand,
15 she screams.

I am a new man.
I snarl at her and bark.
I romp with joy in the bookish dark.

Strand uses many of the 'defining characteristics' of poetry, which will be explored in this chapter, to convey the experience of reading poetry. Using an almost comical tone, Strand suggests that poetry can induce a sort of 'rabid' state within the reader. We don't just read good poetry; we consume it. We may not understand every word, we may puzzle our way through certain metaphors, but, ultimately, a good poem will have an emotional impact on us and illicit a reaction.

ACTIVITY 1: DEFINING POETRY

Consider the following statements made by some of the most well-known English language poets:

'Poetry is the spontaneous overflow of powerful feelings: it takes its origin from emotion recollected in tranquility.'

William Wordsworth

'Poetry is language at its most distilled and most powerful.'

Rita Dove

'Poetry is ordinary language raised to the Nth power. Poetry is boned with ideas, nerved and blooded with emotions, all held together by the delicate, tough skin of words.'

Paul Engle

'If I feel physically as if the top of my head were taken off, I know that is poetry.'

Emily Dickinson

'Genuine poetry can communicate before it is understood.'

TS Eliot

> 1 Consider which of the previous statements best describes the art of poetry.
>
> 2 Write your own definition of poetry. Compare your definition with a classmate's.

What is a poem?

While there may be divergent – and perhaps nebulous – views on what poetry *is* in the abstract sense, there are certain generally agreed-upon conventions of what constitutes a poem as a literary form.

ACTIVITY 2: CONVENTIONS OF POETRY

Before reading any further, make a list of some of the key conventions of poetry that you are familiar with. How does poetry differ from other forms of writing?

You will probably have identified a number of characteristics of a poem in the above activity, such as rhythm and rhyme, sound devices, imagery, figurative language and so on. However, although many poems will possess several of these characteristics, poets do have a tendency to bend – or even break – the rules.

ACTIVITY 3: POETRY OR PROSE?

Read the following two **prose poems**. What elements of poetry are present here? What elements of prose do you recognize?

Bath

by Amy Lowell

The day is fresh-washed and fair, and there is a smell of tulips and narcissus in the air.

The sunshine pours in at the bath-room window and bores through the water in the bath-tub in lathes and planes of greenish-white. It cleaves the water into flaws like a jewel, and cracks it to bright light.

Little spots of sunshine lie on the surface of the water and dance, dance, and their reflections wobble deliciously over the ceiling; a stir of my finger sets them whirring, reeling. I move a foot and the planes of light in the water jar. I lie back and laugh, and let the green-white water, the sun-flawed beryl water, flow over me. The day is almost too bright to bear, the green water covers me from the too bright day. I will lie here awhile and play with the water and the sun spots. The sky is blue and high. A crow flaps by the window, and there is a whiff of tulips and narcissus in the air.

How to Dismantle a Heart

by Rodney Gomez

My mother used to say the heart makes music, but I've never found the keys. Maybe it's the way I was brought into the world: dragged across a river in the night's quiet breathing, trampling through trash and tired runaways as if tearing a window's curtains. We were barred from entry but repeatedly returned, each time becoming a darker part of a tunnel or a truck bed. The sky was so still the stars flickered like carbide lamps. We told time through the landmarks of the dead like cataphiles – the warren of a little girl's murder, the wolf's irrigation pipe. When you see enough unwinding, beating is replaced by the safety of wings. This isn't goodness. The voiceless are never neutral. Bones sway to elegy. Ebony burrows into the earth as a refuge. I grew up, eventually, but the sun was like a cliff with a false bottom: you'd drop and come out the top again. Enough carcasses draped over the dry brush. Enough water towers empty as busted rattles. When you're a child, the heart has a stiff neck and demands to be played. Later, it limps. Before my knees could begin to ache, I crawled to the levee looking for a broken string. Some wayward zil. I stretched my heart over a manhole and drummed it with broken pliers. It wouldn't even quaver. It snapped back into a seed, dry and shriveled and blank.

Try rewriting the above pieces with a 'poetic structure'. Consider carefully where you would break the lines and stanzas. Does this change in structure change the way that you view each piece? Do they 'feel' more poetic when they look like conventional poems?

KEY TERM

Prose poem – poetic writing in prose form.

The line between poetry and prose is in fact a thin one – and one that is very subjective. A novel can sound 'poetic', and a poem can indeed be narrative. Writing in *The Paris Review*, writer and translator Damion Searls offers the following etymological definition: '*Poetry* is from the Greek *poiein*, "to make": a poem is something made, or in English we would more naturally say *crafted*. Yet everyone agrees good prose is well crafted, too. *Prose* means, literally, "straightforward", from the Latin *prosa*, *proversus*, "turned to face forward" (whereas *verse* is all wound up, twisty and snaky, "turned" in every direction except, apparently, forward).' Perhaps it is poetry's inherent ambiguities that distinguish it from prose.

One important difference between poetry and prose is the density of the language; individual words in poetry carry more weight than they tend to do in prose. Another related difference is the number of words; because there are fewer words in a poem, each word has to be chosen very carefully. Reading poetry generally requires a particular kind of imaginative leap to bridge gaps that are left. Poets don't spell things out; they demand that the reader deals directly and extensively in implications.

What are the key aspects to consider in a poem?

There are several elements that shape a poem's meaning. These elements are tools that the poet uses, much like a painter might work with a particular colour palette. It is important not to view these elements in isolation but to consider how they work together to communicate a particular message. The exercises that follow will each focus on a specific element, but it is impossible to consider one element without taking into account others; therefore, it might be a good idea to skim-read the chapter before engaging in the activities. Additionally, we do not want to suggest that you should adopt a linear approach to analysing a poem; you may find that theme is the first thing that jumps out at you, or you may be attuned to picking up on figurative language as you read. The purpose of these exercises is to give you the tools to analyse with more confidence, not to suggest a one-size-fits-all approach.

■ Title

A poem's title is one of its most obvious key elements, and it is perhaps because of this obviousness that it is often overlooked. An effective title can give clues as to the poem's subject matter or communicate an important theme. A title can provide information that is difficult to weave into the body of the poem or it can serve as an ironic contrast to the subject matter itself. The title gives us our first impression of a poem; it is important to stop and consider its significance, perhaps even making predictions, before reading further.

Of course, some titles are deliberately obscure or may hint at something completely different when taken out of context. And some titles may be insignificant – or even absent. Shakespeare's sonnets or Emily Dickinson's poems, for example, are identified by number and first line, respectively; they do not possess titles in the conventional sense.

■ Example: 'Nighttime Fires' by Regina Barreca

Remember the annotated example of this poem in Chapter 1? The following is an example of a student's analysis of the poem's title. The student wrote this before reading the whole poem. Consider how the student examines what themes may be reflected in the poem and what the title might reveal about the speaker.

The title 'Nighttime Fires' conjures up an image of a jovial family sitting around a crackling bonfire. Yet it also plays on the juxtaposition of 'dark' night versus 'light' fire and their relative connotations as 'bad things', suggesting that the contrast between dark and light will be a significant symbol throughout the poem. The simplistic language of the title coupled with the merging of night and time into one word (which echoes childish phrases such as bedtime) also hints that the narrator is of a tender young age and can be viewed as part of the light that shines through the dark.

This student has achieved quite a lot in a relatively short reflection. He or she has made a prediction about the poem's subject matter based on the image associated with the title. The student has also explored the juxtaposition of light and dark suggested in the title. Finally, he or she has considered the point of view of the speaker based on the poet's diction (specifically, the use of childish language).

ACTIVITY 4: CONTEMPLATING TITLES

Consider the following poem titles. What themes do you think they might convey? What predictions can you make about the speaker of these poems?

- 'Death of a Naturalist' by Seamus Heaney
- 'Lady Lazarus' by Sylvia Plath
- 'Queen Kong' by Carol Ann Duffy
- 'Anthem for Doomed Youth' by Wilfred Owen
- 'Funeral Blues' by WH Auden
- 'Nothing Gold Can Stay' by Robert Frost
- 'Mother to Son' by Langston Hughes
- 'A letter to five of the presidents who owned slaves while they were in office' by Clint Smith
- 'For Women Who Are Difficult to Love' by Warsan Shire
- 'Borges and I' by Jorge Luis Borges

In summary, a title serves as an entry point into a poem. Begin with the title of the poem and consider what it suggests about what will follow. Once you have read the poem, go back and reconsider your predictions – you might ask yourself the following questions:

- Are your initial thoughts still relevant?
- Did the subject matter surprise you?
- Are the themes as you predicted?
- Are you left with more questions regarding the poem's title after reading it?

■ Form and structure

Form and **structure** are significant elements of a poem and two of the key features that distinguish poetry from prose. Words, phrases and images do not assemble themselves randomly onto the page; poets carefully consider the placement of these ideas, often choosing a form to complement (or contrast with) the subject matter or theme of the poem.

It is important to remember that form and structure are not the same thing. Structure is an *aspect* of form, but form in and of itself is not structure. We can think of form as a specific type of poem, shaped into a pattern through structural devices such as line and stanza length, rhythmic features (including metre and rhyme) and repetition. The structure of a poem includes the sentence structure, **syntax** and the way the individual lines are arranged.

■ Structural elements

The following features contribute to the structure of a poem:

- stanza
- line
- enjambment
- caesura
- rhythm
- metre.

Below are some examples of how they could be used and how you might include them in your analyses.

A **stanza** is a group of lines. Apart from the individual words, a **line** is the smallest unit of structure within a poem.

A line is not necessarily a sentence. **Enjambment** occurs when an idea carries on from one line to the next – or from one stanza to the next. Unless the punctuation calls for a pause or stop at the end of the line, keep reading until you reach the end of the sentence.

Enjambment can be used for rhythmic purposes or to surprise the reader by delaying a thought or action. Careful consideration should be made of where the poet breaks the line and the emphasis on beginning and end words.

KEY TERMS

Form – a type of text, closely relating to structure. In poetry, we can think of form as a specific type of poem, shaped into a pattern through structural devices such as line and stanza length, rhythmic features (including metre and rhyme) and repetition.

Structure – the way in which a text or poem is organized (it is not the same thing as layout or form).

Syntax – the arrangement of words and phrases in a sentence.

Stanza – a group of lines in a poem.

Line – the smallest unit of structure within a poem. Lines are typically grouped into stanzas.

Enjambment – when an idea or device carries on from one line or stanza to the next.

■ Example: 'We Real Cool' by Gwendolyn Brooks

Gwendolyn Brooks' 'We Real Cool' is an excellent example of how enjambment is employed to achieve a specific effect.

We Real Cool

THE POOL PLAYERS.
SEVEN AT THE GOLDEN SHOVEL.

We real cool. We
Left school. We

Lurk late. We
Strike straight. We

5 Sing sin. We
Thin gin. We

Jazz June. We
Die soon.

Brooks has stated that the 'We' is intended to be spoken softly, with emphasis placed on the action of 'the players' (the collective 'we'). The structure reinforces this intention as the action at the beginning of the line propels the reader forward, with the 'We' at the end almost swallowed up, or absorbed, into the next action.

A **caesura** is a pause within a line of poetry, often created by punctuation such as a comma, semi-colon or dash.

Rhythm is what gives a poem its sound. Rhythm is achieved through a combination of structural elements, including the pattern of stressed and unstressed syllables (a **foot**); the number of feet in a line determines a particular **metre**. Rhythm and metre will be covered in more detail in the context of drama in Chapter 4.

■ Example: *Romeo and Juliet* by William Shakespeare

Notice the way rhythm contributes to meaning in the following extract from Shakespeare's *Romeo and Juliet*. Shakespeare often wrote his plays in verse (this will be explored in more detail in Chapter 4). Here, the regular heartbeat-like rhythm mimics Romeo's euphoric state of mind after his first meeting with Juliet. The second line breaks from the regular iambic pentameter. It starts with a pyrrhic foot (two unstressed syllables), perhaps foreshadowing later tragic events. After the caesura, Romeo's heart literally skips a beat when he says the name 'Juliet', for the rhythm is broken here.

ROMEO   But soft, what light through yonder window breaks?
It is the East, and Juliet is the sun.
(Act 2 Scene 2, 2–3)

KEY TERMS

Caesura – pause within a line of poetry, often created by punctuation such as a comma, semi-colon or dash.

Rhythm – achieved through a combination of structural elements, which gives a poem its sound.

Foot – one unit of metre.

Metre – the arrangement and number of stressed and unstressed syllables in a line of a poem or a verse.

ACTIVITY 5: EXPLORING RHYTHM

Consider the following poem by William Blake. How does rhythm contribute to meaning?

London

by William Blake

I wander thro' each charter'd street,
Near where the charter'd Thames does flow.
And mark in every face I meet
Marks of weakness, marks of woe.

5 In every cry of every Man,
In every Infant's cry of fear,
In every voice: in every ban,
The mind-forg'd manacles I hear.

How the Chimney-sweepers cry
10 Every blackning Church appalls;
And the hapless Soldiers sigh
Runs in blood down Palace walls.

But most thro' midnight streets I hear
How the youthful Harlots curse
15 Blasts the new-born Infants tear
And blights with plagues the Marriage hearse.

■ Form

Poets choose to write using formal structures for many reasons. Form can be seen as a reflection of the age – or a rebellion against it. Miller Williams, in his text *Patterns of Poetry: An Encyclopedia of Forms*, has this to say about form and the age:

> How form relates to the life of the age in which it emerges, or re-emerges, is among the central questions a student of the arts must explore. We can never, probably, say that there was a certain cause or set of causes that led Pope's generation to write in couplets or Wordsworth's generation to turn away from them. But we do know that when a given span of history is dominated by a way of responding to the world – which is to say a way of seeing and hearing and thinking – it eventually cuts across all areas of human expression (Williams 1).

Of course, many poets choose to write in **free verse**, which is the absence of any particular form. When writing about poetry (which will be covered in more detail in Chapter 5), do not make the mistake of stating that a free verse poem does not have any structure. As previously noted, form and structure are not interchangeable, and a poem that is not shaped into a distinctive form will still contain structural elements.

The following are some of the most common forms of poetry, but there are certainly many, many more. If you are interested in formal verse, some good resources to consult include Williams' text or the anthology *Strong Measures: Contemporary American Poetry in Traditional Forms*.

KEY TERM

Free verse – an open form of poetry that has no formal or recognized structure.

KEY TERMS

Iambic pentameter – a line of verse with five metrical feet, each consisting of one short (or unstressed) syllable followed by one long (or stressed) syllable. Shakespeare often wrote in iambic pentameter.

Quatrain – a stanza of four lines.

Rhyme – the repetition of two or more similar sounds, often occurring at the ends of a line in poetry.

Envoi – a short concluding stanza to a sestina.

Elegy: A poem written in response to the death of a person. Traditionally, an elegy is composed of **quatrains** and is written in **iambic pentameter** with an ABAB **rhyme** scheme.

Famous examples: 'In Memory of W.B. Yeats' by WH Auden, 'Dirge Without Music' by Edna St Vincent Millay and 'Elegy Written in a Country Churchyard' by Thomas Gray.

Ode: A lyric poem in praise of a particular subject. The ode originated with the Greeks but was also popular during the English Romantic period. Structurally, its stanza forms and syllable counts vary.

Famous examples: Keats' 'Ode on a Grecian Urn', 'Ode to Beauty' by Ralph Waldo Emerson, 'Ode to a Lemon' by Pablo Neruda.

Terza rima/ottava rima: A poem that is arranged in triplets (three-line stanzas), usually written in iambic pentameter and following the rhyme scheme aba bcb cdc, and so on. A variation of this form is the *ottava rima*, which is composed of eight-line stanzas rhyming *abababcc*.

Famous examples: Dante's *Divine Comedy*, Robert Frost's 'Acquainted with the Night'.

Rondeau: A form of medieval and Renaissance French poetry, characterized by a repeated refrain. The poem usually consists of 10 to 15 lines, with two rhymes, and the 10-line pattern is ABBAABc ABBAc, and the 15-line pattern is AABBA AABc AABAc, with the capital letters representing the repeated refrains and the lowercase letters representing extra lines.

Famous example: John McCrae's 'In Flanders Fields'.

Pantoum: a poem originating in Malaysia; composed of quatrains, with the second and fourth lines of each quatrain repeated as the first and third lines of the next. The second and fourth lines of the final stanza repeat the first and third lines of the stanza.

Famous example: Carolyn Kizer's 'Parent's Pantoum'.

Sestina: A 39-line poem that follows a strict pattern of repetition of the initial six end-words of the first stanza throughout the remaining five six-line stanzas. It ends with a three-line **envoi** which includes all six words.

The order of repetition is as follows (with the letters corresponding to the end-words of each line):

- Stanza 1: ABCDEF
- Stanza 2: FAEBDC
- Stanza 3: CFDABE
- Stanza 4: ECBFAD
- Stanza 5: DEACFB
- Stanza 6: BDFECA
- Stanza 7: (envoi) ECA or ACE

Famous example: Elizabeth Bishop's 'Sestina', Philip Dacey's 'Jill, Afterwards'. (The latter is not a 'pure' sestina, but it is a good example of how a poet successfully manipulates form.)

Sonnet: A 14-line poem, usually based on the subject or theme of love. There are two main types of sonnets: the Italian (or Petrarchan) and the English (or Shakespearean).

KEY TERMS	Italian (Petrarchan) sonnet	English (Shakespearean) sonnet
Octet – the first eight lines of a sonnet. **Sestet** – the last six lines of a sonnet.	■ 14 lines are divided into an **octet** (8 lines) and a **sestet** (6 lines) ■ a turn (in narrative or tone), or 'volta', occurs between the eighth and ninth lines ■ rhyme scheme of abbaabba cdecde or cdcdcd	■ 14 lines structured in three quatrains and a couplet ■ the volta usually occurs between the 12th and 13th lines ■ follows a rhyme scheme of ababcdcdefefgg

Famous examples: sonnets by Petrarch (and Sir Thomas Wyatt), Shakespeare, Spenser, and Edna St Vincent Millay. 'Composed Upon Westminster Bridge' by William Wordsworth.

Villanelle: A 19-line poem with two repeating rhymes and two refrains. The poem is made up of five three-line stanzas and a final quatrain, with the first and third lines of the first stanza repeating alternately in the following stanzas. These two refrain lines form the final couplet in the quatrain.

With the capital letters representing the refrains and the lowercase letters representing the individual rhymed lines, the pattern can be expressed as A1 b A2 / a b A1 / a b A2 / a b A1 / a b A2 / a b A1 A2.

Famous examples: Elizabeth Bishop's 'One Art', Sylvia Plath's 'Mad Girl's Love Song'.

When approaching contemporary poetry, one must consider the significance of form in relation to meaning. Ask yourself, why *this* form for this particular poem? WS Merwin's answer to this question is 'the poem itself' (Dacey and Jauss 2). In other words, Merwin is saying that the poem should dictate the form, not the other way around.

■ Example: 'America' by Claude McKay

Claude McKay's 'America' is an interesting example of how form can contribute to meaning. McKay was a key figure in the Harlem Renaissance, and this poem relays the experience of a black man in 1920s America.

America

Although she feeds me bread of bitterness,
And sinks into my throat her tiger's tooth,
Stealing my breath of life, I will confess
I love this cultured hell that tests my youth.
5 Her vigor flows like tides into my blood,
Giving me strength erect against her hate,
Her bigness sweeps my being like a flood.
Yet, as a rebel fronts a king in state,
I stand within her walls with not a shred
10 Of terror, malice, not a word of jeer.
Darkly I gaze into the days ahead,
And see her might and granite wonders there,
Beneath the touch of Time's unerring hand,
Like priceless treasures sinking in the sand.

The sonnet form was traditionally reserved for expressing romantic sentiments. McKay initially surprises the reader with negative images – of bitterness, of a 'hell that tests [the speaker's] youth'. However, despite facing hate and feeling overwhelmed ('Her bigness sweeps my being like a flood'), the speaker stands 'within her walls with not a shred / Of terror', seeing instead the promise in America. The poem adheres to the structure of an English sonnet (perhaps an ironic choice?), with a regular rhythm and metre (iambic pentameter) and an ABAB CDCD EFEF GG rhyme scheme.

ACTIVITY 6: IDENTIFYING FORM

Identify the form of each of the following poems. It might be helpful to mark the structural features that you notice. Once you have identified the form, consider the effect of this choice on the poem as a whole. How does it complement (or contrast with) certain themes? How successfully does the poet conform to the structure of the chosen form? For what purposes might he or she deviate from the standard conventions of the form?

Poem A

We Wear the Mask

by Paul Laurence Dunbar

We wear the mask that grins and lies,
It hides our cheeks and shades our eyes,—
This debt we pay to human guile;
With torn and bleeding hearts we smile,
5   And mouth with myriad subtleties.

Why should the world be over-wise,
In counting all our tears and sighs?
Nay, let them only see us, while
        We wear the mask.

10   We smile, but, O great Christ, our cries
To thee from tortured souls arise.
We sing, but oh the clay is vile
Beneath our feet, and long the mile;
But let the world dream otherwise,
15   We wear the mask!

Poem B

Anne Hathaway

by Carol Ann Duffy

'Item I gyve unto my wief my second best bed...'
(from Shakespeare's will)

The bed we loved in was a spinning world
of forests, castles, torchlight, cliff-tops, seas
where he would dive for pearls. My lover's words
were shooting stars which fell to earth as kisses
5   on these lips; my body now a softer rhyme
to his, now echo, assonance; his touch

a verb dancing in the centre of a noun.
Some nights I dreamed he'd written me, the bed
a page beneath his writer's hands. Romance
10 and drama played by touch, by scent, by taste.
In the other bed, the best, our guests dozed on,
dribbling their prose. My living laughing love–
I hold him in the casket of my widow's head
as he held me upon that next best bed.

Poem C

Do Not Go Gentle Into That Good Night

by Dylan Thomas

Do not go gentle into that good night,
Old age should burn and rave at close of day;
Rage, rage against the dying of the light.

Though wise men at their end know dark is right,
5   Because their words had forked no lightning they
Do not go gentle into that good night.

Good men, the last wave by, crying how bright
Their frail deeds might have danced in a green bay,
Rage, rage against the dying of the light.

10 Wild men who caught and sang the sun in flight,
And learn, too late, they grieved it on its way,
Do not go gentle into that good night.

Grave men, near death, who see with blinding sight
Blind eyes could blaze like meteors and be gay,
15 Rage, rage against the dying of the light.

And you, my father, there on the sad height,
Curse, bless, me now with your fierce tears, I pray.
Do not go gentle into that good night.
Rage, rage against the dying of the light.

Poem D

Incident

by Natasha Trethewey

We tell the story every year—
how we peered from the windows, shades drawn—
though nothing really happened,
the charred grass now green again.

5   We peered from the windows, shades drawn,
at the cross trussed like a Christmas tree,

the charred grass still green. Then
we darkened our rooms, lit the hurricane lamps.

At the cross trussed like a Christmas tree,
10 a few men gathered, white as angels in their gowns.
We darkened our rooms and lit hurricane lamps,
the wicks trembling in their fonts of oil.

It seemed the angels had gathered, white men in their gowns.
When they were done, they left quietly. No one came.
15 The wicks trembled all night in their fonts of oil;
by morning the flames had all dimmed.

When they were done, the men left quietly. No one came.
Nothing really happened.
By morning all the flames had dimmed.
20 We tell the story every year.

Poem E

O Captain! My Captain!

by Walt Whitman

O Captain! my Captain! our fearful trip is done,
The ship has weather'd every rack, the prize we sought is won,
The port is near, the bells I hear, the people all exulting,
While follow eyes the steady keel, the vessel grim and daring;
5   But O heart! heart! heart!
                O the bleeding drops of red,
                    Where on the deck my Captain lies,
                        Fallen cold and dead.

O Captain! my Captain! rise up and hear the bells;
10 Rise up—for you the flag is flung—for you the bugle trills,
For you bouquets and ribbon'd wreaths—for you the shores a-crowding,
For you they call, the swaying mass, their eager faces turning;
                Here Captain! dear father!
                  This arm beneath your head!
15   It is some dream that on the deck,
                      You've fallen cold and dead.

My Captain does not answer, his lips are pale and still,
My father does not feel my arm, he has no pulse nor will,
The ship is anchor'd safe and sound, its voyage closed and done,
20 From fearful trip the victor ship comes in with object won;
                Exult O shores, and ring O bells!
                  But I with mournful tread,
                    Walk the deck my Captain lies,
                        Fallen cold and dead.

Poem F

The Painter
by John Ashbery

Sitting between the sea and the buildings
He enjoyed painting the sea's portrait.
But just as children imagine a prayer
Is merely silence, he expected his subject
5 To rush up the sand, and, seizing a brush,
Plaster its own portrait on the canvas.

So there was never any paint on his canvas
Until the people who lived in the buildings
Put him to work: "Try using the brush
10 As a means to an end. Select, for a portrait,
Something less angry and large, and more subject
To a painter's moods, or, perhaps, to a prayer."

How could he explain to them his prayer
That nature, not art, might usurp the canvas?
15 He chose his wife for a new subject,
Making her vast, like ruined buildings,
As if, forgetting itself, the portrait
Had expressed itself without a brush.

Slightly encouraged, he dipped his brush
20 In the sea, murmuring a heartfelt prayer:
"My soul, when I paint this next portrait
Let it be you who wrecks the canvas."
The news spread like wildfire through the buildings:
He had gone back to the sea for his subject.

25 Imagine a painter crucified by his subject!
Too exhausted even to lift his brush,
He provoked some artists leaning from the buildings
To malicious mirth: "We haven't a prayer
Now, of putting ourselves on canvas,
30 Or getting the sea to sit for a portrait!"

Others declared it a self-portrait.
Finally all indications of a subject
Began to fade, leaving the canvas
Perfectly white. He put down the brush.
35 At once a howl, that was also a prayer,
Arose from the overcrowded buildings.

They tossed him, the portrait, from the tallest of the buildings;
And the sea devoured the canvas and the brush
As though his subject had decided to remain a prayer.

Poem G

To Autumn

by John Keats

Season of mists and mellow fruitfulness,
   Close bosom-friend of the maturing sun;
Conspiring with him how to load and bless
   With fruit the vines that round the thatch-eves run;
5 To bend with apples the moss'd cottage-trees,
   And fill all fruit with ripeness to the core;
    To swell the gourd, and plump the hazel shells
   With a sweet kernel; to set budding more,
And still more, later flowers for the bees,
10 Until they think warm days will never cease,
    For summer has o'er-brimm'd their clammy cells.

Who hath not seen thee oft amid thy store?
   Sometimes whoever seeks abroad may find
Thee sitting careless on a granary floor,
15   Thy hair soft-lifted by the winnowing wind;
Or on a half-reap'd furrow sound asleep,
   Drows'd with the fume of poppies, while thy hook
    Spares the next swath and all its twined flowers:
And sometimes like a gleaner thou dost keep
20   Steady thy laden head across a brook;
   Or by a cyder-press, with patient look,
    Thou watchest the last oozings hours by hours.

Where are the songs of spring? Ay, Where are they?
   Think not of them, thou hast thy music too,—
25 While barred clouds bloom the soft-dying day,
   And touch the stubble-plains with rosy hue;
Then in a wailful choir the small gnats mourn
   Among the river sallows, borne aloft
    Or sinking as the light wind lives or dies;
30 And full-grown lambs loud bleat from hilly bourn;
   Hedge-crickets sing; and now with treble soft
   The red-breast whistles from a garden-croft;
    And gathering swallows twitter in the skies.

CREATIVE EXTENSION: USING FORM

Try your own hand at one of the poetic forms, using the prompts below.

1   Write an ode to an inanimate object.

2   Write a sonnet expressing an emotion other than love (for example, gratitude, amusement, disgust, fear).

3   Write a sestina using the following words: sky, swim, red, mask, glow, empty.

4   Write two individual end-rhymed lines of a poem. Exchange your lines with a partner. Use each other's lines to write a villanelle.

■ Voice, tone and mood

The voice of a poem is like the narrator in a work of prose. This voice can be a 'tangible', intimate first-person voice or it can be a more omniscient, third-person voice. It is important to remember to refer to the voice as *the speaker* of a poem. We cannot assume that the speaker is the poet; many poets adopt a **persona**, much like a novelist might create a character who serves as the narrator.

Tone and **mood** are elements which are related to voice. Tone refers to the attitude of the speaker or poet. Mood, or atmosphere, is influenced by tone. For example, if a speaker's tone is angry, this might create a tense mood.

■ Example: 'Daddy' by Sylvia Plath

'Daddy' by Sylvia Plath is an example of a poem with a very distinctive tone. The poem is told through the voice of a first-person speaker. (Many students often assume that the speaker is Plath herself. Refer to the note on page 51 on the pitfalls of considering the biography of the poet when analysing a poem.)

If we make a prediction based on the title, we might assume that the speaker is a child as 'Daddy' is an affectionate name often used by younger children. However, as we read the poem, we quickly realize that the speaker is reflecting on a contentious relationship with her father from an adult perspective. This mature point of view is contrasted with the poem's sing-song-like rhythm, evocative of a nursery rhyme, and with the use of rhyme and assonance (devices that will be explored in more detail later in the chapter). We can characterize the tone of the poem as aggressive or confrontational; this is supported through the use of imperatives ('You do not do, you do not do'); the many references to the Holocaust and associated images of torture ('a love of the rack and the screw'); and the use of plosives (for example, 'The boot in the face, the brute / Brute heart of a brute like you.'). This aggressive or confrontational tone makes us as readers feel uncomfortable or vulnerable.

KEY TERMS

Persona – the voice or person chosen by the author to tell the narrative.

Tone – the attitude of the writer or speaker towards his or her subject.

Mood – the feeling that is evoked in the reader (or audience) as a result of the tone that is set.

Daddy

> You do not do, you do not do
> Any more, black shoe
> In which I have lived like a foot
> For thirty years, poor and white,
> 5   Barely daring to breathe or Achoo.
>
> Daddy, I have had to kill you.
> You died before I had time—

Marble-heavy, a bag full of God,
Ghastly statue with one gray toe
10   Big as a Frisco seal

And a head in the freakish Atlantic
Where it pours bean green over blue
In the waters off beautiful Nauset.
I used to pray to recover you.
15   Ach, du.

In the German tongue, in the Polish town
Scraped flat by the roller
Of wars, wars, wars.
But the name of the town is common.
20   My Polack friend

Says there are a dozen or two.
So I never could tell where you
Put your foot, your root,
I never could talk to you.
25   The tongue stuck in my jaw.

It stuck in a barb wire snare.
Ich, ich, ich, ich,
I could hardly speak.
I thought every German was you.
30   And the language obscene

An engine, an engine
Chuffing me off like a Jew.
A Jew to Dachau, Auschwitz, Belsen.
I began to talk like a Jew.
35   I think I may well be a Jew.

The snows of the Tyrol, the clear beer of Vienna
Are not very pure or true.
With my gipsy ancestress and my weird luck
And my Taroc pack and my Taroc pack
40   I may be a bit of a Jew.

I have always been scared of *you*,
With your Luftwaffe, your gobbledygoo.
And your neat mustache
And your Aryan eye, bright blue.
45   Panzer-man, panzer-man, O You–

Not God but a swastika
So black no sky could squeak through.
Every woman adores a Fascist,
The boot in the face, the brute
50   Brute heart of a brute like you.

You stand at the blackboard, daddy,
In the picture I have of you,
A cleft in your chin instead of your foot
But no less a devil for that, no not
55 Any less the black man who

Bit my pretty red heart in two.
I was ten when they buried you.
At twenty I tried to die
And get back, back, back to you.
60 I thought even the bones would do.

But they pulled me out of the sack,
And they stuck me together with glue.
And then I knew what to do.
I made a model of you,
65 A man in black with a Meinkampf look

And a love of the rack and the screw.
And I said I do, I do.
So daddy, I'm finally through.
The black telephone's off at the root,
70 The voices just can't worm through.

If I've killed one man, I've killed two—
The vampire who said he was you
And drank my blood for a year,
Seven years, if you want to know.
75 Daddy, you can lie back now.

There's a stake in your fat black heart
And the villagers never liked you.
They are dancing and stamping on you.
They always *knew* it was you.
80 Daddy, daddy, you bastard, I'm through.

ACTIVITY 7: EXAMINING TONE

Using the analysis of 'Daddy' by Sylvia Plath as a model, consider how tone is conveyed in the following poem by Sharon Olds. Use the accompanying questions to guide you through your analysis.

I Go Back to May 1937

by Sharon Olds

I see them standing at the formal gates of their colleges,
I see my father strolling out
under the ochre sandstone arch, the
red tiles glinting like bent
5 plates of blood behind his head, I

see my mother with a few light books at her hip
standing at the pillar made of tiny bricks,
the wrought-iron gate still open behind her, its
sword-tips aglow in the May air,
10 they are about to graduate, they are about to get married,
they are kids, they are dumb, all they know is they are
innocent, they would never hurt anybody.
I want to go up to them and say Stop,
don't do it—she's the wrong woman,
15 he's the wrong man, you are going to do things
you cannot imagine you would ever do,
you are going to do bad things to children,
you are going to suffer in ways you have not heard of,
you are going to want to die. I want to go
20 up to them there in the late May sunlight and say it,
her hungry pretty face turning to me,
her pitiful beautiful untouched body,
his arrogant handsome face turning to me,
his pitiful beautiful untouched body,
25 but I don't do it. I want to live. I
take them up like the male and female
paper dolls and bang them together
at the hips, like chips of flint, as if to
strike sparks from them, I say
30 Do what you are going to do, and I will tell about it.

1 Sum up the speaker's attitude in one or two words. Identify specific words or phrases from the poem which reflect this attitude.

2 What sort of mood or atmosphere is created by the speaker's tone? In other words, how do you, as the reader, feel when reading the poem?

3 How does repetition reinforce tone or mood?

■ Diction

One of the things that distinguishes poetry from prose is its economy of language; that is, the ability to communicate often profound emotions and universal themes in relatively few words. Diction, or word choice, is perhaps the poet's most important tool when crafting a poem. Diction conveys tone, or attitude, and establishes mood. Diction also reflects the poet's unique style. Even the slightest change to word choice can alter the effect on the reader.

Diction can be broken down into different categories, some of which are outlined on the next page. It is important when writing about diction to identify the specific aspect of diction you are referring to; this precision will allow you to demonstrate greater knowledge and appreciation of language.

KEY TERMS

Jargon – words that are used in a specific context that may be difficult to understand, often involving technical terminology.

Colloquialism – the use of informal or everyday language.

Denotation – the literal, dictionary definition of a word.

Connotation – the ideas provoked beyond the literal meaning.

Cacophony – a harsh or unpleasant sound.

Euphony – a sound that is pleasant to the ear.

■ Vocabulary

Specific vocabulary reflects a particular style. For example, multisyllabic Latin-based words as opposed to shorter, punchier Anglo-Saxon words would suggest a more formal, elevated style. The use of **jargon**, slang or **colloquialisms** might also reveal certain things about the speaker's personality.

■ Denotation vs connotation

Words have both **denotative** (literal) and **connotative** (emotional) meanings. The word 'home' is a good example of a word that has both a denotative and a connotative meaning; literally, a home is a place where one lives, but emotionally the word conjures up feelings of comfort, family and security.

■ Concrete vs abstract words

Concrete language refers to things that we can physically observe (for example, table, book, sky). Abstract language refers to intangible ideas like love, truth, sadness and so on. A poet may choose to immerse the readers in a physical experience, allowing them to draw their own emotional conclusions, or may choose to connect on an emotional level, leaving the physical world within the poem vague.

■ Verb choice

A poet's choice of verbs can have a significant impact on the way a poem 'moves'. The use of passive verbs (for example, state-of-being verbs like am, is, are, was or verbs ending in *–ing*) can make a poem feel static, whereas more active verbs can add a sense of energy or movement to a poem. Skilful poets will use verbs in unexpected ways, such as using familiar verbs in unfamiliar contexts or creating verbs out of nouns.

■ Cacophonous vs euphonious words (sound)

Cacophony is defined as a harsh or unpleasant sound. Cacophonous words are characterized by harsh consonants such as *c* or *k, d, g, p, ch* and so on; 'cacophony' itself is an example of such disharmonious sounds, as are the words 'cackle', 'gargle' and 'gnarly'. In contrast, **euphony** (sound that is pleasant to the ear) is achieved through vowels and soft consonants such as *l, m, n, s, v* and so on. The first line of Keats' 'To Autumn' is a great example of euphonious language: 'Season of mists and mellow fruitfulness …'

■ Figurative language

The choice to use direct language or to reveal emotions more subtly through figurative language is another important tool at the poet's disposal. Different types of figurative language will be explored in more detail on page 41.

■ Example: '12th November: Winter Honey' by Sean Borodale

Sean Borodale's poem, from his collection entitled *Bee Journal*, contains many of the aspects of diction that have been addressed here. A brief analysis is provided, which can serve as a model for the activity that follows.

12th November: Winter Honey

To be honest, this is dark stuff; mud, tang
of bitter battery-tasting honey. The woods are in it.

Rot, decayed conglomerates, old garlic leaf, tongue
wretched

5   by dead tastes, stubborn crystal, like rock. Ingredients:

ivy, sweat, testosterone, the blood of mites. Something
human
in this flavour surely.

Had all the clamber, twist and grip
10   of light-starved roots, and beetle borehole dust.

Deciduous flare of dead leaf,
bright lights leached out like gypsum almost, alabaster
ghost.

Do not think this unkind, the effect is slow
15   and salty in the mouth. A body's widow in her dying
year.

It is bleak with taste and like meat, gamey.

This is the offal of the flowers' nectar.
The sleep of ancient insects runs on this.

20   Giant's Causeway hexagons we smeared on buttered toast
or just the pellets gouged straight from wax to mouth.

Try this addiction:
compounds of starched-cold, lichen-grey light. What else seeps
out?

25   Much work, one bee, ten thousand flowers a day,
to make three teaspoons-worth of this
disconcerting
solid broth
of forest flora full of fox. Immune to wood shade now.

ANALYSING DICTION

✔ **Vocabulary:** There is quite a lot of scientific vocabulary used in the poem ('conglomerates', 'testosterone', 'Deciduous', 'gypsum', 'offal', 'flora'), suggesting that the speaker is perhaps a scientist or naturalist. It is clear that, whoever the speaker is, he is performing the role of 'observer'.

✔ **Concrete vs abstract words:** Much of the language in the poem is concrete, for example, his list of 'ingredients', emphasizing the immediacy of the experience (tasting honey). This concrete language is reinforced by the title, which roots us in a very specific time. Line 2 ('The woods are in it.') could be viewed as a concrete image; literally, the elements of the woods intermingle to create the taste of winter honey. But the line could also be seen as an abstraction; if we consider the connotation of the word 'woods' (another element of diction), we might have mystical, almost fairy tale-like associations, thus giving us a sense that the honey itself is full of the magic of the woods.

✔ **Verb choice:** The interesting thing about this poem is the lack of active verbs; in fact, many of the sentences are fragments, reflecting the immediate, fleeting observations of the speaker. Because the poem is focused on relaying one single experience through imagery, the majority of the language consists of concrete nouns and some adjectives.

✔ **Cacophonous vs euphonious words:** Borodale employs several examples of cacophony. The language itself is hard to swallow, just the like the honey that it is describing: 'mud, tang / of bitter battery-tasting honey', 'forest flora full of fox'.

✔ **Figurative language:** Borodale makes extensive use of figurative language; in particular, metaphors. Apart from the title, he only refers to the honey directly once (in line 2). Referring to the honeycomb as 'Giant's Causeway hexagons' gives it an almost mystical, otherworldly quality. Likewise, the 'disconcerting / solid broth / of forest flora full of fox' evokes an image of disgust; we could almost associate the image with that of a witch's brew.

ACTIVITY 8: EXPLORING DICTION

What aspects of diction does Heaney employ in the following poem and to what effect? Consider what the choice of diction tells us about the speaker at various points in the poem.

Death of a Naturalist

by Seamus Heaney

All year the flax-dam festered in the heart
Of the townland; green and heavy headed
Flax had rotted there, weighted down by huge sods.
Daily it sweltered in the punishing sun.
5 Bubbles gargled delicately, bluebottles
Wove a strong gauze of sound around the smell.
There were dragonflies, spotted butterflies,
But best of all was the warm thick slobber
Of frogspawn that grew like clotted water
10 In the shade of the banks. Here, every spring
I would fill jampotfuls of the jellied
Specks to range on window sills at home,
On shelves at school, and wait and watch until
The fattening dots burst, into nimble
15 Swimming tadpoles. Miss Walls would tell us how
The daddy frog was called a bullfrog
And how he croaked and how the mammy frog
Laid hundreds of little eggs and this was
Frogspawn. You could tell the weather by frogs too
20 For they were yellow in the sun and brown
In rain.

Then one hot day when fields were rank
With cowdung in the grass the angry frogs

> Invaded the flax-dam; I ducked through hedges
> 25 To a coarse croaking that I had not heard
> Before. The air was thick with a bass chorus.
> Right down the dam gross bellied frogs were cocked
> On sods; their loose necks pulsed like sails. Some hopped:
> The slap and plop were obscene threats. Some sat
> 30 Poised like mud grenades, their blunt heads farting.
> I sickened, turned, and ran. The great slime kings
> Were gathered there for vengeance and I knew
> That if I dipped my hand the spawn would clutch it.

■ Translation's effect on diction

Poetry may feature in your study of works in translation. When you study a translated work, it is important to remember that you are not reading the words of the author, but of the translator. Translation itself is an art which involves the manipulation of words, phrases and sentence structures in order to convey the same ideas within a different linguistic and cultural context. As a result, the original connotation is sometimes lost when one word or image is translated to another.

■ Example: 'Passerò per Piazza di Spagna' by Cesare Pavese (Italian)

Below are two versions of a translation of the Italian poem 'Passerò per Piazza di Spagna' by Cesare Pavese. (If Italian happens to be your mother tongue, you may wish to refer to the original poem.) These translations were produced by students in a classroom exercise focused on diction, not by professional translators. Note the subtle differences in diction in each version, some of which we will explore in more detail. You will likely notice additional examples and instances where sentence structure, punctuation and line breaks vary, each having a different effect on the meaning of the text; for the purposes of this exercise, we are only focusing on word choice.

I will pass by Piazza di Spagna

The skies will be clear.
The path will open
Onto hills of pines and stones.
The roar of the streets
5 Won't taint the still air.
The flowers, splashed
With colour, will ogle
The fountains, like merry
Damsels. The stairs,
10 The balconies, the swallows
Will sing in the sun.
That path will open,
Those stones will sing,
My heart will beat, leaping
15 Like the water in the fountains –
This will be the voice

Through Piazza di Spagna

Cloudless the sky shall be.
The roads will open onto
Hills of trees and stones.
The tumult of the streets
5 Won't alter that still air.
The flowers bursting
with glow glimpsing like jocund girls
at the fountains.
The stairs, the terraces, the sparrows
10 all singing in the sun.
Open the path,
Let the stones rejoice
And my heart will skip and swing
Like the rising fountain's waters –
15 This the voice
That shall soar your steps.

Ascending your steps.
The windows will know
The smell of stone
20 And of the morning air.
A door will open.
The roar of the streets
Will be the roar of my heart
When the light is lost.

25 You will be there – still and clear.

The windows shall taste
The scent of mist and morning air.
Throw open the door.
20 The ferment of the streets
Shall be the ferment of the heart
Lost in a place without light.

You – firm and fair.

Blue: Immediately, we have a difference in word choice. Student A on the left has chosen to describe the skies as 'clear', while Student B on the right has opted for the word 'cloudless'. Both seem to be saying the same thing, but the word 'cloudless' evokes a certain mood or atmosphere. Cloudy skies are usually associated with gloominess or oppression, so perhaps the translator (on behalf of the poet) is trying to suggest an optimistic mood.

Pink: The words 'roar' and 'tumult' have very different connotations. 'Roar' reflects the sounds of the streets and has animalistic associations. 'Tumult' can refer to sound but also suggests 'chaos or disorder'. The streets are therefore characterized slightly differently with each word that is used.

Green: Here again we have two words with very different connotations. To 'taint' means to contaminate, pollute or spoil, whereas to 'alter' means to change. The negative connotation of 'taint' is a contrast to the more neutral connotation of 'alter'.

Yellow: These are interesting choices as each student has employed figurative language in different ways. Student A has begun the image with a more literal statement ('My heart will beat'), followed by use of personification to paint a picture of the speaker's heart 'leaping / Like the water in the fountains'. Student B has avoided the literal and gone straight for the figurative image of the heart skipping and swinging; notice the use of alliteration here as well. 'Skip' and 'swing' have a more playful, lyrical connotation than 'beating' or 'leaping', which feel slightly more aggressive.

> **KEY TERM**
>
> **Imagery** – a technique employed to convey emotion using language that appeals to the senses.

■ Imagery

Imagery is language that appeals to the senses. Rather than rely on narrative as a novelist might do, poets use imagery as a way of conveying emotion. Although the word 'imagery' derives from the root 'image', there are several different types of imagery, not just those that appeal to the sense of sight.

■ Visual imagery

Visual imagery is imagery that appeals to the sense of sight. In Ezra Pound's two-line imagist poem 'In a Station of the Metro', the language is stripped back to its most economical, providing a single snapshot or visual image of a scene in a Paris metro station.

This extract from 'The Fish' by Elizabeth Bishop is another good example. Here, the imagery paints a vivid portrait of a fish:

> ## The Fish
> **by Elizabeth Bishop**
> Here and there
> his brown skin hung in strips

> like ancient wallpaper,
> and its pattern of darker brown
> was like wallpaper:
> shapes like full-blown roses
> stained and lost through age.
> He was speckled with barnacles,
> fine rosettes of lime,
> and infested
> with tiny white sea-lice,
> and underneath two or three
> rags of green weed hung down.

■ Auditory imagery

Auditory imagery is imagery that appeals to the sense of sound. 'The Machinist, Teaching His Daughter to Play the Piano' by BH Fairchild is an excellent example of how a poet uses sound imagery to bring a poem to life, as in this extract from the poem:

> … these gestures of voice and hands
> suspended over the keyboard
> that move like the lathe in its turning
>
> toward music, the wind dragging the hoist chain, the ring
> of iron on iron in the holding rack.

■ Olfactory imagery

Olfactory imagery is imagery that appeals to the sense of smell. These lines from John Montague's 'The Water Carrier' are a good example:

> You stood until the bucket brimmed
> Inhaling the musty smell of unpicked berries,
> That heavy greenness fostered by water.

■ Gustatory imagery

Gustatory imagery is imagery that appeals to the sense of taste. For example, Seamus Heaney invokes a sense of taste in this extract from his poem 'Blackberry Picking':

> You ate that first one and its flesh was sweet
> Like thickened wine: summer's blood was in it
> Leaving stains upon the tongue and lust for
> Picking.

■ Tactile imagery

Tactile imagery is imagery that appeals to the sense of touch. For example, Heaney also makes interesting use of tactile imagery in 'Blackberry Picking', as this extract shows:

> Our hands were peppered
> With thorn pricks, our palms sticky as Bluebeard's.

Note: Bluebeard is an allusion to the 17th-century French folktale about a wealthy yet violent man (Bluebeard) who had a habit of murdering his wives.

■ Kinaesthetic imagery

Kinaesthetic imagery is imagery that appeals to the sense of movement. For example, in the opening two stanzas of Wilfred Owen's 'Dulce et Decorum Est' the kinaesthetic imagery relays the feeling of fatigue experienced by First World War soldiers.

■ Example: 'Double Dutch' by Gregory Pardlo

Double Dutch

The girls turning double-dutch
bob & weave like boxers pulling
punches, shadowing each other,
sparring across the slack cord
5 casting parabolas in the air. They
whip quick as an infant's pulse
and the jumper, before she
enters the winking, nods in time
as if she has a notion to share,
10 waiting her chance to speak. But she's
anticipating the upbeat
like a bandleader counting off
the tune they are about to swing into.
The jumper stair-steps into mid-air
15 as if she's jumping rope in low-gravity,
training for a lunar mission. Airborne a moment
long enough to fit a second thought in,
she looks caught in the mouth bones of a fish
as she flutter-floats into motion
20 like a figure in a stack of time-lapse photos
thumbed alive. Once inside,
the bells tied to her shoestrings rouse the gods
who've lain in the dust since the Dutch
acquired Manhattan. How she dances
25 patterns like a dust-heavy bee retracing
its travels in scale before the hive. How
the whole stunning contraption of girl and rope
slaps and scoops like a paddle boat.
Her misted skin arranges the light
30 with each adjustment and flex. Now heather-
hued, now sheen, light listing on the fulcrum
of a wrist and the bare jutted joints of elbow

and knee, and the faceted surfaces of muscle,
surfaces fracturing and reforming
35 like a sun-tickled sleeve of running water.
She makes jewelry of herself and garlands
the ground with shadows.

'Double Dutch' captures a specific moment in time: a young girl jumping 'double dutch'. The poem relies on extensive visual imagery to present the reader with an image, much like a photograph. Pardlo also uses kinaesthetic imagery to invoke a sense of movement, reflecting the experience of the jumper. For example, we can almost feel the weightlessness in the following lines: 'The jumper stair-steps into mid-air / as if she's jumping rope in low-gravity, / training for a lunar mission.' And in these lines Pardlo compares the jump-roper's movements to that of an insect: 'How she dances / patterns like a dust-heavy bee retracing / its travels in scale before the hive.'

As an aside, if we think back to how form and structure can shape meaning, this is an excellent example of how free verse is employed with purpose. Pardlo captures one moment within this poem; thus, the one-stanza free-verse structure is appropriate. The use of enjambment is equally fitting; the continuous 'motion' of ideas mimics the movement of the rope-jumper.

ACTIVITY 9: REFLECTING ON IMAGERY

Cold Knap Lake

by Gillian Clarke

We once watched a crowd
pull a drowned child from the lake.
Blue-lipped and dressed in water's long green silk
she lay for dead.

5 Then kneeling on the earth,
a heroine, her red head bowed,
her wartime cotton frock soaked,
my mother gave a stranger's child her breath.
The crowd stood silent,
10 drawn by the dread of it.

The child breathed, bleating
and rosy in my mother's hands.
My father took her home to a poor house
and watched her thrashed for almost drowning.

15 Was I there?
Or is that troubled surface something else
shadowy under the dipped fingers of willows
where satiny mud blooms in cloudiness
after the treading, heavy webs of swans
20 as their wings beat and whistle on the air?

All lost things lie under closing water
in that lake with the poor man's daughter.

1   What images initially strike you in this poem? Can you identify the type of imagery that Clarke uses?

2   What emotions are conveyed through the imagery that is used? For example, 'bleating' is an animalistic word, characteristic of sheep, goats or calves. How does knowing this detail contribute to the emotions in the third stanza?

3   Consider contrasts, especially those connected to colour. What is the effect of these images?

4   Note examples of tactile imagery. How do these images contribute to the theme of memory and remembrance?

■ Figurative language

Poets often rely on figurative language to imply meaning rather than simply stating the literal. Because we often expect this in a poem, it can be tempting to jump to the figurative level before establishing a solid understanding of the literal (more on this on page 52). There are many different types of figurative language, which are outlined below.

■ Metaphors and similes

Metaphors and **similes** are a comparison of two unlike things. The poem 'The Country Shaped like a Butterfly's Wing' by Bob Orr is full of metaphors and similes. The title itself is a reference to Orr's native New Zealand; Orr makes an unusual comparison between the geographical shape of New Zealand and a butterfly's wing as a way of romanticising a sense of place.

■ Personification

Personification is giving human characteristics to inanimate objects. A good example of personification is Emily Dickinson's poem 'Because I could not stop for Death'. Here in the first stanza, she effectively personifies death:

> Because I could not stop for Death –
> He kindly stopped for me –
> The Carriage held but just Ourselves –
> And Immortality.

This is not to be confused with **anthropomorphism**, which is the attribution of human characteristics to an animal.

■ Hyperbole

Hyperbole is exaggeration for dramatic effect. In the opening lines of William Wordsworth's 'Composed Upon Westminster Bridge', he exaggerates the beauty of London and its effect on the speaker:

> Earth has not anything to show more fair:
> Dull would he be of soul who could pass by
> A sight so touching in its majesty …

KEY TERMS

Metaphor – a comparison between two things.

Simile – a comparison of two things using like or as.

Personification – giving human characteristics to inanimate objects.

Anthropomorphism – the attribution of human characteristics or behaviour to an animal.

Hyperbole – exaggeration to make a situation seem more dramatic or humorous.

KEY TERMS

Metonymy – a figure of speech in which the name of an object or concept is replaced with a word which is closely related to the original.

Synecdoche – the naming of a part for the whole or the whole for the part.

Symbol – a comparison between something the author wants the reader to think about and another element.

Allusion – a reference in literature to another piece of literature, art, music or history.

■ Metonymy

Metonymy is a figure of speech in which the name of an object or concept is replaced with a word which is closely related to the original meaning. For example, In Robert Frost's 'Out, Out', a boy has cut himself with a saw. The speaker describes him as holding his bleeding hand up 'as if to keep / The life from spilling.' Here, 'blood' is substituted with 'life' – literally, it is the blood that is spilling from him.

■ Synecdoche

Similar to metonymy, **synecdoche** is the naming of a part for the whole or the whole for the part.

Here is an example from Samuel Taylor Coleridge's 'The Rime of the Ancient Mariner', where Coleridge uses 'wave' instead of 'sea'.

> The western wave was all a-flame.
> The day was well nigh done!
> Almost upon the western wave
> Rested the broad bright Sun.

■ Symbol

A **symbol** is an object used to represent an idea. For example, in 'The Black Lace Fan My Mother Gave Me' by Eavan Boland, a daughter reflects on the significance of a fan, which represents to her, the speaker, the whole development of her parents' relationship with each other.

■ Allusion

Allusion is a reference in literature to another work of literature, art, music or history. Allusions appear frequently in the work of poets. Anne Sexton's *Transformations* is a collection of re-tellings of classic Grimms' Fairy Tales. Louise Glück's 'Meadowlands' makes extensive references to Greek myths like *The Odyssey* to explore the topic of marriage. Many of Sylvia Plath's poems, particularly those in *Ariel*, are peppered with allusions to Greek myths, the Bible and Nazi Germany, among other literary, religious and historical references.

■ Example of figurative language

Blood Dazzler (2008) is a collection of poetry by Patricia Smith which centres around Hurricane Katrina in 2005. Many of the poems contain examples of figurative language, while Smith also adopts many personas throughout the collection, including the hurricane itself. This is the first poem in the collection.

5 P.M., Tuesday, August 23, 2005

by Patricia Smith

"Data from an Air Force reserve unit reconnaissance aircraft… along with observations from the Bahamas and nearby ships… indicate the broad low pressure area over the southeastern Bahamas has become organized enough to be classified as tropic depression twelve."
NATIONAL HURRICANE CENTER

A muted thread of gray light, hovering ocean,
becomes throat, pulls in wriggle, anemone, kelp,

widens with the want of it. I become
a mouth, thrashing hair, an overdone eye. How dare
5 the water belittle my thirst, treat me as just
another
small
disturbance,

try to feed me
10 from the bottom of its hand?

I will require praise,
unbridled winds to define my body,
a crime behind my teeth
because

15 every woman begins as weather,
sips slow thunder, knows her hip. Every woman
harbors a chaos, can
wait for it, straddling a fever.

For now,
20 I console myself with small furies,
those dips in my dawning system. I pull in
a bored breath. The brine shivers.

The speaker is the storm that will become Hurricane Katrina, personified as a woman. The many references to body parts (for example, throat, mouth, hair, eye) give the storm human-like characteristics, emphasizing the power the storm wields over humanity. The use of assertive language such as 'How dare / the water belittle my thirst, treat me as just / another / small / disturbance' and 'I will require praise' further characterizes the storm as a powerful and demanding force, reinforcing a key theme of the destructive power of nature.

ACTIVITY 10: ANALYSING METAPHOR

Blessing

by Imtiaz Dharker

The skin cracks like a pod.
There never is enough water.

Imagine the drip of it,
the small splash, echo
5 in a tin mug,
the voice of a kindly god.

Sometimes, the sudden rush
of fortune. The municipal pipe bursts,
silver crashes to the ground
10 and the flow has found
a roar of tongues. From the huts,

> a congregation: every man woman
> child for streets around
> butts in, with pots,
> 15 brass, copper, aluminium,
> plastic buckets,
> frantic hands,
>
> and naked children
> screaming in the liquid sun,
> 20 their highlights polished to perfection,
> flashing light,
> as the blessing sings
> over their small bones.

1 Consider the metaphors that Dharker uses to describe water, beginning with the title. Which one do you think is most effective? Why?

2 What other examples of figurative language can you identify in the poem?

■ Sound devices

Poetry is an aural art. Originally, poetry was written to be read aloud, to be *heard* rather than *read*. It is important to remember that, when reading a poem, sound is as important as meaning; indeed, sound often *shapes* meaning in poetry.

There are several ways that poets can manipulate sound. The following are some of the most common sound devices.

■ Alliteration

Alliteration is the repetition of initial consonant sounds. For example, in 'Let America Be America Again' by Langston Hughes, the line 'Let America be the dream the dreamers dreamed …' is a good example of alliteration. The repetition of the letter 'd' has an authoritative, affirmative sound to it, a bit like a drum-beat.

■ Assonance

Assonance is the repetition of vowel sounds within words. In 'No Encore', Betty Adcock takes on the persona of a magician's assistant. The repetitive 'o' sounds in the following stanza create a mysterious mood and suggest a melancholy tone associated with the sound 'oh'.

> Late or soon a guttering silence will ring down
> a curtain like woven smoke on thickening air.
> The audience will strain to see what's there,
> the old magician nowhere to be found.

■ Consonance

Consonance is the repetition of consonant sounds within words. In *Hamlet*, Shakespeare uses the repetition of the 's' sound (also called 'sibilance', which will be explored in more detail in the next example) to create a dream-like effect; there is also a sinister undertone to the sound, which reflects Hamlet's state of mind in this particular scene.

KEY TERMS

Alliteration – the repetition of initial consonant sounds.

Assonance – the repetition of vowel sounds within words.

Consonance – the repetition of consonant sounds within words.

> HAMLET   To be, or not to be: that is the question:
> Whether 'tis nobler in the mind to suffer
> The slings and arrows of outrageous fortune
> Or to take arms against a sea of troubles,
> And by opposing end them?—To die,—to sleep,—
> No more; and by a sleep to say we end
> The heartache, and the thousand natural shocks
> That flesh is heir to,—'tis a consummation
> Devoutly to be wish'd. To die,—to sleep;—
> To sleep: perchance to dream:—ay, there's the rub;
>
> (Act 3 Scene 1, 55–64)

■ Sibilance

Sibilance is the repetition of 's' sounds. WB Yeats' 'The Lake Isle of Innisfree' makes extensive use of 's' and 'sh' sounds to create a sense of peace and calm often associated with water, as in the following line from the second stanza: 'And I shall have some peace there, for peace comes dropping slow.'

■ Onomatopoeia

Onomatopoeia is a word which sounds like the noise that it makes. For example, bang, crash, plop, zoom. Seamus Heaney's 'Death of a Naturalist', explored previously, is full of child-like examples of onomatopoeia, such as 'gargled', 'burst', 'croaked', 'farting'. This use of language reflects the speaker's changing tone and point of view.

■ Rhyme

Rhyme is corresponding sounds in words. There are many different types of rhymes, the most common of which are:

- end rhymes (those at the ends of lines of poetry)

- internal rhymes (words that rhyme within a single line of poetry)

- slant rhymes (words that share a vowel sound or consonant sound, also called half rhymes or partial rhymes; for example, thumb and gun)

- eye rhymes (words that look the same but are pronounced differently; for example, move and love)

■ Repetition

Repetition is the repeated use of a sound, word, phrase or sentence within a poem. Repetition is both a structural element and a sound device.

■ Example of sound devices

Liz Lochhead is a contemporary Scottish poet, playwright, translator and broadcaster. It is perhaps because of Lochhead's many roles within the world of the arts that she is so attuned to the importance of sound in shaping meaning.

The first thing you might notice as you read her poem 'Men Talk' is the inconsistency of punctuation. This is no accident or mistake. Read the poem to the punctuation (not to the end of the line or stanza) and you will notice that the breathlessness that you feel as a reader mimics women's speech patterns as Lochhead describes them in the poem. In contrast, men's speech habits are reflected in a simple declarative sentence ('Men Talk.') and used sparingly in comparison. (If you can find a performance of the poem from Lochhead online, it's interesting to consider which words or phrases she emphasizes.)

> **KEY TERMS**
>
> **Sibilance** – the repetition of 's' sounds.
>
> **Onomatopoeia** – a word which sounds like the noise that it makes. For example: bang, crash, plop, zoom.
>
> **Repetition** – the repeated use of a word, phrase or image to draw attention to it.

Men Talk (Rap)

by Liz Lochhead

Women
Rabbit rabbit rabbit women
Tattle and titter Women prattle
Women waffle and witter
5   Men Talk. Men Talk.

Women into Girl Talk
About Women's Trouble
Trivia 'n' Small Talk
They yap and they babble

10   Men Talk. Men Talk.

Women gossip Women giggle
Women niggle-niggle-niggle
Men Talk.

Women yatter
15   Women chatter
Women chew the fat, women spill the beans
Women aint been takin'
The oh-so Good Advice in them
Women's Magazines.
20   A Man Likes a Good Listener.

Oh yeah
I like A Woman
Who likes me enough
Not to nitpick
25   Not to nag and
Not to interrupt 'cause I call that treason
A woman with the Good Grace
To be struck dumb
By me Sweet Reason. Yes –

30   A Man Likes a Good Listener
A Real
Man
Likes a Real Good Listener

Women yap yap yap
35   Verbal Diarrhoea is a Female Disease
Women she spread she rumours round she
Like Philadelphia Cream Cheese

Oh
Bossy Women Gossip
40   Girlish Women Giggle
Women natter, women nag
Women niggle niggle niggle

>   Men Talk.
>
>   Men
> 45 Think First.
>   Speak Later
>   Men Talk.

Now that you have read the poem, you will have picked up on some examples of onomatopoeia (for example, 'tattle', 'titter', 'prattle'). All of these words, which sound childish, are used to characterize how women 'talk'. Men, on the other hand, are only given two words to characterize their speaking habits: 'talk' and 'speak', which have neutral connotations. Lochhead uses repetition to reinforce the idea that women speak incessantly and perhaps unnecessarily: 'Women / Rabbit rabbit rabbit', 'Women niggle-niggle-niggle'. The use of alliteration and rhyme creates a sort of playful, sing-song-like rhythm (as indicated in the title's classification of the poem as a 'rap'), which is perhaps deliberately chosen to reflect the speaker's light-hearted attitude towards women's speech habits (mostly likely tinged with irony).

ACTIVITY 11: CONSIDERING SOUND

My Rival's House

by Liz Lochhead

>   is peopled with many surfaces.
>   Ormolu* and gilt, slipper satin,
>   lush velvet couches,
>   cushions so stiff you can't sink in.
> 5   Tables polished clear enough to see distortions in.
>
>   We take our shoes off at her door,
>   shuffle stocking-soled, tiptoe – the parquet floor
>   is beautiful and its surface must
>   be protected. Dust-
> 10 cover, drawn shade,
>   won't let the surface colour fade.
>
>   Silver sugar-tongs and silver salver,
>   my rival serves us tea.
>   She glosses over him and me.
> 15 I am all edges, a surface, a shell
>   and yet my rival thinks she means me well.
>   But what squirms beneath her surface I can tell.
>   Soon, my rival
>   capped tooth, polished nail
> 20 will fight, fight foul for her survival.
>   Deferential, daughterly, I sip
>   and thank her nicely for each bitter cup.
>
>   And I have much to thank her for.
>   This son she bore –

25 first blood to her –
     never, never can escape scot free
     the sour potluck of family.
     And oh how close
     this family that furnishes my rival's place.

30 Lady of the house.
     Queen bee.
     She is far more unconscious,
     far more dangerous than me.
     Listen, I was always my own worst enemy.
35 She has taken even this from me.

     She dishes up her dreams for breakfast.
     Dinner, and her salt tears pepper our soup.
     She won't
     give up.

* ormolu: a gold-coloured metal used in decoration and making ornaments

1 Sibilance is employed throughout this poem. Identify examples of sibilance and comment on its effects.

2 Comment on the use and effects of rhyme in the poem.

KEY TERM

Theme – an overarching idea or concept.

■ Theme

A **theme** is an overarching idea or concept. Not to be confused with a subject, a theme is more specific. For example, love is a subject, but a theme would be 'the destructive power of love' (think *Romeo and Juliet*). A theme is universal and can be applied to other poems or works of literature. Theme is usually conveyed through a combination of all of the other elements at work in a poem: form and structure, voice, figurative language, sound devices and so on.

■ Example: 'The Contract Says: We'd Like the Conversation to Be Bilingual' by Ada Limón

The Contract Says: We'd Like the Conversation to Be Bilingual

    When you come, bring your brown-
    ness so we can be sure to please

    the funders. Will you check this
    box; we're applying for a grant.

5 Do you have any poems that speak
    to troubled teens? Bilingual is best.

    Would you like to come to dinner
    with the patrons and sip Patrón?

    Will you tell us the stories that make

10   us uncomfortable, but not complicit?

Don't read the one where you
are just like us. Born to a green house,

garden, don't tell us how you picked
tomatoes and ate them in the dirt

15   watching vultures pick apart another
bird's bones in the road. Tell us the one

about your father stealing hubcaps
after a colleague said that's what his

kind did. Tell us how he came
20   to the meeting wearing a poncho

and tried to sell the man his hubcaps
back. Don't mention your father

was a teacher, spoke English, loved
making beer, loved baseball, tell us

25   again about the poncho, the hubcaps,
how he stole them, how he did the thing

he was trying to prove he didn't do.

The title gives us our first clue as to the subject matter that will be explored in the poem: race and identity. After we have read the poem, we can zoom in on a more specific theme related to the subject, such as 'individuals can sometimes be treated as tokens by those who look to profit from their identity'. This theme is reinforced by the content of the poem, but it is also interesting to consider how form and structure help reinforce this theme.

The syntax of the title reflects 'the conversation' that the contract requests; a colon separates the more omniscient voice in the first clause ('The Contract Says') from the 'voice' of the contract in the second clause ('We'd Like the Conversation to Be Bilingual'). The colon acts as a sort of physical barrier between the two voices. The structure of the poem, arranged in couplets, reflects the two-way relationship of a conversation, but this is an ironic choice since the rest of the poem is only told from the point of view of the contractor, with a mixture of questions and imperative statements ('Tell us how …', 'Don't mention …'). The final stanza is one line on its own, breaking from the previous pattern. We could view this line as symbolic of the isolation that the subject of the poem feels as a result of being treated as a token. We could also see this line as an attempt by the subject to reclaim a sense of singular identity.

An interview with the poet on National Public Radio gives us further insight into her intentions. In addition to the broad theme of diversity versus inclusion, Limón states that: 'I think there's another level to that where audience members or readers want you also to perform your pain. And I'm – I struggle with that sometimes because I really want writers of colour to be given the permission to write about joy and gratitude and ordinary things as opposed to always getting up there, dancing at our bruises.' (NPR Choice Page.) So the poem could also reflect the relationship between a poet (or artist) and his or her audience.

ACTIVITY 12: EXPLORING THEME

Planting a Sequoia

by Dana Gioia

All afternoon my brothers and I have worked in the orchard,
Digging this hole, laying you into it, carefully packing the soil.
Rain blackened the horizon, but cold winds kept it over the Pacific,
And the sky above us stayed the dull grey
5 Of an old year coming to an end.

In Sicily a father plants a tree to celebrate his first son's birth—
An olive or a fig tree—a sign that the earth has one more life to bear.
I would have done the same, proudly laying new stock into my father's
    orchard,
A green sapling rising among the twisted apple boughs,
10 A promise of new fruit in other autumns.

But today we kneel in the cold planting you, our native giant,
Defying the practical custom of our fathers,
Wrapping in your roots a lock of hair, a piece of an infant's birth cord,
All that remains above earth of a first-born son,
15 A few stray atoms brought back to the elements.

We will give you what we can—our labor and our soil,
Water drawn from the earth when the skies fail,
Nights scented with the ocean fog, days softened by the circuit of bees.
We plant you in the corner of the grove, bathed in western light,
20 A slender shoot against the sunset.

And when our family is no more, all of his unborn brothers dead,
Every niece and nephew scattered, the house torn down,
His mother's beauty ashes in the air,
I want you to stand among strangers, all young and ephemeral to you,
25 Silently keeping the secret of your birth.

1 Gioia deals with universal subjects such as life and death in his poem. Look closer and state a specific theme that is linked to each of those overarching ideas.

2 How does imagery or figurative language reinforce the themes that you have identified?

3 Comment on the significance of structure in relation to theme.

■ Considering a poem's context

One final aspect that should be considered when analysing a poem is its context – within a specific collection and within the wider body of the poet's work. When dealing with unseen poems in an exam-like situation, you will not have this information, as only the poem itself is provided. However, when you are studying poetry within the classroom it is important to take into account how a particular poem fits into the wider context of the poet's work. Some things to think about when considering context include, but are not limited to:

■ When was the poem written in relation to other notable poems that the poet has written? Is it an early poem? A late poem? If it is an early poem, how has the poet's style evolved since the poem was written? If it is a later poem, what characterizes the poet's style at this stage in his or her career? For example, did the poet use more traditional forms at this early stage, or did he or she experiment more with verse forms and structures? Was the language less formal at an earlier stage?

■ Where is the poem placed within a specific collection? Is it the first poem? Is it the last poem? Why might this be significant? For example, Seamus Heaney's collection entitled *Death of a Naturalist* (1966) begins with the poem 'Digging', which sort of acts as a metaphor for the 'digging' that the reader will do as he or she explores the collection. The poem also reflects some of the overarching themes that will be present in the rest of the collection, such as family bonds, heritage and traditions; connection to nature and the land; and the power of writing. The arrangement of poems within a collection is also significant to the work of Sylvia Plath. After Plath's suicide in 1963, her estranged husband Ted Hughes published her final manuscript, *Ariel*, changing the order of the poems, omitting some and adding others; in 2004, a 'new' version of *Ariel* was published, restoring Plath's original arrangement.

■ Does the poem reflect certain themes the poet is known for or contain symbols, motifs or other elements of language which are representative of the poet's wider body of work? In short, what characterizes the poet's style, and how does this particular poem reflect that?

A note on the biography of the poet: While it may be interesting to examine the life of a poet, your analysis of the work should not rest too heavily on elements of the poet's biography. To use the example of Sylvia Plath again, students often like to try to connect everything in her poems to her husband's infidelity or to her death by suicide, while overlooking elements of language and technique. Think back to the section on voice; more often than not, the poet is not the speaker. Even if there are autobiographical elements in a poem (Plath was labelled a 'confessional poet' by many critics), the poem itself should not be read as a truthful account of something that happened in the poet's life. Relying on conjecture will not allow you to demonstrate a sophisticated appreciation of language, form and structure, which is what you should be aiming for.

Poetry and a guided analysis

You will be studying various poems over the course of your studies in language and literature and you will be using what you study for several different IB assessments. Chapter 5 of this book will discuss in detail how to write about literary works whenever you are dealing with whole texts. You will, however, be asked to write about a poem or prose passage you have never seen before for Paper 1. Because your time is limited, you will not have time to look for every element that has been explored in this chapter, but here are some tips for how to proceed.

FIVE TIPS FOR TACKLING UNSEEN POEMS
1 Read the poem several times! You should read it at least three times:
a once for structure and organization
b once for sound and rhythm
c once for meaning.

2 In order to appreciate the metaphorical level of a poem and develop an individual interpretation, you must first understand the poem at a literal level. Try to write a one- or two-sentence summary of what is happening in the poem after your first reading; think about what the narrative or the emotional experience being conveyed is.

3 Don't try to force an interpretation that isn't supported by the language. Instead, let the language of the poem guide you towards your interpretation.

4 Don't neglect sound. It's easy to forget this aspect, especially in an exam situation, but remember that poems are meant to be *heard*.

5 Don't spend so much time focusing on the individual parts of the poem that you miss out on the big picture. When analysing a poem, always consider how the parts contribute to the whole.

And a bonus tip:

6 Don't expect to 'get' everything about a poem. Most poems have multiple layers and multiple ways of being interpreted. Focus on trying to extract two or three key points from the poem and go from there.

■ Pulling it all together

The features explored above should not be viewed as a tick-list. The criteria for Paper 1 requires you to demonstrate both knowledge *and* understanding of the given poem (or extract). These two skills are not interchangeable. If you simply identify the various parts of the poem, you may be able to demonstrate some knowledge of the poem, but without considering how those parts contribute to the whole, you will not be able to demonstrate much understanding. The ability to comment on the *effects* of the poet's choices, as opposed to just *recognizing* those choices, is the difference between a superficial analysis and a sophisticated analysis.

Think back to 'Nighttime Fires', the poem in the annotation example from Chapter 1 and in the title analysis earlier in this chapter. See below how the student's analysis has focused on a few key points and pulled everything together to demonstrate an appreciation for Barreca's craft as a poet. Consider how the student demonstrates both knowledge *and* understanding of the poem.

In her poem 'Nighttime Fires', Regina Barreca creates an evocative depiction of a strange and disturbing childhood remembrance. This haunting narrative recounts a family routine where the speaker's father, unemployed, aimless and disillusioned with society, excitedly rouses his wife and children to follow the wailing fire engines and watch late night house fires. Through the use of subtle metaphors, childlike language and shifting tones, Barreca draws a portrait of a man broken by failure, envy and a sense of injustice, and exposes to the reader the ugly human desire to watch those more successful crumble.

The fiery destruction of the houses in wealthy neighbourhoods longed for by the speaker's father can be interpreted as a metaphor for his state of mind. He finds retribution for the wrongs committed against him by society in watching others, whose 'Cadillacs' and 'curved driveways' taunt him with their comparative success, experience loss and trauma – 'his face lit up in the heat given off by destruction like something was being made, or was being set right'. The father's emotionally damaged state is perhaps best exemplified in the metaphor of the last line where his eyes are 'like hallways filled with smoke'. He himself is like the smouldering ruins of the burned homes he is drawn to, left increasingly empty and devastated after each vengeful, voyeuristic outing.

The poem uses familiar and nostalgic language to create a soothing, innocent mood that lies in stark contrast to the disturbing nature of the poem's events. In using the childlike term 'nighttime' the poem's title, 'Nighttime Fires' suggests a warm and cosy atmosphere perhaps set around an evening campfire. The implicated fire seems comforting rather than dangerous. The nostalgic language continues, fondly describing the children's 'pyjamas and running noses' and showing the giddy excitement the children feel as they 'longed for burnt wood and a smell of flames high into the sky'. The narrator affectionately refers to their bitter father as 'my old man'. The emergency fire engines speeding through the dark city are remembered as a 'festival, carnival'. This disconnect between the mood evoked and the actual events of the memories show how oblivious the children were to the unusual behaviour displayed by their father and tolerated by their mother. The distant sentimentality of this perspective allows the reader to make an independent judgement of the poem's subject without much speaker bias. The now adult speaker struggles with what previously they didn't understand.

In the second half of the poem, the tone shifts to become more solemn and wistful, returning to the attitude of the speaker in the poem's opening lines. The poem began with the poet recalling their father, who had been killing time in the middle of the night, spurred to action by the call of the siren. Like the beautiful yet dangerous creatures of Greek mythology who lured sailors to shipwreck, the fire engine's siren seems to have an irresistible effect on the speaker's father who is also drawn to destruction. The family was all pulled together and united by the father's dark obsession. The normally distant parent 'who never held us' would share his voyeurism with the children pointing things out to them, but 'when it was finally over' and 'nothing else could burn', 'the glow of the nighttime fire' no longer unites the family. The mother drifts off to sleep; the children huddle 'behind', separated from their parents; and the father is again withdrawn and perhaps like the house they've left in ruins, he too is ready to collapse. This shifting tone reveals the effects the father's actions have on his family and reveal the emotionally detached state of the father and its effect on his family. The family is only intimate when caught up in an exciting ordeal when the father is able to openly express the harsh internal feelings pent up inside. Once these sentiments have been expended, he, and with him his family, returns to his isolated state. This reveals to the reader the extent to which the father's withdrawal and depression dominate the family dynamic.

Ultimately it is the innocent yet aware perspective which makes this poem so startling. Through the study of the speaker's father and his actions, the poem magnifies uncomfortable aspects of human nature: jealousy and vindictiveness. The reader is left discomforted at the detachment with which the family celebrates others' losses and the translation of that detachment to the family dynamic where the only sense of intimacy is through shared experience rather than emotional connection.

Consider what this student has achieved: she has not picked apart every aspect of the poem; rather, she has focused on three key points which she develops in detail, using specific evidence from the poem to support her analysis. She considers the use of extended metaphor; the effects of diction (specifically, words and phrases with nostalgic connotations); and the shifting tone of the speaker. She ties all of these elements together to paint a picture of the emotional state of the father and comment on larger themes. Another student may offer a different analysis, and this would be valid. This student's response is focused and relies on the language of the poem to support her points.

ACTIVITY 13: INDEPENDENT ANALYSIS

Now that you have had the chance to focus on the individual elements of a poem in the previous exercises, try to pull everything together and annotate the following poem. Consider how the poet uses different tools to create meaning. Use the accompanying questions to guide you through the exercise; if they are not helpful, feel free to use one of the strategies outlined in Chapter 1.

Five Lemons

by Grevel Lindop

Here are five lemons from the poet's garden,
the colour of white gold and icy sunshine,
flooded with green around the pointed nipples.
My younger daughter cuts one into quarters,
5   careful of fingers, bites the white-furred pith out,
devours the quartz-white segments with her eyes shut,
sighing and swaying in the sharp enjoyment.

Here are four lemons from the poet's garden:
one perched on three, a perfect tetrahedron.
10   The poet's widow showed me where to pick them,
kindly and shrewd, helping me find the best ones,
holding the branch down while I snapped the stalks off,
the cold breeze in our faces from the mountain.
We'll halve this one and squeeze it over couscous.

15   Here are three lemons from the poet's garden
still in the bowl, turned in a neat triangle,
yellower now. My elder daughter chooses,
after long thought, one for her still-life painting,
the twisted leaves like green airplane-propellers
20   with a Cezanne pear and a Braque violin,
fractured into art-deco Cubist slices.

Here are two lemons from the poet's garden
below his tall house on the terraced hillside,
red earth black-pitted with his fallen olives
25   between the gnarled trunks trailing silver foliage,
beside the boulders of the dusty torrent
rainless above that sea of sparkling turquoise.
The juice is perfect for a tuna salad.

Here is a lemon from the poet's garden,
30   the last of them. Long is the poet gone,
silent his grave on the hilltop under the cypress,
long the shadows drawn by moon and sun

out from the low walls and high gate of the graveyard.
I press the waxy peel to my face and breathe it.
35 There are no words for what the fragrance tells me.

1 What is happening in the poem – on a literal level?

2 Consider the possible figurative significance of the lemons.

3 Comment on the use of descriptive detail (colour, shape, scent, texture and so on) in the poem.

4 Examine the use of the different senses in the poem.

5 Explore the irregularity within the poem (for example, the uneven number of stanzas, the uneven number of lines in the stanza, uneven number of syllables in the lines).

6 Consider the complexities or even ironies of the last stanza.

Resources for additional study

There are a number of resources available on and off-line to supplement your study of poetry. Stephen Fry's *The Ode Less Travelled* is a witty, accessible book that covers aspects of form and metre, with an emphasis on guiding readers towards writing their own poetry. A slightly older text, *A Poetry Handbook* by Pulitzer Prize winning poet Mary Oliver, has a similar aim.

Poetry Foundation (**www.poetryfoundation.org**) and **www.poets.org** are both useful websites devoted to the enjoyment and study of poetry. Here you will find poems and guides to poems, biographical information on poets, glossaries of poetic terms, information about poetry competitions, and more.

Works cited

'Ada Limon On Poetry Collection, "The Carrying"', *NPR*, 19 August 2018, Web, accessed 7 December 2018 **www.npr.org/2018/08/19/639997901/ada-limon-on-poetry-collection-the-carrying**

Adcock, Betty, 'No Encore', *Rough Fugue*, Louisiana State University Press, 2017 (print).

Ashbery, John, 'The Painter', *The Mooring of Starting Out: The First Five Books of Poetry*, Ecco Press, 1997 (print).

Bishop, Elizabeth, 'The Fish', *Poems*, New York, Farrar, Straus and Giroux, 2011 (print).

Blake, William, 'London', *Poetry Foundation*, Web, accessed 7 December 2018, **https://www.poetryfoundation.org/poems/43673/london-56d222777e969**

Borodale, Sean, '12th November: Winter Honey', *Bee Journal*, Vintage Classics, 2016 (print).

Brooks, Gwendolyn, 'We Real Cool', *Selected Poems*, Harper Collins Publishers, 2006 (print).

Brooks, Gwendolyn, and Stavros, George, 'An Interview with Gwendolyn Brooks', *Contemporary Literature*, vol. 11, no. 1, 1970, p. 1., doi:10.2307/1207502.

Clarke, Gillian, 'Cold Knap Lake', *Letting in the Rumour*, Fyfield Books, 1989 (print).

Coleridge, Samuel Taylor, 'The Rime of the Ancient Mariner (Text of 1834)', *Poetry Foundation*, Web, accessed 7 December 2018, **www.poetryfoundation.org/poems/43997/the-rime-of-the-ancient-mariner-text-of-1834**

Collins, Billy, 'Introduction to Poetry', *The Apple that Astonished Paris*, University of Arkansas Press, 1988 (print).

Dacey, Philip, and Jauss, David, *Strong Measures: Contemporary American Poetry in Traditional Forms*, Longman, 1986 (print).

Dharker, Imtiaz, 'Blessing (Poem)', *Genius*, Web, accessed 7 December 2018, **https://genius.com/Imtiaz-dharker-blessing-poem-annotated**

Dickinson, Emily, 'Because I Could Not Stop for Death', *Poetry Foundation*, Web, accessed 7 December 2018, **www.poetryfoundation.org/poems/47652/because-i-could-not-stop-for-death-479**

Duffy, Carol Ann, 'Anne Hathaway', *The World's Wife*, Picador, 2010 (print).

Dunbar, Paul Laurence, 'We Wear the Mask', *The Complete Poems of Paul Laurence Dunbar*, CreateSpace Independent Publishing Platform, 2015 (print).

Fairchild, BH, 'The Machinist, Teaching His Daughter to Play the Piano', *The Art of the Lathe*, Alicejamesbooks, 1998 (print).

FredTheMister, 'Liz Lochhead-Men Talk.wmv.' *YouTube*, YouTube, 26 March 2010, Web, accessed 7 December 2018, **www.youtube.com/watch?v=SUhlskKe6BY**

Frost, Robert, 'Out, Out', *Poetry Foundation*, Web, accessed 7 December 2018, **www.poetryfoundation.org/poems/53087/out-out**

Gioia, Dana, 'Planting a Sequoia', *The Gods of Winter*, Peterloo Poets, 1991 (print).

Gomez, Rodney, 'How to Dismantle a Heart', *Citizens of the Mausoleum*, Sundress Publications, 2018 (print).

Heaney, Seamus, 'Blackberry Picking', *Death of a Naturalist*, Faber & Faber, 2006 (print).

Heaney, Seamus, 'Death of a Naturalist', *Death of a Naturalist*, Faber & Faber, 2006 (print).

Hughes, Langston, 'Let America Be America Again', *The Collected Poems of Langston Hughes*, Alfred A. Knopf, Inc., 1994 (print).

Keats, John, 'To Autumn', *Poetry Foundation*, Web, accessed 7 December 2018, **www.poetryfoundation.org/poems/44484/to-autumn**

Limón, Ada, 'The Contract Says: We'd Like the Conversation To Be Bilingual', *The Carrying*, Milkweed Editions, 2018 (print).

Lindop, Grevel, 'Five Lemons', *Playing With Fire*, Carcanet Press Ltd, 2006 (print).

Lochhead, Liz, 'My Rival's House', *A Choosing: Selected Poems,* Polygon, 2011 (print).

Lowell, Amy, 'Bath', *The Complete Poetical Works of Amy Lowell*, Houghton Mifflin Company, 1955 (print).

McKay, Claude, 'America', *Poets.org*, Academy of American Poets, 8 August 2017, Web, accessed 7 December 2018, **www.poets.org/poetsorg/poem/america-2**

Montague, John, 'The Water Carrier', *Collected Poems*, Gallery Press, 1995 (print).

Olds, Sharon, 'I Go Back to May 1937', *Strike Sparks: Selected Poems 1980–2002*, Alfred A. Knopf, 2004 (print).

Orr, Bob, 'A Country Shaped like a Butterfly's Wing', *Valparaiso*, Auckland University Press, 2002 (print).

Pardlo, Gregory, 'Double Dutch', *Totem*, The American Poetry Review, 2007.

Pavese, Cesare, 'Passerò per Piazza Di Spagna', VIVIT, Web, accessed 19 April 2019, **www.viv-it.org/schede/passerò-piazza-di-spagna**

Plath, Sylvia, 'Daddy', *Ariel: The Restored Edition*, Faber and Faber Limited, 2007 (print).

Searls, D, 'Write Tight', *The Paris Review*, 2018, Web, accessed 3 October 2018, **https://www.theparisreview.org/blog/2015/04/21/write-tight/**

Shakespeare, William, *Hamlet*, Richard Andrews ed., Cambridge, Cambridge University Press, 2014.

Shakespeare, William, *Romeo and Juliet*, Rex Gibson *et al.*, eds., Cambridge University Press, 2014.

Smith, Patricia, '5 P.M., Tuesday, August 23, 2005', *Blood Dazzler*, Coffee House Press, 2008 (print).

Strand, Mark, 'Eating Poetry', *Selected Poems*, Alfred A. Knopf, 1979 (print).

Thomas, Dylan, 'Do Not Go Gentle Into That Good Night', *The Poems of Dylan Thomas*, New Directions, 1952 (print).

Trethewey, Natasha, 'Incident', *Native Guard*, Mariner Books, 2007 (print).

Whitman, Walt, 'O Captain! My Captain!', *Leaves of Grass.* Createspace Independent Publishing Platform, 2009 (print).

Williams, Miller, *Patterns of Poetry*, Baton Rouge: Louisiana State University Press, 1987 (print).

Wordsworth, William, 'Composed Upon Westminster Bridge', *Poetry Foundation*, Web, accessed 7 December 2018, **https://www.poetryfoundation.org/poems/45514/composed-upon-westminster-bridge-september-3-1802**

'Quotes About Poetry', Writerswrite.com, 2018, Web, accessed 4 October 2018, **https://www.writerswrite.com/poetry/quotes/**

Yeats, WB, 'The Lake Isle of Innisfree', *The Collected Poems of W. B. Yeats*, Wordsworth Poetry Library, 2000 (print).

Approaches to prose

How does prose differ from poetry?

Prose fiction looks quite different on the page from virtually all poetry (though you might occasionally find a poem which looks a lot like a paragraph). The major difference between prose and poetry, however, is not the way it looks, but the fact that prose fiction always involves some sort of story – a series of events told by a narrator for some purpose. Some poems, such as 'Ithaca' by Carol Ann Duffy, also tell stories, but they do so in a fundamentally different way, relying on language which is as sparse as it possibly can be, so that each word carries tremendous weight in the poem as a whole. Refer to the section on prose poetry in Chapter 2 (pages 16–17) for a reminder of similarities and differences. In prose, authors use many of the same strategies that poets use, but prose is not nearly as dense as poetry, and generally requires less work on the part of the reader to work out the intricately created meanings. Both are art forms, but they are different forms. In this chapter, we will look at some of the basic elements of prose and how you might use them to help you understand what the author is doing in the novel or short story.

Understanding the narrator

Understanding the narrator of any literary text will take you a long way towards a sophisticated understanding of that text. The reason for the importance of the narrator is that, although it might be tempting to think of the narrator as the author, in fact, all narrators are creations of an author. This means that readers who assume that the narrator is the author, or even that the narrator speaks directly for the author, make an error. Narrators are not the authors themselves. Instead, all narrators are tools used by the authors as an important means of creating the effect that they want, and many narrators are actually characters in their own right. In order to be able to appreciate the effect, the reader's first job, then, is to work out *how* the author has employed his or her tool.

■ The reliability of the narrator

Reliable narrators know the true story and tell that story. Reliable narrators know the truth and tell the truth. **Unreliable narrators**, on the other hand, believe that they are telling the story exactly as it happened, but for any one of a number of reasons that we will investigate a little later, they are wrong. The concept of reliability was developed by critic Wayne Booth and was first introduced in his book *The Rhetoric of Fiction,* published in 1969. One important idea for you to know is that under Booth's definition, a narrator who lies, that is one who knows the true story and tells it as something else for whatever reason, is not an unreliable narrator. An unreliable narrator believes that he or she is telling the truth.

■ Third-person narration

Third-person narrators are commonly the most reliable narrators. Readers are inclined to believe third-person narrators because those narrators are not developed as characters in the story. They are usually presented as being **omniscient**, which we recognize because they are capable of knowing not only the actions characters undertake, but also his or her thoughts, feelings and motivations.

This passage from Charles Dickens' *Hard Times* features what is possibly the most familiar type of narrator: the third-person omniscient narrator. There are quite a variety of third-person narrators but this is a truly omniscient narrator who knows the thoughts and feelings of all the characters in the novel. In this example, the narrator opens with the kind of classic third-person narrative description with which we are so familiar.

> The scene was a plain, bare, monotonous vault of a school-room, and the speaker's square forefinger emphasized his observations by underscoring every sentence with a line on the schoolmaster's sleeve. The emphasis was helped by the speaker's square wall of a forehead, which had his eyebrows
> 5 for its base, while his eyes found commodious cellarage in two dark caves, overshadowed by the wall. The emphasis was helped by the speaker's mouth, which was wide, thin, and hard set. The emphasis was helped by the speaker's voice, which was inflexible, dry, and dictatorial. The emphasis was helped by the speaker's hair, which bristled on the skirts of his bald head, a plantation of
> 10 firs to keep the wind from its shining surface, all covered with knobs, like the crust of a plum pie, as if the head had scarcely warehouse-room for the hard facts stored inside. The speaker's obstinate carriage, square coat, square legs, square shoulders,—nay, his very neckcloth, trained to take him by the throat with an unaccommodating grasp, like a stubborn fact, as it was,—all
> 15 helped the emphasis. (3)

This narrator knows all about the place where the action is going to happen, and includes a great many details about the character – down to the shape of his mouth, the sound of his voice and the way that his tie fits around his neck.

In the short opening chapters to this novel, Dickens' narrator moves from character to character, giving us an assessment of each one's mindset. He begins with Thomas Gradgrind, moves on to Sissy – Cecelia Jupe – then to Mr M'Choakumchild, Mr Bounderby and Mrs Gradgrind (*Hard Times* pp. 3–15). The narrator sees inside the heads of all the characters and can report them to us accurately.

Even such a narrator as this one, though, needs to be examined carefully, because they do not as a rule content themselves with just reporting facts. A discerning reader will pick up on commentary the narrator slips in, guiding us to think of the characters and events in a certain way. Take this passage, also from *Hard Times*:

> There were five young Gradgrinds, and they were models every one. They had been lectured at, from their tenderest years; coursed, like little hares. Almost as soon as they could run alone, they had been made to run to the lecture-room. The first object with which they had an association, or of which
> 5 they had a remembrance, was a large black board with a dry Ogre chalking ghastly white figures on it.
>
> Not that they knew, by name or nature, anything about an Ogre. Fact forbid! I only use the word to express a monster in a lecturing castle, with Heaven knows how many heads manipulated into one, taking childhood captive, and
> 10 dragging it into gloomy statistical dens by the hair. (9)

The tone of this excerpt clues us to the attitude the narrator has towards Thomas Gradgrind. First, the narrator calls Gradgrind, in his role as teacher, an 'Ogre' (line 5). He also uses the word 'ghastly' to describe what Gradgrind writes on the board. The strongly negative connotation of both of those words tell us that the narrator disapproves of Gradgrind's actions. In the second paragraph, the 'Fact forbid!' and especially the exclamation mark, indicates a kind of false horror with which we are all familiar. The final image, on lines 9–10, of the children being dragged by their hair into a dark cave adds to the potent negativity of the description, and we are left with the clear understanding that this narrator thinks that what Mr Gradgrind considers to be 'education' is actually an abomination.

Even with a seemingly innocuous third-person narrator, then, you must be alert for clues as to the narrator's intentions. If you pay attention closely to the tone, the vocabulary that the narrator uses, as well as the images and metaphors, you will understand how the author, through the narrator, is guiding you to a particular reaction to the characters and events of the work.

■ Free indirect speech

KEY TERM

Free indirect speech – a narrative trick whereby the narrator is expressing a character's thoughts without quotation marks, so that we hear the thoughts not as reported by an onlooker or listener, but in their unedited form, as the characters themselves experience them.

Free indirect speech is a narrative trick, the invention of which has long been attributed to Jane Austen. Her narrators clearly have access to the thoughts of some or all of the characters in the novels; however, unlike Dickens's narrators, they do not simply report thoughts and then comment on the personalities and behaviours of the characters. Instead, Austen's narrators rely heavily on a technique of speaking the characters' thoughts without quotation marks, so that we hear the thoughts not as reported by an onlooker or listener, but in their unedited form, as the characters themselves experience them. When we have access to thoughts in that form, we have the opportunity to assess for ourselves the ways in which the thinker of those thoughts might be deluded, confused or wrong.

■ *Emma* by Jane Austen

One of the main plots in Austen's *Emma* is Emma's plan to marry off her friend Harriet to a man whom she, Emma, thinks suitable. She fixes first on Mr Elton, and actively encourages Harriet to consider Mr Elton as a likely suitor. In one scene, Emma engages in a little subterfuge: she pretends that her shoe has been damaged and that she cannot walk home again unless she can get a piece of ribbon to fix it. This 'accident' occurs, conveniently, just outside Mr Elton's house, and he, when appealed to, naturally invites the two young ladies in. Emma leaves with the housekeeper to fix the shoe, leaving Harriet alone with Mr Elton. The narrator provides us with this recounting of Emma's thoughts upon her returning to Harriet:

> The lovers were standing together at one of the windows. It had a most favourable aspect; and, for half a minute, Emma felt the glory of having schemed successfully. But it would not do; he had not come to the point. He had been most agreeable, most delightful. He had told Harriet that he had seen
> 5 them go by, and had purposefully followed them; other little gallantries and allusions had been dropped, but nothing serious.
>
> 'Cautious, very cautious,' thought Emma; 'he advances inch by inch, and will hazard nothing until he believes himself secure.'
>
> Still, however, though everything had not been accomplished by her
> 10 ingenious device, she could not but flatter herself that it had been the occasion of much present enjoyment to both, and must be leading them forward to the great event. (112)

This passage shows us the difference between the narrator's reporting actual thoughts, almost as dialogue; this is free indirect speech. Lines 7–8 are the words that Emma thinks, which we know because of the quotation marks. Lines 1–6 are free indirect speech: we know that these are Emma's thoughts rather than the narrator reporting facts, because those thoughts are actually quite misguided. Astute readers will have already picked up on the fact, elsewhere, that Mr Elton is in love with Emma (in fact, he proposes marriage to her a short time later), and it is Emma who has deluded herself into thinking that her wishes for the match between Harriet and Mr Elton are going to be fulfilled. The narrator does not have to tell us that Emma is deluded; we know this because of our knowledge of Mr Elton's true wishes, and because Emma's thoughts are so arrogant. It is Emma who, in line 1, calls Harriet and Mr Elton 'lovers', not the narrator. It is Emma who 'felt the glory of having schemed successfully'. We know the kind of trick that Emma used to get Mr Elton alone with Harriet is not really something of which she ought to be proud. If, indeed, Mr Elton were in love with Harriet he would not need Emma to trick him into seeking Harriet out. And it is Emma who, in lines 9–11 is feeling very pleased with herself. We recognize someone who is arrogant and who is apparently far more interested in her own perceived achievements than she is in the happiness of her supposed friend. The use of the free indirect speech allows the author, through the narrator, to guide us to understanding that Emma is interfering where she really has no business to interfere, and to suspect that things are not going to work out for Emma and her plans.

In both of these examples, and indeed in virtually all third-person narratives, we trust the third-person narrators because of his or her omniscience. It's a convention with which we as readers are quite familiar. Your job as a reader of the vast majority of third-person narratives is not to decide whether the narrator is trustworthy, but rather to decide what clues the narrator is giving you as to the author's purpose, and to the attitudes we are expected to take towards the characters and their actions.

■ First-person narration

First-person narrators, on the other hand, are not to be trusted nearly so readily. First-person narrators are characters in the stories they tell – at least in a minor role. As actual characters, they are subject to all the flaws and foibles to which humans are vulnerable. That means we, as readers, have to be on the lookout for a variety of potential problems which can undermine the narrator's reliability, such as the following:

- The narrator might be lying.

- The narrator might have a mental health condition.

- The narrator might be so emotionally invested in one or more of the characters that he or she is driven to view the events in a biased way.

- The narrator might not know the whole story (this is almost certainly true – who among us knows all the truth of any situation in which we find ourselves?) and might not realize the extent of his or her own ignorance.

- The narrator might be extremely arrogant, unable to believe that he or she could possibly be wrong about anything.

- The narrator might be suffering from extreme duress due, for example, to the loss of a loved one, and might be emotionally unable to face the truth.

- The narrator might be trying to convince him or herself that the story is true because he or she wants or needs, badly, to believe it.

These are not the only forces that might operate on a narrator to keep him or her from telling the truth, but they are a good representative list. The fun of reading a first-person narrative is, first, in figuring out whether the narrator is reliable and second, if they are not, determining the cause of the unreliability. Very often the author is actually giving us a story about the narrator, while the narrator is giving us a story about something else.

■ *The Good Soldier* by Ford Madox Ford

The Good Soldier by Ford Madox Ford is a typical portrayal of an unreliable narrator. The narrator is a man who has suffered a great shock. We learn, right at the beginning of the novel, that his wife has recently died and he has just discovered that she had, for nine years, been having an affair with the man whom he, the narrator, previously considered to be his best friend.

> This is the saddest story I have ever heard. We had known the Ashburnhams for nine seasons of the town of Nauheim with an extreme intimacy—or, rather, with an acquaintanceship as loose and easy and yet as close as a good glove's with your hand. My wife and I knew Captain and Mrs Ashburnham as
> 5 well as it was possible to know anybody, and yet, in another sense, we knew nothing at all about them. This is, I believe, a state of things only possible with English people of whom, till today, when I sit down to puzzle out what I know of this sad affair, I knew nothing whatsoever.

This is the first paragraph of the novel, and you can already see the unreliability of the narrator. He contradicts himself several times over the degree of knowledge he has of his friends of nine years, calling it in turns 'intimacy', 'acquaintanceship' and like a glove on one's hand. He says he knew them as well as it is possible to know others, and then he immediately says that he didn't know them at all. Any time you encounter this kind of muddled thinking, you should immediately begin asking yourself whether the narrator is unreliable and to what degree.

The Good Soldier turns out to be the story of the narrator and his reaction to events much more than it is the story of Edward Ashburnham and Mrs Dowell. The latter is the story the narrator thought he was telling. The former is the story the author is telling.

In order to discover and understand an unreliable narrator, you, as reader, must ask yourself some questions:

1   **Why is this narrator telling the story? What has prompted him or her to speak?** You might discover that the narrator has a large personal stake in the events. In the example above, the narrator has been driven to speech by the shock of the discovery of the betrayal he suffered at the hands of his wife and his friend.

2   **What does the narrator want to achieve by telling the story?** You might discover a situation in which the narrator stands to gain personally from the story being understood in a particular way. In the case of *The Good Soldier,* the narrator, Dowell, wants very badly to talk away the reality he cannot face. He is trying to figure out a way to make the truth go away.

3   **How involved was the narrator in the actual events of the story?** If the narrator's involvement was highly personal there is a strong possibility that his or her perspective will be distorted by bias. In the case of *The Good Soldier,* of course, Dowell is himself the injured party and his world view has been challenged dramatically through a traumatic experience. Such a person is very likely to be unable to see the situation clearly.

4   **Are there any clues to the narrator's unreliability in the style and/or content of the narrative?** Dowell contradicts himself over and over throughout the novel. He also clearly misinterprets the behaviour of the people he is talking about: he insists that Edward Ashburnham is the finest of men, but he also reports the series of adulterous affairs in which Ashburnham has been engaged for years – including with Dowell's wife. The judgement that such a man is a 'fine' person is not rational.

Don't worry if you can't answer all of the questions or if you can't answer them in order. Discovering the answer to one question might very well lead you to be able to answer another. You might find that the third and fourth questions give you the easiest access to the answers to the first two.

ACTIVITY 1: ANALYSING 'WHY I LIVE AT THE P.O.' BY EUDORA WELTY

Here are the opening two paragraphs from 'Why I Live at the P.O.' This is the story of a woman we know only as 'Sister', who has a job at the local post office and who has recently moved in there to stay. The story is her explanation of why she has done so.

Read the two paragraphs and look for clues about to Sister's unreliability. Ask yourself the four questions listed in the green box on page 61, and see how many of them you can answer. Once you have decided for yourself, you can read the explanatory notes at the end of this book.

> I was getting along fine with Mama, Papa-Daddy and Uncle Rondo until my sister Stella-Rondo just separated from her husband and came back home again. Mr. Whitaker! Of course I went with Mr. Whitaker first, when he first appeared here in China Grove, taking 'Pose Yourself' photos, and Stella-Rondo broke us up. Told him I was one-sided. Bigger on one side than the
> 5   other, which is a deliberate, calculated falsehood: I'm the same. Stella-Rondo is exactly twelve months to the day younger than I am and for that reason she's spoiled.
>
> She's always had anything in the world she wanted and then she'd throw it away. Papa-Daddy gave her this gorgeous Add-a-Pearl necklace when she was eight years old and she threw it away playing baseball when she was nine, with only two pearls. (89)

■ Final notes about the first-person narrator

Although it is true that many first-person narrators are unreliable to some degree, it is not true of all of them. Some first-person narrators are balanced, insightful characters who are fully aware of the story they are telling and of his or her own role and stake in it – they are highly reliable. Free indirect speech, because it is so similar to first-person narration, can also reveal unreliability – as it did in the example of *Emma* earlier in the chapter. However, we should note that it is not the narrator who is unreliable, it is the character of Emma. Carried to extremes, free indirect speech can result in a third-person narrator who might be seen as being unreliable, because that third-person narrator is actually giving the reader direct access to the thinking of an unreliable character. Some of Katherine Mansfield's short stories, such as 'Bliss', create just such an effect (Murphy and Walsh).

One example of a text with a highly reliable first-person narrator is *Ready Player One*, by Ernest Cline. Here are the opening paragraphs:

> Everyone my age remembers where they were and what they were doing when they first heard about the contest. I was sitting in my hideout watching cartoons when the news bulletin broke in on my video feed announcing that James Halliday had died during the night.
>
> 5   I'd heard of Halliday, of course. Everyone had. He was the videogame designer responsible for creating the OASIS, a massively multiplayer online game that had gradually evolved into the globally networked virtual reality most of humanity now used on a daily basis. The unprecedented success of the OASIS had made Halliday one of the wealthiest people in the world.
>
> 10 At first, I couldn't understand why the media was making such a big deal of the billionaire's death. After all, the people of Planet Earth had other concerns. The ongoing energy crisis. Catastrophic climate change. Widespread famine, poverty, and disease. Half a dozen wars.

The narrator is speaking about events from his past, which means that there has been time for reflection and for the narrator to develop perspective. He is also knowledgeable about the history of how his society has come to be the way it is, and he is aware of the kinds of serious global problems that humanity is suffering from. He demonstrates that he can make judgements about the relative importance of the death of a famous game designer and poverty, disease, and wars. All of these signify that the narrator is self-aware and trustworthy.

Another reliable first-person narrator is this one, from *The Book Thief* by Markus Zusak.

> When the coughing stopped, there was nothing but the nothingness of life moving on with a shuffle, or a near-silent twitch. A suddenness found its way onto his lips then, which were a corroded brown colour, and peeling, like old paint. In desperate need of redoing.
>
> 5 Their mother was asleep.
>
> I entered the train.
>
> My feet stepped through the cluttered aisle and my palm was over his mouth in an instant.
>
> No-one noticed. The train galloped on. Except the girl.
>
> 10 With one eye open, one still in a dream, the book thief – also known as Liesel Meminger – could see without question that her younger brother Werner was now sideways and dead.
>
> His blue eyes stared at the floor. Seeing nothing. (17)

The narrator of this novel, as this scene reveals, is Death himself. In this incarnation, Death arrives at the scene of every death and collects the soul to carry it into the afterlife. He's actually portrayed as a rather benign and sympathetic character. He doesn't cause the deaths; indeed, he has no control over any death. Instead, it's his job to gather the souls in. We trust his information because we accept the **conceit** of Death as a god-like figure who can believably know everything about everyone. He would have to be omniscient, in order to know when and how everyone is going to die.

■ Second-person narration

If you look up a definition of **second-person narration**, you are likely to find that it's the term used to describe narrators who address his or her story directly to an audience using 'you'. That definition is not really precise, however, because many first-person narrators address a 'you', either real or imaginary. Dowell, in *The Good Soldier*, which we looked at earlier, tells his story to an imagined audience. He sometimes describes them as reading his words and he sometimes describes them as sitting in a room with him, listening to him speak. In another example, the narrator, Sarah Ann, in 'My Sister's Marriage' by Cynthia Marshall Rich, also addresses a listener, one who, we think, is entirely imaginary. We still think of these stories as being narrated in the first person because the predominant focus is on the perceptions of that first-person narrator.

A better definition of second-person narration is that it is the use of 'you' which suggests that the 'you' is the person who has had the experiences being described. Even under this narrower definition, second-person narration is, to some degree, imprecise since 'you' cannot possibly tell the story. Rather, second-person narration has a first-person narrator behind it. The degree to which the narrator identifies his or her own personal involvement may vary from text to text, but in most cases, the pronoun 'I' is as prominent as the pronoun 'you'. What this complicated relationship between 'you' and 'I' means for the reader is that you, as reader, must be alert for the possibility of unreliability, just as you are with a first-person narrator.

■ What's the difference between first- and second-person narrators?

The interesting question for you as the reader is that of who that 'you' is supposed to refer to. The narrator tells the story as if 'you' (whoever that may be) are the one who has experienced the events, but this is clearly not true. The literal you, the real live reader, can never be the 'you' to whom the narrator refers. The narrator does not exist in the real world (see page 57 about distinguishing between narrator and author), and the narrator, therefore, has no idea that you exist. The 'you' is some person, real or imagined, in the narrator's world. The two most likely effects of the use of that 'you' are:

1 **To universalize the experience**. You are probably accustomed to this effect from everyday colloquial English, in which speakers use 'you' to mean 'anyone' or 'everyone'. Someone might say, for example, 'You know when you go into town during the holidays and it's really crowded and you can't find anywhere to park?' This statement is not meant to refer to a specific instance in which you, the actual listener, actually went to the town and couldn't find a parking place. It refers to a common experience that virtually everyone has had. Second-person narration sometimes has that same effect. The narrator uses it in order to draw in the audience by calling on universal experiences.

2 **To distance the narrator from his or her own personal experiences** which have been painful or traumatic, or which for another reason feel somehow alien. This can make it seem as if those experiences happened to someone else.

ACTIVITY 2: EXAMPLE FROM *THE NIGHT CIRCUS* BY ERIN MORGENSTERN

Read the following extract from *The Night Circus* and see if you can decide whether the use of the second-person narration is because the narrator is trying to universalize an experience or because he is trying to distance himself from the action. Give reasons for your choice and use the text to support your answer. When you are done, you can read the explanatory notes at the end of the book.

> 'What kind of circus is only open at night?' people ask. No one has a proper answer, yet as dusk approaches there is a substantial crowd of spectators gathering outside the gates.
>
> You are amongst them, of course. Your curiosity got the better of you, as curiosity is wont to do. You stand in the fading light, your scarf around your neck pulled up against the chilly evening
> 5 breeze, waiting to see for yourself exactly what kind of circus only opens once the sun sets.
>
> The ticket booth clearly visible behind the gates is closed and barred. The tents are stilled, save for when they ripple ever so slightly in the wind. The only movements within the circus is the clock that ticks by the passing minutes, if such a wonder of sculpture can even be called a clock.
>
> The circus looks abandoned and empty. But you think perhaps you can smell caramel
> 10 wafting through the evening breeze, beneath the crisp scent of the autumn leaves. A subtle sweetness at the edges of the cold. (3)

■ A final observation about narrators

You will be a much more skilled reader of prose fiction if you understand thoroughly that narrators are not authors.

Keep a lookout for changes in narration. Many works of literature contain shifts in narrative perspective – the narrator changes in written letters (see *Pride and Prejudice* by Jane Austen), lengthy sections in which the main narrator quotes another character (see *The Great Gatsby* by F Scott Fitzgerald) or actual shifts in narrator from one chapter to the next (see *As I Lay Dying* by William Faulkner). One of the great pleasures of reading is the puzzle of the narrator(s): figuring out what his or her (or their!) real agenda is can be extremely satisfying.

ACTIVITY 3: ANALYSING 'MY SISTER'S MARRIAGE' BY CYNTHIA MARSHALL RICH

Read the following extract from the short story, 'My Sister's Marriage'. Identify the type of narrator and comment on his or her reliability. Provide the evidence from the passage which supports your findings. When you are done, you can read the explanatory notes at the end of this book.

> When my mother died she left just Olive and me to take care of Father. Yesterday when I burned the package of Olive's letters that left only me. I know that you'll side with my sister in all of this because you're only outsiders, and strangers can afford to sympathize with young love, and with whatever sounds daring and romantic, without
> 5 thinking what it does to all the other people involved. I don't want you to hate my sister – I don't hate her – but I do want you to see that we're happier this way, Father and I, and as for Olive, she made her choice. (197)

Characters

■ What is a character?

All readers are used to encountering characters in novels and short stories, but we don't always think deeply about what the difference is between a character in a work of fiction and a real person in the real world. The important thing to remember is that characters are *not* real people. They are collections of features, actions, words, thoughts and, most importantly, motivations. If you take a close look at the descriptions of characters in literary prose, you will find that the descriptions focus very little on the appearance of the characters. You would be hard put to draw your favourite characters from the text alone – this is why people form such strong opinions, both good and bad, about casting choices when books are made into films. Instead, we get descriptions of some physical features, combined with descriptions of character traits.

Take a look again at the description of the schoolmaster, Thomas Gradgrind, from *Hard Times* on page 58. We get a strong sense of Gradgrind as a person, and especially what he cares about. That is the key to understanding characters: what they care about will tell us why they behave the way they behave and, by extension, what the author wants us to understand about people like that.

■ How characters can contribute to meaning

Another important job that you have as a reader is to figure out what each character wants, and then to connect that desire to his or her behaviour. Take, for example, the description of Jay Gatsby in our first introduction to that character from *The Great Gatsby*, by F Scott Fitzgerald:

> But I didn't call to him for he gave a sudden intimation that he was content to be alone—he stretched out his arms toward the dark water in a curious way, and as far as I was from him I could have sworn he was trembling. Involuntarily I glanced seaward—there was nothing to be seen except a single green
> 5 light, minute and far away, that might have been the end of the dock. When I looked once more for Mr. Gatsby, he had gone, and I was alone again in the unquiet darkness. (25–26)

We get an image of Gatsby reaching out his arms and trembling as he gazes on a green light at the end of a dock – both the reach and the trembling convey a deep desire for something. We learn later that the light is the light at the end of Daisy's dock, so we can understand that the dream that drives Jay Gatsby is the dream of possessing Daisy Buchanan.

One other helpful strategy for understanding characters is to look at the ways in which they change – or fail to change – over the course of the story. Generally speaking, there are three kinds of change that a character might undergo:

- **in knowledge**

- **in fortune**

- **in morality**.

While characters cannot really undergo a change in knowledge that results in their having *less* knowledge (short of significant brain damage), their fortune can change either for the better or the worse, as can their moral characters.

'Fortune' in this context does not refer specifically to money, though gaining or losing money might be part of a character's change in fortune. A change in fortune means, more generally, any change in the circumstances of a character's life: a change from illness to health, a change in social status, a change from single to married, a change in the country in which the character lives or a change from life to death are all examples of changes in fortune. When characters change in positive ways, they are generally successful and the ending of the story is also generally positive. When they change in negative ways, or even more interestingly, fail to change when they should, we often have a tragedy.

Jay Gatsby provides us with a great example of how failure to change results in tragedy. Gatsby experiences dramatic changes in his general fortune over the course of his life; he began life as the son of poor parents and he ends up with a vast fortune and the kind of material goods that his parents never even dreamed of for him. Most of that change, however, takes place before the story the narrator, Nick Carraway, is telling. The main events of the novel occur during one year Carraway spent in New York and in this time, Gatsby's fortune and lifestyle do not change. He does end up dead, though, so the change in his fortune is ultimate and irretrievable.

Interestingly, the reason he ends up dead is that he fails to gain either knowledge or improved moral character. Throughout the novel, Gatsby deludes himself that he can shape the world any way he wishes. We saw earlier that the dream that drives Jay Gatsby is the dream of possessing Daisy Buchanan. He thinks that all he needs to achieve his goal is money – that if he just has enough money, Daisy will come to him, and that it won't matter how he got it. Gatsby is wrong on both counts, and his inability to see the world in any different way means that he causes Daisy to turn from him in disgust over his criminal behaviour, and that he cannot recover from her loss. His failure to grow into a decent, moral character and his failure to understand that what he wants from the world – to turn time back five years – is impossible, and it leads, in Gatsby's case, to tragedy.

ACTIVITY 4: ANALYSING A PASSAGE FROM *A CHRISTMAS CAROL* BY CHARLES DICKENS

Read the following extract from Charles Dickens' *A Christmas Carol* and consider the description of the main character Ebenezer Scrooge. Answer the questions that follow the extract and remember to support your answers with evidence from the text. After you have answered the questions, you can read the commentary at the end of this book.

Oh! But he was a tight-fisted hand at the grindstone, Scrooge! a squeezing, wrenching, grasping, scraping, clutching, covetous, old sinner! Hard and sharp as flint, from which no steel had ever struck out generous fire; secret, and self-contained, and solitary as an oyster. The cold within him froze his old features, nipped his pointed nose, shrivelled his cheek, stiffened his gait; made his
5 eyes red, his thin lips blue; and spoke out shrewdly in his grating voice. A frosty rime was on his head, and on his eyebrows, and his wiry chin. He carried his own low temperature always about with him; he iced his office in the dog-days; and didn't thaw it one degree at Christmas.

External heat and cold had little influence on Scrooge. No warmth could warm, no wintry weather chill him. No wind that blew was bitterer than he, no falling snow was more intent upon its
10 purpose, no pelting rain less open to entreaty. Foul weather didn't know where to have him. The heaviest rain, and snow, and hail, and sleet, could boast of the advantage over him in only one respect. They often 'came down' handsomely, and Scrooge never did.

1 What do you learn about Scrooge's physical appearance?

2 What do you learn about Scrooge's personality and moral character?

3 What do you learn about what Scrooge's motivations are?

■ Ghosts as characters

Ghosts are particularly interesting characters; ghosts who appear in novels or short stories exist in a way that they do not exist in the real world outside of fiction. We might expect to encounter ghosts only in fantasy novels, where they can participate in the action just as any other character can; however, they do appear from time to time in much more realistic literary fiction, in which case we have to account for their presence.

In mainstream fiction, ghosts take on one of two roles: they are either symbolic or they are imagined by other characters. In both instances, they are very often manifestations of the memory or guilt of another character. Some famous examples of literary novels with ghosts are: *Beloved* by Toni Morrison, *Lincoln at the Bardo* by George Saunders and *Sing, Unburied, Sing* by Jesmyn Ward.

If you encounter a ghost, then your job is to figure out whether the ghost is intended to be a literal character, or if the author is using the ghost to reveal something important about other characters' feelings and experiences. If the ghost appears to be an actual character, then treat it as you would any other character: try to figure out what its motivations are and check to see whether the character of the ghost changes in any way from the beginning of the story to the end. In either case, you can evaluate the other characters' reactions to the ghost, and that will tell you a great deal about their frame of mind. Changes in a ghost which a character has been carrying with him or her will also indicate a change in that character's mental or emotional state.

■ Final comment about character

One final consideration when you are trying to analyse character is to identify any conflict in which each character (and particularly the main character) is involved. Characters are commonly in conflict with each other, or with external forces, and that conflict is often the cause of the events in the story. We saw in the section on narrators that they can sometimes be in conflict with themselves – even though they may not realize it – because they want to believe something that is not true. When you are trying to assess character change, you will need to be able to determine *how* that character acted in the face of conflict, as well as *why* that character either triumphed or failed.

Structure

Unlike poetry, prose does not have a set of recognizable structures that we can use as starting points for analysis. However, each work of prose does naturally have a structure fundamental to that work. As readers, we have to figure out how each work of prose is structured. Stories can be structured in chronological order, they can rely on flashbacks, on a particular order based on chapter titles, on a series of changing settings and so on.

In Diane Setterfield's *The Thirteenth Tale*, Setterfield gives us two distinct narrators: Vida Winter, a famous (fictional) novelist and Margaret Leigh, the amateur biographer that Vida Winter has chosen to write her (Winter's) story. The two stories develop in alternating chapters. In *As I Lay Dying*, William Faulkner created 15 separate narrators, all of whom tell the same story from a different perspective. Each chapter is entitled with the name of the particular narrator telling that section. *Their Eyes Were Watching God*, by Zora Neale Hurston, uses an extended flashback, and the events in the flashback move from place to place. *Like Water for Chocolate*, by Laura Esquivel, has 12 sections, one for each month of the year. Esquivel also uses recipes between chapters to help develop images and ideas. The possibilities for structures you might find in a prose work of fiction are endless.

■ *Pride and Prejudice* by Jane Austen

Pride and Prejudice is structured around a series of different communities through which the two main characters, Elizabeth and Darcy, pass. At each site, their relationship develops a little more. In the first section of the novel, the action takes place in Elizabeth's home territory. In that environment, Elizabeth feels confident, secure and infallible. In that situation, she feels quite justified in rejecting Mr Darcy as being too cold and selfish to deserve her attention. Darcy, on the other hand, seeing Elizabeth only against the background of her rude and uncouth family, rejects any possibility of connecting himself to her.

The next environment in which they encounter each other is the neighbourhood of Rosings, the home of Darcy's aunt. In that environment, Darcy is forced to see, in his aunt's treatment of Elizabeth, that rudeness is not a matter of social status, but of character. In her turn, Elizabeth, in that neighbourhood, learns the truth of Darcy's ill-treatment at the hands of Mr Wickham. Out of her own secure environment, she is more open to recognizing her own errors of judgement.

The third meeting between Elizabeth and Darcy takes place at his home, Pemberley. There, they meet in the absence of either family (except for Elizabeth's very respectable aunt and uncle). Here, they can both be seen at their best. The action moves back to Elizabeth's home for the end of the novel, but this time, both Elizabeth and Darcy have changed from the beginning of the novel, and so they are immune to the negative forces which kept them apart in the beginning.

Numerous novels other than *Pride and Prejudice* also rely on a structure based on a quest but your job as reader is to take each work as it comes and to figure out what the author is doing. You can examine the structure by asking yourself the following questions:

KEY TERMS

In medias res – the structural technique of beginning a story in the middle of the action and then going back to the beginning later.

Quest – a journey which results in significant change.

TIPS FOR IDENTIFYING STRUCTURE

1 Do the chapter headings or titles suggest a particular order of events?

2 When does the book begin relative to the events of the story? Is the narrator talking soon after the events, during them or much later?

3 Is the order of events chronological, or are there flashbacks? The term **in medias res** refers to the structural technique of beginning the story in the middle and then going back to the beginning later.

4 Is there a journey? If so, is it a **quest**? You can find out more about quest from reading Joseph Campbell's work, *Hero With a Thousand Faces*, on 'the hero's journey'.

5 What other patterns can you see in the way that the events of the story have been arranged into a narrative?

6 Are the events in the different sections divided into types – one type per section?

7   Do the characters change from section to section?

8   Do the events somehow escalate in importance or drama from section to section?

9   What can recognizing these sections contribute to my understanding of what the author is up to?

■ Stream of consciousness

One type of narration that really influences the structure of a work is **stream of consciousness**. A stream-of-consciousness narration is one in which the narrator just says whatever comes into his or her head as he or she thinks it. This strategy affects structure because the order of events is not planned in advance and can seem somewhat random, although it really is not. The metaphor is of a stream, not of an avalanche! The thoughts lead inevitably one to the next; they don't all spill out in a random explosion of ideas. Your job, when reading a stream-of-consciousness narration, is to consider how the events relate to each other. Ask yourself why one thought lead to the next thought. One very famous example of a stream-of-consciousness narration is William Faulkner's *Light in August.* Here is an extract:

> The brother worked in the mill. All the men in the village worked in the mill or for it. It was cutting pine. It had been there seven years and in seven years more it would destroy all the timber within its reach. Then some of the machinery and most of the men who ran it and existed because of and
> 5   for it would be loaded onto freight cars and moved away. But some of the machinery would be left, since new pieces could always be bought on the installment plan—gaunt, staring, motionless wheels rising from mounds of brick rubble and ragged weeds with a quality profoundly astonishing, and gutted boilers lifting their rusting and unsmoking stacks with an air stubborn,
> 10 baffled and bemused upon a stumppocked scene of profound and peaceful desolation, unplowed, untilled, gutting slowly into red and choked ravines beneath the long quiet rains of autumn and the galloping fury of vernal equinoxes. (4)

Notice how the passage begins with the brother, but then immediately passes on to all the men who worked in the mill, and then on to the mill itself, ending, eventually, with a description of the effect of the machines on the environment of the village. You can get great insight into how the mind of a narrator works by examining the pathways his or her stream of consciousness takes.

■ Final observations about structure

Structure in prose can sometimes be difficult to recognize. Its role in creating meaning will be more important in some works than in others. If you can find a structure, then think about how it helps you understand the work, but if you can't find one, move on to examining the other elements described in this chapter. You can often come up with an excellent and insightful interpretation without being able to identify a particular structure, and, furthermore, examining the other elements might help you recognize the structure that is there.

Plot

In its most basic form, the **plot** in a work of prose fiction is a sequence of interrelated events. You may be familiar with a simple five-stage plot structure proposed by Gustav

Freytag as a modification of Aristotle's triangular model for plots ('An Online Resource Guide for Freytag's Pyramid'). **Freytag's pyramid** includes an introduction, rising action, climax, falling action and resolution. This map can be a useful guide to help you identify parts of a literary prose work; however, it tends to be pretty simplistic and will not really work for a lengthy or complicated novel or story. It can still help you identify some elements of, say, a novel, but alone will not help you understand nuances. Allen Tilley at the University of North Florida proposed a more complicated model which is called the **plot snake**, and which involves a series of what Freytag called rising and falling actions with an ultimate resolution. This model reminds us that most narratives are not simple matters of one conflict with one crisis and one resolution.

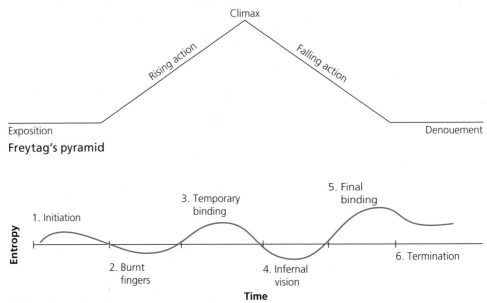

Freytag's pyramid

The plot snake

Notice that this kind of model for plot is really about structure, which is addressed on page 67.

Another way to think of plot is to categorize the kinds of stories that people write: comedy, tragedy, quest, rags to riches, love stories and so on. A third way to think of plot is the idea that plot always revolves around **conflict**, and you are probably familiar with basic kinds of conflicts: man vs man, man vs nature, and man vs self. (By 'man', of course, we mean human! The traditional nomenclature does not imply that women cannot be involved in conflicts.)

■ Final comments about plot

The plot is, of course, at the centre of any story; however, paradoxically, just identifying a list of important events will not do much to help you understand the author's purpose. Instead, detangling the elements of narrative that are the underpinning to plot will reveal much more. The sections in this chapter on narrator, characters and structure give you specific strategies for understanding significant elements of what we normally call plot, because those elements of prose work together to comprise the plot. The plot is made up of the characters' actions, which are driven by their motivations, and the order in which we get those events is determined by the narrator, who has motivations of his or her own, which affect how we are told the story.

Setting

Setting is a lot more than just the place where the events of the story happen. Authors choose their settings carefully, just as they choose their narrators, characters and events.

KEY TERMS

Freytag's pyramid – a way of looking at plot that includes an introduction, rising action, climax, falling action and resolution.

Entropy – a state of disorder.

Plot snake – a series of rising and falling actions with a resolution.

Conflict – a struggle between two opposing forces.

Setting – the place where events of the story happen.

KEY TERMS

Functions of setting – the role that a setting plays in conveying meaning.

Mood – the feeling that is evoked in the reader (or audience) as a result of the tone that is set.

Symbolic – setting which functions as a symbol.

Sympathetic – setting that functions as a reflection of a change in the character's mood.

Supernatural – setting that functions either to aid or to hinder a character's actions, but without exhibiting any will – it helps or hinders simply by existing.

We, as readers, can expect that the author did not choose the setting at random, and so we can expect it to have some significance to the author's meaning. You can, therefore, analyse the setting in terms of how it functions in any particular work of literature. There are seven basic **functions of setting** (Sharpe).

- **Background**: all settings function as background, but this is not an interesting function for literary analysis.

- **Characterization**: the setting around a character can help the reader to understand the nature of that character. Very often when a setting functions to characterize someone, that character has created the setting themselves and that is why the setting reflects his or her nature. For example, Ebenezer Scrooge's cold office is an example of a setting characterizing a person: Scrooge is not a warm, friendly or comfortable person. His freezing cold office reflects that.

- **Mood**: the setting can reflect the mood of the characters in that setting. Weather is often a good tool for this, and one common example is the use of rain to reflect characters' sadness. The setting often foreshadows the mood.

- **Symbolic**: the setting can function as a symbol for something in the story. Characterization and mood are subsets of symbols, where the character or the character's mood is symbolized, but setting can also function symbolically in many other ways. Doorways and windows can symbolize freedom or entrapment, depending on whether they are open or closed. Water – especially immersion in and emergence from, symbolizes rebirth. (The roots of that symbol are in the fact that human babies are born out of water.) The water and the green light we saw in the scene from *The Great Gatsby* (see page 65) are symbols of Gatsby's desire, and, ultimately, of his failure to achieve it. The water, which would symbolize his rebirth into a new man had he been able to enter and arise from it, acts instead as a barrier keeping him from Daisy.

- **Sympathetic**: the setting can function as a symbol for a character's mood, but it does so by changing after the character's mood is established. This function is much rarer than the others; the trick for readers is to establish that the character's mood changes first, and then something in the setting changes. In the scene in *The Great Gatsby* in which Jay Gatsby and Daisy Buchanan come face to face for the first time in five years, it is raining. The two characters are awkward and uncomfortable with each other. But after a while, they get over their embarrassment and re-establish their relationship, and then the sun comes out. The sun coming out can be seen as a sympathetic function of setting, because the weather changes in response, apparently, to the mood of the two characters.

- **Supernatural**: the setting can intervene in the action either to help it along or to hinder it. The critical point here is that if the function is supernatural, the setting does not have any will or take any action – it is just there. For example, if a criminal being pursued runs down an alley where there is a huge wall that traps him, and the police catch up, the wall performs a supernatural function of setting. If the criminal runs down the blind alley and finds a ladder against the wall so he can climb up and pull the ladder up behind him, that would still be a supernatural function of setting. In the first example, the setting blocks the character; in the second, it helps the character. The bay in the Gatsby example can also be seen to be performing a supernatural function of setting, as it keeps Gatsby from getting to where he wants to be.

- **Actant**: this is the most active function of setting. If the setting performs an actant function, it acts as a character. You will be familiar with this function of setting from fantasy and science fiction: the Whomping Willow in the Harry Potter books is an example of the actant function of setting. The difference between actant and supernatural is that actant settings actually take action.

In order to determine the relevant function of setting, just work your way through the list. Don't concern yourself with the background function, but ask yourself if each of the others could be in play in a particular setting. Don't stop looking if you find one function; the same setting could have several functions.

■ *The Underground Railroad* by Colson Whitehead

The **symbolic** function of setting is probably the most common and often the most interesting function of setting you will encounter in a literary prose work. In Colson Whitehead's novel about slaves escaping the horrors of the southern plantations via the underground railroad, he didn't use the term 'underground railroad' simply as a metaphor: instead, he physicalized it. Throughout the novel, an actual train runs underneath the cities and towns, and the escaping slaves are taken down into the tunnels to board the train and be taken to their next destination.

> The stairs led onto a small platform. The black mouths of the gigantic tunnel opened at either end. It must have been twenty feet tall, walls lined with dark and light colored stones in an alternating pattern. The sheer industry that had made such a project possible. Cora and Caesar noticed the rails. Two
> 5 steel rails ran the visible length of the tunnel, pinned into the dirt by wooden crossties. The steel ran south and north presumably, springing from some inconceivable source and shooting toward a miraculous terminus. Someone had been thoughtful enough to arrange a small bench on the platform. Cora felt dizzy and sat down. (67)

The **characterization** and **mood** functions are not relevant in this passage; the train does not stand for any particular character, nor is there anything in the description of the train tunnel that suggests an emotional state. For that same reason, the setting will not have a **sympathetic** function.

The **symbolism**, however, is rich and interesting. Dark, underground areas are commonly associated with danger, evil or even hell. In this case, however, the descent down the stairs into the darkness is a journey towards freedom. The darkness, instead of symbolizing evil, symbolizes protection and security; it is the darkness in which the hunted cannot be seen. The rails are made of steel, which can be seen as a symbol of strength – and of human-made strength. It is by the power of humankind that the slaves are going to escape to freedom, if they do. The rails are described as running from south to north, and traditionally the south is a symbol of confusion or trouble. A journey northward, then, is a journey away from trouble. The ends of the tunnel are described as 'mouths', which is a somewhat ominous symbol: those who ride through the tunnel are, in a symbolic sense, eaten. They do, however, arrive at the other end, into the light. As in the story of Jonah and the whale, the exit from the tunnel will mean a rebirth into a world of light, and light is a traditional symbol of knowledge, wisdom and freedom.

There is an interesting decision for you to make with regard to the underground train and the **supernatural** and **actant** functions of setting. Certainly, the train (which does not appear in this particular passage, but which is obviously coming) carries the slaves towards freedom, so the supernatural function is undeniable. The train helps the characters achieve their goal. An interesting question remains, however: can we see the train as an actual character with a sort of will of its own? You will have to read the whole book to decide for yourself whether that is a viable interpretation; however, the possibility is suggested in this passage by the mention of the mouth, which relates the train and tunnel to something alive.

ACTIVITY 5: ANALYSING A PASSAGE FROM *WUTHERING HEIGHTS* BY EMILY BRONTË

The following passage from *Wuthering Heights*, by Emily Brontë, occurs at the beginning of the novel, when the narrator is describing his first visit to the home of his landlord, Mr Heathcliff. Read the extract and determine which of the functions of setting are used. Check each of the six functions of setting (other than background) and decide if it is at work here. Be sure you can provide textual evidence for your interpretations. When you have finished, read the explanatory notes at the end of this book.

> Wuthering Heights is the name of Mr. Heathcliff's dwelling. 'Wuthering' being a significant provincial adjective, descriptive of the atmospheric tumult to which its station is exposed in stormy weather. Pure, bracing ventilation they must have up there at all times, indeed: one may guess the power of the north wind blowing over the edge, by the excessive slant of a few stunted firs at the
> 5   end of the house; and by a range of gaunt thorns all stretching their limbs one way, as if craving alms of the sun. Happily, the architect had foresight to build it strong: the narrow windows are deeply set in the wall, and the corners defended with large jutting stones.

■ Final comments on setting

There are two things for you to remember as you try to interpret the function of settings in a prose work:

1 Settings can perform many different functions, as we saw in the two examples above.

2 Since the setting nearly always changes throughout the course of a text, you need to be alert to how the different settings function differently.

Literary elements

With the exception of versification – stanza structure and formal metre – all of the literary elements that occur in poetry, and which you can analyse as part of your effort to understand and interpret the content, occur in prose as well. As you read, keep your eye and ear tuned to the possibility that the language being used might be instances of imagery, allusion, figurative language or other literary elements. Novels are significantly longer than poems, of course (and so are most short stories), so you should not expect to notice or interpret every literary element in the text, but the more attuned you are to discovering what's there, the richer and more sophisticated your interpretation of the text will be.

■ *Frankenstein in Baghdad* by Ahmed Saadawi

The first thing you should notice about this prizewinning novel is its title. We have a direct allusion to Mary Shelley's famous novel, *Frankenstein*, and so we know right away that we had better be familiar with the basic story of Dr Frankenstein, an ambitious scientist, and his monster. In Shelley's version, Dr Frankenstein creates a living creature in his science lab and imbues it with a spark of life. The novel is, at least in part, a morality tale about humankind's attempt to play God and to take charge over processes which determine the life and death of humankind. Most people probably have a mental image of Frankenstein's monster: a creature comprised of various random body parts which have been roughly stitched together; the 1931 movie version, directed by James Whale, gave us the monster with the bolts sticking out of his neck (Whale). We know that as we read Saadawi's novel, we will need to check his monster against our idea of Shelley's and consider what similarities, and especially what differences, there are.

As it happens, Saadawi's version of *Frankenstein* is quite different from Shelley's. Hadi is a junk collector who creates his 'monster' out of body parts which are left after explosions in Baghdad, and he does not intend to animate his compiled body, which he calls 'the Whatsitsname'; quite the opposite. Saadawi has given us an **ironic** take on *Frankenstein*.

KEY TERM

Irony – using words or phrases to convey an intended meaning different to the literal meaning or in contrast to the expected meaning.

Hadi constructs the body out of unrelated parts because he wants to give those parts a proper burial. The body is animated by the spirit of 21-year-old Hasib Mohamed Jaafar, who was killed in yet another bombing, and who has been seeking a body because nothing was left of his own after a garbage truck blew up. Similar to Shelley's monster, however, the Whatsitsname moves through Baghdad wreaking havoc and killing people who have themselves been responsible for chaos and destruction.

One further difference between the two books is that the Whatsitsname was built from body parts of very diverse people – men, women, Muslims, Christians, people of different cultures, races and religions (Saadawi 146–7). One idea conveyed by this multi-cultural monster is that all people in Iraq are equally likely to be victims of a senseless war, and all people, regardless of class, gender, race or religion require vengeance – or justice.

Given the quite different motivations that we find in *Frankenstein in Baghdad* from those in the original *Frankenstein*, we know, as readers, that we are seeking different ideas from those of Shelley's: this story is not about humankind's dangerous hubris; rather, it is a story about the meaningless destruction wrought by war. Saadawi has taken the allusion to *Frankenstein* and he has upended our expectations so that he can shed new light on the old problem of senseless violence.

In addition to the **literary allusion**, we ought to investigate the **historical allusion** to Baghdad. The novel is set in the time following the US invasion of Iraq, and so we will be better readers of this novel if we know something about what happened in Baghdad – both in terms of the violence and in terms of the military presence and the power wielded by both American and Iraqi forces.

Those two allusions reveal major ideas in the novel as a whole, but we can also find numerous passages in the novel in which other literary features provide us with insight into what Saadawi is doing. Here is an example from Chapter 6:

> Saidi's car approached an imposing gate flanked by enormous concrete walls of a kind Mahmoud had never seen before in the streets of Baghdad. Night had fallen, and Saidi had taken a series of turns in Jadriya to avoid a traffic jam, so Mahmoud no longer knew where they were. The gate opened, and
> 5 they drove down a long, deserted street lined with busy eucalyptus trees. The farther they went, the quieter it became. The sound of the traffic and the police sirens faded into the distance.
>
> At the end of the street they turned into a side lane, and Mahmoud saw police cars parked alongside an American Hummer and some civilian cars. A
> 10 man in uniform waved them into a parking space.
>
> Mahmoud and Saidi got out of the car and were escorted into a two-story building by a man in civilian clothes. Saidi turned to Mahmoud. 'So, you don't have any appointments or anything' he said with his usual smile. 'Today we're going to have lunch together.'
>
> 15 They went into a grand office, and as soon as they entered, Mahmoud could smell an apple-scented air freshener. (74)

■ Elements of a quest

This passage contains several literary elements that can help us to a richer understanding of what is happening. To begin with, we have a journey by car. Anytime you encounter a journey in a literary text, you should ask yourself whether you are discovering the makings of a quest. A quest is a journey which results in significant change. We do not have, in this passage alone, enough information to establish how significant this journey might be, but we know from the mention of the car that we should keep a lookout for further indicators. You can learn more about the elements of a quest by reading Joseph Campbell's work, *Hero With a Thousand Faces*. Many online sites explain 'the hero's journey' in detail; this one from the University of California has a nice condensed version at **http://web.archive.org/web/20100118100900/http://orias.berkeley.edu/hero/**.

- ■ **Imagery**

  The imagery in lines 1–5 create a sense of isolation from a familiar environment. In this case, Mahmoud does not even recognize the type of wall, so these concrete walls suggest that the travellers have journeyed into the unknown. Additionally, walls are naturally a barrier, whether to keep something in or out. In this case, the journey seems to be into the area contained by the walls, so for the time that Mahmoud and Saidi are here, they will be contained by the walls, apart from their usual environment.

- ■ **Symbolism**

  Trees very often function as significant symbols. When reading western literature, you should always be alert to any mention of a tree which might be an allusion to the tree of knowledge in the Garden of Eden. In this novel, however, we want to be careful about making such a leap of interpretation, since the author and the context of the work are Arabic. Nevertheless, we are told on line 9 that there are Americans present (and earlier in the novel we have been introduced to some Christians), so we should still consider whether the mention of the trees on line 5, and, perhaps more significantly, the mention of the apple scent on line 16, should be considered in terms of the story of the Garden of Eden.

  Eucalyptus trees are not the usual symbol for the tree in the Garden of Eden, but Eucalyptus trees *are* traditional symbols of healing and purity or protection ('Eucalyptus'). The tree is very fast growing and, although not indigenous to the Middle East, it has been planted in Iraq as a means of fighting desertification, that is, keeping the desert from encroaching further and further throughout the country and for reducing the damage caused by sandstorms ('Iraqi Green Belt Fights Desertification').

- ■ **Religious allusion**

  The Qur'an does have a garden story which features the illicit eating of fruit of a forbidden tree. As in the Bible, the fruit is not actually specified; the association of apples with the fruit of the tree of knowledge has a long history, though (think of the symbol of apples as a gift for teachers or as a symbol for teaching). The mention of apple-scented air freshener in the extract might reasonably be seen to suggest that there is knowledge in this place which is not necessarily available outside it, and we are not sure yet whether the knowledge is that of sin and evil, as represented by the Christian Bible, or that of 'immortality and power that does not waste away' (Aslam) as represented by the Qur'an. Possibly both will come into play in this novel. The idea of 'fresh air' adds to this impression that there are new ideas and new knowledge in this place. As readers, then, reading about the apple-scented air, we are cued to keep on the lookout for the kind of knowledge and ideas that are in this place, guarded by those unfamiliar concrete walls.

  One final observation about the apple scent: notice that it is only the scent that we get, not the actual apple. The apple is invisible, accessible only by smell. That fact suggests that the knowledge is either unsubstantial, maybe something that will turn out not to be knowledge after all, or that it is hidden from visitors – or both. We will have to read more to find out.

Given all the elements of this passage, then: the walls, the foreign trees, the apple scent and the journey, we are beginning to get a picture of a place which might serve in this story as somewhere that is safeguarding some important information, but which might be in the service of friends or enemies – we cannot yet be sure. In fact, we find out later that this place is the Department of Pursuit and Tracking – an agency which is mentioned in the introduction to the novel. A government report, which serves as the introduction, tells us that the people who staffed that agency had overstepped their authority, and instead of documenting and archiving important information, had been employing astrologers and fortune-tellers (Saadawi 3). Clearly, then, our assumptions about secret knowledge intended for protection would seem to be true – though not, perhaps in the way we expected. To find out whether the agency was indeed acting in the best interest of the country, we will need to read the rest of the novel.

■ Observations about interpreting literary elements

From our experience analysing the passage from *Frankenstein in Baghdad*, we can make some generalizations about how to approach the interpretation of literary elements in prose fiction. First, we need to be alert to the presence of many literary elements. In the extract on page 74, we found elements of a quest, important imagery, symbolism and religious allusion. Secondly, we need to interpret what we find in the context of the other iterary elements we find, and in the context of the work as a whole. The literary elements have to make sense together. Finally, we should be alert to how the author might have deliberately upended our expectations. In *Frankenstein in Baghdad*, we don't have the traditional Frankenstein monster, and in the passage we examined closely, we don't have the traditional use of the religious symbols of the tree of knowledge and the fruit, or apple.

ACTIVITY 6: ANALYSING A PASSAGE FROM 'THE STORY OF AN HOUR' BY KATE CHOPIN

Now you try it. Read the following extract from the short story 'The Story of an Hour' by Kate Chopin and see if you can discover elements which have metaphorical or symbolic meaning. Look for:

a   significant objects

b   significant images

c   repeated elements.

To interpret the significance of these items, try two things:

1   Consider the features of the object which stand for something else (as we did with the features of a eucalyptus tree mentioned on page 75) and then determine which of those features might apply in a metaphorical or symbolic way.

2   Ask yourself what these objects or images might mean in the context of a story about a woman whose husband has died.

After you have read the story and tried to identify significant literary elements, you can turn to the end of this book for a discussion of some of the things a sophisticated reader might have noticed. The extract occurs in the story right after the main character, Louise Mallard, has been told of the death of her husband. The whole story is very short. It is in the public domain and you can read it online by scanning the QR code shown.

> She did not hear the story as many women have heard the same, with a paralyzed inability to accept its significance. She wept at once, with sudden, wild abandonment, in her sister's arms. When the storm of grief had spent itself she went away to her room alone. She would have no one follow her. There stood, facing the open window, a comfortable, roomy armchair. Into this she sank,
> 5   pressed down by a physical exhaustion that haunted her body and seemed to reach into her soul. She could see in the open square before her house the tops of trees that were all aquiver with the new spring life. The delicious breath of rain was in the air. In the street below a peddler was crying his wares. The notes of a distant song which some one was singing reached her faintly, and countless sparrows were twittering in the eaves.
> 10   There were patches of blue sky showinghere and there through the clouds that had met and piled one above the other in the west facing her window.

■ A note on works in translation

Saadawi wrote his novel in Arabic, and it has been translated into English by Jonathan Wright. Any time you read a work in translation, you must always keep in mind the fact that you are not reading the words the author wrote. Effective translation is a very difficult task, and even the very best translators (of whom Mr Wright may very well be one!) cannot recreate the entirety of a literary work with all its nuances, implications and cultural information. Some words cannot be translated as single words, for instance, and must be replaced with a phrase. Humour may not translate at all.

If you have access to a native speaker of the language in which a text was originally written, you could endeavour to engage in a discussion about a paragraph or more – say the opening of the novel – to see what the native speaker thinks about the quality of the translation, but you must, of course, deal with the text that you have in front of you, and you should treat it seriously as a work of literature in its own right. You can trust that a professional translator has got the story right, and that objects which appear in the translation appeared in the original. You can, therefore, trust that the symbols and allusions are intended, and so you can use them to form your understanding of the text. That being said, however, whenever you are working to understand a symbol or allusion in a text you are reading in translation, you must work to consider the interpretation from the perspective of the cultural context in which the author writes.

Review the translation activity in Chapter 2 (pages 36–37) for a good example of how translation affects a text.

Interpreting non-fiction prose

Since all four literary forms – poetry, drama, prose fiction and non-fiction – are available for inclusion on Exam Paper 1, students at both Higher Level and Standard Level are very likely to encounter a non-fiction passage for the guided analysis task; therefore, you are quite likely to study at least one non-fiction work over the course of your literature programme. With the exception of the unreliable narrator, all of the techniques that have been explored over the course of this chapter apply to the study of literary non-fiction.

In literary non-fiction, such as the literary essay, memoir or autobiography, we assume that the narrator is reliable, even if it is first-person, because the narrator will come as close to being the author's direct voice as it is possible to get. It is useful to remember, however, that even in autobiography and memoir, the voice of the narrator is still a voice which can only represent part of the author's worldview, ideas, beliefs and attitudes. Think about how much of your whole nature and life experience you reveal in any one paper you write – very little. The same is true of authors of literary non-fiction. What we get from a memoir or autobiography is the narrator who is a character in which only certain aspects of the author's personality and worldview are implied or described. You would not be able to describe the author in great detail from reading a memoir – especially in essay form – just as we saw earlier that we cannot create fully developed drawings or descriptions of characters in novels and short stories. Only those features which are salient to the story at hand are mentioned.

Because the narrator is highly reliable, it is generally not useful to try to analyse the role of the narrator as a tool in creating meaning.

All other strategies, however, from structure, to character development, to allusion, figurative language, setting and so on, may be present in a non-fiction work. Here is an example from EB White's essay, 'Death of a Pig':

> Once in a while something slips – one of the actors goes up in his lines and the whole performance stumbles and halts. My pig simply failed to show up for a meal. The alarm spread rapidly. The classic outline of the tragedy was lost. I found myself cast suddenly in the role of pig's friend and physician – a
> 5 farcical character with an enema bag for a prop. I had a presentiment, the very first afternoon, that the play would never regain its balance and that my sympathies were now wholly with the pig. This was slapstick – the sort of dramatic treatment which instantly appealed to my old dachshund, Fred, who joined the vigil, held the bag, and, when all was over, presided at the
> 10 interment. When we slid the body into the grave, we both wore shaken to the core. The loss we felt was not the loss of ham but the loss of pig. He had evidently become precious to me, not that he represented a distant nourishment in a hungry time, but that he had suffered in a suffering world. But I'm running ahead of my story and shall have to go back. (White *Atlantic*)

Starting in lines 1–2, the passage features a metaphor of life as a play with people, and even the pig, as actors playing roles. White uses the language of the theatre to make his point about how the normal routine of his life was disrupted: he moves from tragedy to farce to slapstick. Additionally, the dog, Fred, appears as a symbol of Cerberus, the mythological dog who guards the entrance to hell. In this version, we see Fred presiding over the burial of the pig in line 9.

ACTIVITY 7: LITERARY ELEMENTS IN ALICE WALKER'S 'CRIMES AGAINST DOG'

Read the following extract from Walker's essay. The whole story is about her relationship with her dog, Marley, from the time she first got her and over many years together. Find as many literary elements as you can in the passage, and justify them with text from the passage. Consider the title as well. Once you have done your analysis, you can look at the commentary at the end of this book.

> On entering a place where animals are bred, my first thoughts are always about enslavement. Force. Captivity. I looked at the black and the chocolate labs who were Marley's parents and felt sad for them. They looked healthy enough, but who knew whether, left to themselves, they would choose to have litter after litter of offspring? I wondered how painful it was to part with
> 5 each litter. I spoke to both parents, let them sniff my hand. Take in the quality of my being. I asked permission to look at their young. The mother moved a little away from her brood, all crawling over her blindly feeling for a teat; the father actually looked rather proud. My friend joked about offering him a cigar. (81–82)

Prose and a guided analysis

You will be studying various prose works over the course of your literature course and you will be using what you study on several different IB assessments. Chapter 5 of this book will discuss in detail how to write about literary works whenever you are dealing with whole works. You will, however, be asked for Paper 1, to write about a poem or prose passage you have never seen before. If you choose to write about prose, you will treat the passage essentially as an entire short story. Because your time is limited, you will not have time to look for every element that has been explored in this chapter, but here are some tips for how to proceed:

FIVE TIPS FOR DEALING WITH PROSE ON A GUIDED ANALYSIS

1 When you get a prose passage on Paper 1, it will be an excerpt from a longer work – a novel or short story or non-fiction work. You are not, however, expected to know the longer work, so treat the passage as a stand-alone text.

2 Consider the nature of the narrator first. If the narration is third-person, you can probably move on to other elements for interpretation. If the narration is first-person, you should try to determine whether the narrator is reliable or not. You will, of course, have to stick with the information in the passage, so if you can't tell that the narrator is unreliable, don't worry about it and move on.

3 You can try to determine the structure of the passage. Ask yourself what is happening in each paragraph, or if the passage seems to move from one topic to another to another.

4 Look for as many literary strategies as you can: symbol, metaphor, allusion, imagery, setting and character development.

5 Once you have identified as many elements for interpretation as you can, do not stop at simply identifying them and establishing their presence in the text. You must always explain how the presence of that strategy helps you understand the meaning of the passage.

Bonus tip:

6 You will not be able to write about everything that is going on in a prose passage in the time you have allotted for the exam paper. An important part of your process, then, will be to choose which elements in the passage are the most important in terms of conveying the author's meaning. If you can discuss the three or four most important literary strategies in terms of what they contribute to meaning, you will be doing very well.

■ Final thoughts

Two more important considerations about the interpretation of literary elements in any prose work:

1 You, as an individual reader, might not know everything you need to know in order to pick up on all the imagery, allusions, metaphors, symbols and so on which might be embedded in a text. So one of your jobs, as you read, is to keep asking yourself: 'Could there be a greater significance to this thing than I realize?' You may have to look things up in order to educate yourself. Maybe you don't know anything about eucalyptus trees or about apples. Many objects which might seem, on the surface, to be simple objects, have very interesting symbolic meanings, so it's worth your while to look them up and see what you might learn. If you are a western reader reading non-western texts, you will need to learn as much as you can about the religion and culture relevant to the text, and if you are a non-western reader reading western texts, you will need to learn about western religion, particularly common stories from Christianity. Don't worry that you might miss something; you will. Your job is to be alert to possibilities, to keep asking questions about what things might mean, and to be open to learning something new that might help you understand the novel or short story you are reading.

2 We've seen from our analysis of both *Frankenstein in Baghdad* and 'The Story of an Hour' that the authors worked against our expectations. That approach is a very common one – authors don't aim to tell stories that have already been told, so whenever you discover an allusion or a symbol that has a common meaning, you need to be alert to the ways in which the author may have deliberately undermined your expectations. One of the most important reading skills for you to develop is the skill of being open-minded so that you don't miss something important because it was actually not what you were expecting to read!

Conclusion

This chapter has armed you with a toolkit of approaches to use in your effort to interpret any literary work: novel, short story or non-fiction. We have, however, kept to the most common strategies for the most common type of narrative. You may find that works, especially those written in the 20th or 21st century, have been constructed deliberately to violate the conventions which have been in place for several centuries. You can, therefore, find works in which the characters appear to be aware of their own fictionality and speak to their authors, in which the author declares him or herself to be the narrator, in which the author has tried to eliminate plot and so on. These works are the exception rather than the rule, however. You can approach the interpretation of any work with the strategies in this chapter in mind, and if you discover something very unusual, you can alter your thinking to accommodate what the author has done.

ACTIVITY 8: ANALYSING A SHORT STORY BY RICHARD POWERS

The following short story by Richard Powers was commissioned by *Wired* magazine. The challenge given to many science fiction or fantasy writers was to write a story in six words. Your job is to apply what you've learned in this chapter to analyse the story. Answer the questions which follow the story, and support your answers with evidence from the text. When you have finished, you can check the explanatory notes at the end of this book.

> Lie-detector eyeglasses perfected: civilization collapses. (Powers, *Wired*)

1   What type of narrator did Powers create? Can you tell whether the narrator has any bias or is the narrator highly reliable?

2   Who are the characters in the story? (Tip: the characters may be implied, rather than overtly named or described.)

3   What do the characters care about?

4   What actions do the characters take?

5   What is the basic plot?

6   How is the story structured?

7   Can you tell anything about setting?

8   Do you recognize any standard literary strategies in use here?

Resources for additional study

Some excellent sources to help you learn more about symbolic elements in prose are Thomas C Foster's books: *How to Read Literature Like a Professor* and *How to Read Novels Like a Professor*.

Wayne C Booth's *Rhetoric of Fiction* is an outstanding study of how fiction works; however, it is a formal academic book and is quite long. The chapter on unreliable narrators, however, is well worth reading, even for the casual student of how to read fiction.

Joseph Campbell's book, *Hero With a Thousand Faces,* is an excellent resource for helping you learn both structures and symbols that are embedded in numerous literary texts.

The authors of this book have also written a skills text to accompany the IB Language and Literature course: *Textual Analysis for English Language and Literature for the IB Diploma: Skills for Success*. In that book, skills for reading and interpreting non-fiction texts are covered in much greater depth than they have been here.

Works cited

Aslam, Imaani, 'Adam & Eve In The Quran', *The Revival*, 23 April 2010, 23:52, Web, accessed 21 September 2018, **www.therevival.co.uk/article/adam-eve-quran**

Austen, Jane, *Emma*, London, CRW Publishing, 2003 (print).

Austen, Jane, *Pride and Prejudice*, Clare West, ed., Oxford, Oxford University Press, 2008 (print).

Booth, Wayne C., *The Rhetoric of Fiction*, Chicago: University of Chicago Press, 2008 (print).

Brontë, Emily, *Wuthering Heights*, Project Gutenberg, Web, accessed 10 May 2019. **https://www.gutenberg.org/files/768/768-h/768-h.htm**

Campbell, Joseph, *The Hero with a Thousand Faces*, Yogi Impressions, 2017 (print).

Chopin, Kate, 'The Story of an Hour', *Webtexts*, Virginia Commonwealth University, Web, accessed 22 September 2018, **http://archive.vcu.edu/english/engweb/webtexts/hour/**

Cline, Ernest, *Ready Player One*, New York: Broadway Books, 2018 (print).

Dickens, Charles, *A Christmas Carol*, Project Gutenberg, 11 August 2004, Web, accessed 18 September 2018, **www.gutenberg.org/files/46/46-h/46-h.htm**

Dickens, Charles, *Hard Times*, Project Gutenberg, 20 January 1997, Web, accessed 15 September 2018, **www.gutenberg.org/files/786/786-h/786-h.htm**

Duffy, Carol Ann, 'Ithaca', *Rapture*, London: Picador, 2005 (print).

Esquivel, Laura, *Like Water for Chocolate: a Novel in Monthly Installments, with Recipes, Romances, and Home Remedies*, New York: Doubleday, 1989 (print).

'Eucalyptus', *The Joy of Plants*, The Flower Council of Holland, Web, accessed 20 September 2018, **www.thejoyofplants.co.uk/eucalyptus**

Faulkner, William, *As I Lay Dying: Authoritative Text, Backgrounds and Contexts, Criticism*, Michael Edward Gorra ed., New York, NY: Norton, 2010, (print).

Faulkner, William, *Light in August*, Noel Polk and Joseph Blottner, eds., Vintage Books, 1990 (print).

Fitzgerald, F Scott, *The Great Gatsby*, with an introduction by Matthew Joseph Bruccoli, Collier Books, 1992 (print).

Ford, Ford Madox, *Good Soldier: A Tale of Passion*, Bantam, 1991 (print).

Foster, Thomas C, *How to Read Novels like a Professor*, New York: Harper, 2008 (print).

Hurston, Zora Neale, *Their Eyes Were Watching God; with an introduction by Holly Eley*, London: Virago, 2004 (print).

International Baccalaureate Organization, *Language A Literature Guide: First Assessment 2021*, Cardiff, Wales: International Baccalaureate Organization, 2019 (print).

'Iraqi Green Belt Fights Desertification', *Ecology Global Network*, Ecology Communications Group, 13 June 2012, Web, accessed 20 September 2018, **www.ecology.com/2012/06/14/iraqi-green-belt-fights-desertification/**

'Monomyth home', Office of Resources for International and Area Studies (ORIAS), 13 November 2007, Web, accessed 20 September 2018, **http://web.archive.org/web/20100118100900/http://orias.berkeley.edu/hero/**

Morgenstern, Erin, *The Night Circus*, Vintage, 2016 (print).

Morrison, Toni, *Beloved*, Vintage, 2016 (print).

Murphy, Terence Patrick, and Kelly S Walsh, 'Unreliable Third Person Narration? The Case of Katherine Mansfield', *Journal of Literary Semantics*, De Gruyter, 10 April 2017, Web, accessed 16 September 2018, **www.degruyter.com/view/j/jlse.2017.46.issue-1/jls-2017-0005/jls-2017-0005.xml**

Perry, Sarah, '*Frankenstein in Baghdad* by Ahmed Saadawi review – strange, violent and wickedly funny' *The Guardian*, Guardian News and Media, 16 February 2018, Web, accessed 22 September 2018, **https://www.theguardian.com/books/2018/feb/16/frankenstein-in-baghdad-by-ahmed-saadawi-review**

'An Online Resource Guide to Freytag's Pyramid', Quick Base, Web, accessed 18 September 2018, **www.quickbase.com/articles/an-online-resource-guide-to-freytags-pyramid**

Rich, Cynthia Marshall, 'My Sister's Marriage', *Points of View: An Anthology of Short Stories*, Mentor, 1966, (print) (pages 185–197).

Rowling, Joanne K, *Harry Potter / Harry Potter and the Chamber of Secrets*, Hamburg: Petersen, 2000, (print).

Powers, Richard, (Untitled) 'Very Short Stories', *Wired*, Conde Nast, 1 November 2006, 12:00, Web, accessed 25 September 2018, **www.wired.com/2006/11/very-short-stories/**

Saadawi, Ahmed, *Frankenstein in Baghdad*, translated by Jonathan Wright, Penguin Books, 2018 (print).

Saunders, George, *Lincoln in the Bardo*, Thorndike Press, 2017 (print).

Setterfield, Diane, *The Thirteenth Tale*, London: Orion, 2013 (print).

Sharpe, Jack, 'Teaching IB English HL', IB Teacher Training Workshop. IB Teacher Training, October 1999, St. Pete's Beach, Tradewinds Resort.

Shelley, Mary, *Frankenstein: A Norton Critical Edition*, New York: W.W. Norton & Company, 2012 (print).

Talib, Ismail S, 'Narrative Theory: A Brief Introduction', National University of Singapore, 2004, Web, accessed 15 September 2018, **courses.nus.edu.sg/course/ellibst/NarrativeTheory/chapt6.htm**

Tilley, Allen, '(Plot Snake) Documents', Univeristy of North Florida, 2005, Web, accessed 18 September 2018, **www.unf.edu/~atilley/documents.htm**

Walker, Alice, 'Crimes Against Dog', *We Are the Ones We Have Been Waiting for: Inner Light in a Time of Darkness: Meditations.* New Press, 2007 (print).

Ward, Jesmyn, *Sing, Unburied, Sing*, Bloomsbury Publishing, 2018 (print).

Welty, Eudora, 'Why I Live at the P.O.', *A Curtain of Green and Other Stories*, Harvest Books, 1979, (print) (pages 89–110).

Whale, James, director, *Frankenstein*, Universal Pictures, 1931.

White, EB, 'Death of a Pig', *The Atlantic*, Atlantic Media Company, January 1948 issue, Web, accessed 23 September 2018, **www.theatlantic.com/magazine/archive/1948/01/death-pig/309203/**

Whitehead, Colson, *The Underground Railroad*, Random House Inc, 2018 (print).

Zusak, Markus, *The Book Thief (Young Adult)*, Alfred A. Knopf Pub., 2006 (print). [p74–98]

4 Approaches to drama

What is drama?

When we talk about drama as a form, we are referring to plays – works of any length which are intended to be performed so that audiences see actions and hear words, rather than reading them. Since all four literary forms can appear on your guided analysis paper, you can expect to study drama as part of your Literature course.

■ How does drama differ from poetry and prose?

The major difference between drama and the other two forms of literature that we've investigated so far is that drama very rarely has a narrator. We'll look at the exceptions later in this chapter; however, first we'll explore how to interpret the most common form of drama – that without a narrator.

■ A note about reading vs watching a play

Plays are, of course, written to be performed. The **playwright**, therefore, can be assumed to have been writing with the assumption that an audience will see and hear the story, rather than read it. The playscript is intended for a director and cast to use as instructions, as it were, about what the audience should see and hear. Nevertheless, there is a great deal of room for interpretation. For example, playwrights can differ wildly in terms of how much description they give for what the scene should look like or how the actors should deliver the lines.

■ Interpreting the stage directions

In some scripts, the **stage directions** are sparse. William Shakespeare's plays, famously, have very few stage directions – at least in the first published collection (the First Folio published in 1623). You may find, though, that you are reading one of his plays from an edition to which an editor has added a great many stage directions which he or she has inferred from the text. In the original published version, though, the author's voice telling directors and actors what to do is markedly lacking.

Other playwrights, however, provide lengthy and detailed stage directions. Eugene O'Neill, in *Long Day's Journey Into Night*, for example, wrote long descriptions of what he intended the characters to be like and how all the settings ought to look. Directors and actors then decide how closely they are going to stick to the playwright's instructions.

When a playwright provides very few instructions, those which are present seem to take on a greater significance. Despite the dearth of stage directions in Shakespeare's plays in general, we do find the occasional one. In *The Winter's Tale,* for example, there is a very famous direction in Act 3 Scene 2: 'Exit, pursued by a bear' (Act 3, Scene 3, line 62). This direction is quite famous because it is so strange, and because it poses such a problem for performance. Does one use a real bear? A stuffed bear? A person in a bear costume? The director must consider what effect any of these choices would have on the audience and choose on that basis. In general, it's common to find that striking and unusual stage directions are more likely to be honoured by a director, as they seem to add more to meaning than lengthy, detailed descriptions do.

When you are watching a staged version of a play, therefore, you are seeing a director's interpretation of the stage directions. When you are reading the play, however, *you* are the person who must interpret the stage directions and decide how important they are in terms of helping you understand the playwright's intentions.

ACTIVITY 1: STAGE DIRECTIONS FROM *A RAISIN IN THE SUN* BY LORRAINE HANSBERRY

Read the following stage direction from *A Raisin in the Sun*, Act 1 Scene 1 and comment on what you think is the important information you get about the characters or other elements of the play. When you are done, you can review the commentary at the end of this book.

> [*His sister BENEATHA enters. She is about twenty, as slim and intense as her brother. She is not as pretty as her sister-in-law, but her lean, almost intellectual face has a handsomeness of its own. She wears a bright-red flannel nightie, and her thick hair stands wildly about her head. Her speech is a mixture of many things; it is different from the rest of the family's insofar as*
> 5   *education has permeated her sense of English—and perhaps the Midwest rather than the South has finally—at last—won out in her inflection; but not altogether, because over all of it is a soft slurring and transformed use of vowels which is the decided influence of the Southside. She passes through the room without looking at either RUTH or WALTER and goes to the outside door and looks, a little blindly, out to the bathroom. She sees that it has been lost to the*
> 10   *Johnsons. She closes the door with a sleepy vengeance and crosses to the table and sits down a little defeated.*] (19)

Interpreting the rest of the text

■ Familiar approaches to interpretation

All of the literary strategies we have investigated with poetry and prose can be applied to the interpretation of drama **except** interpreting the role and reliability of the narrator. You need to be on the lookout for: figurative language such as metaphor and symbolism, allusion, irony, functions of setting, character development and so on.

As a brief example, look at the balcony scene in *Romeo and Juliet* (Act 2 Scene 2). The setting functions symbolically because Juliet is physically higher than Romeo, which reflects how he sees her. It also functions supernaturally, as, initially, the fact that she is on the balcony is a barrier to Romeo getting what he wants. Ironically, though, the fact that there are features present that allow Romeo to climb up to Juliet (directors might choose to use a trellis or a tree, for example) means that a portion of the setting also performs a supernatural function, aiding Romeo to get up to Juliet's level. At that point the symbolism also changes: when they are together on the balcony, they are physically equal, and that can be seen to symbolize the budding relationship between them. Directors often choose to have rose bushes present in this scene, as roses reflect the famous line: 'What's in a name? That which we call a rose / By any other word would smell as sweet.' (Act 2 Scene 2, 45–6). Where that is the case, we also have the rose as a symbol of love. Even if the director chooses not to physicalize the idea of the rose, it is there in the text as a metaphor.

So, you can see that you must bring all the skills you have developed so far when looking at poetry and prose to the interpretation of drama.

ACTIVITY 2: LITERARY ELEMENTS IN *A RAISIN IN THE SUN*

Read the following passage from *A Raisin in the Sun* and comment on as many literary elements as you can find. When you have finished, you may look at the commentary at the end of the book.

	BENEATHA	Me? ... Me? ... Me, I'm nothing ... Me. When I was very small ... we used to take our sleds out in the wintertime and the only hills we had were the ice-covered stone steps of some houses down the street. And we used to fill them in with snow and make
5		them smooth and slide down them all day ... and it was very dangerous, you know ... far too steep ... and sure enough one day a kid named Rufus came down too fast and hit the sidewalk and we saw his face just split open right there in front of us ... And I remember standing there looking at his bloody open face
10		thinking that was the end of Rufus. But the ambulance came and they took him to the hospital and they fixed the broken bones and they sewed it all up ... and the next time I saw Rufus he just had a little line down the middle of his face ... I never got over that ...
15	ASAGAI	What?
	BENEATHA	That that was what one person could do for another, fix him up—sew up the problem, make him all right again. That was the most marvelous thing in the world ... I wanted to do that. I always thought it was the one concrete thing in the world that
20		a human being could do. Fix up the sick, you know—and make them whole again. This was truly being God ... (116–117)

◼ The structure of drama

We considered how the structure of a prose work can contribute to meaning; the same is even more true with drama. As a starting point (using *Romeo and Juliet* as our example), drama has a structure that consists of the following components:

- **Opening balance**: the situation in the fictional world at the beginning of the play. People might not be happy, but there is a status quo to which the characters have been accustomed. In *Romeo and Juliet*, the opening balance is a situation in which the two families, Capulet and Montague, have been feuding for some time and in which Prince Escalus has decreed that the fighting in the streets must stop.

- **Disturbance**: something happens to upset the balance and force the characters to deal with an unexpected problem. The Capulet and Montague servants open the play by starting a fight, in defiance of the prince's order.

- **Protagonist**: the character who has the plan for dealing with the disturbance. The plan should have two important aspects:

  - ☐ an objective which is the resolution of the problem

  - ☐ steps to be taken.

  Prince Escalus is the protagonist here. He tries to stop the fighting permanently by threatening to have anyone who starts another fight killed. His plan, therefore, is to use that threat and the steps he takes are to announce the threat, then to meet with the heads of the families to ensure that they understand him. (Note that this is surprising; many people would likely think of Romeo as the protagonist in this play, but the Romeo and Juliet love story is actually a second plot and not the one that opens the play.)

- **Antagonist**: not every play has an antagonist, but many do. An antagonist is a character who is working consciously to stop the protagonist from implementing his or her plan. In *Romeo and Juliet*, it is debatable whether or not there is an antagonist; we could say that Tybalt, who starts the next fight, is antagonistic to the prince's

KEY TERMS

Obstacle – in drama, something that already exists in the fictional situation, which interferes with the protagonist's ability to implement his or her plan.

Fabula – a fictional world created by the writer.

Complication – in drama, something that arises as a result of the protagonist's effort to implement the plan, and which interferes with the ability to employ the plan effectively.

Climax – in drama, the final complication that determines whether the plan is going to be successful or not.

Resolution – in drama, the outcome that brings a new balance.

Suspense – a feeling from the audience when waiting for an outcome.

Dramatic irony – when the audience knows something that the characters in the play do not.

plan, however, he does so in the heat of anger and not specifically in order to defy the prince.

- **Obstacles:** an obstacle is something that already exists in the fictional situation, the **fabula**, which interferes with the protagonist's ability to implement the plan. There might be one or more obstacles. An obstacle to Prince Escalus' plan is the hatred that the two families have for each other – and especially Tybalt's hatred for Romeo. That hatred existed before the prince implemented his plan, so it is an obstacle, rather than a complication.

- **Complications:** a complication is something that arises as a result of the protagonist's effort to implement the plan, and which interferes with the ability to employ the plan effectively. A complication that arises in *Romeo and Juliet* is that when it is time for the prince to order the consequence he promised, he can't do so, as it was Tybalt, the prince's own relative, who started the fight. Since Tybalt is dead already, Romeo is left to be punished. The prince decides that since Romeo did not start the fight, he will be banished rather than killed.

- **Climax:** the climax is the final complication that determines whether the plan is going to be successful or not. If the climax can be dealt with effectively, the plan will succeed. If it cannot, the plan will fail. There is an interesting question with *Romeo and Juliet*, as to what we might call the climax. The puzzle for the audience arises because Shakespeare deftly weaves the second plot, the love and death of Romeo and Juliet, into the first plot – the feud. As we eventually find out, the feud ends when Romeo and Juliet kill themselves, so we can say that the climax is the scene in the tomb during which that happens. That is the action which directly causes the end of the feud, which is what the prince initially wanted. Ironically, his plan was not the reason for his goal being met.

- **Resolution:** the resolution is the outcome and brings a new balance. If the plan ultimately succeeds in solving the problem, then we are likely to have a happy ending. If the plan does not solve the problem, we are likely to have an unhappy ending. Keep in mind, however, that the protagonist might have had a bad plan – in that case, even if the plan succeeded then the ending might, ironically, be unhappy. In *Romeo and Juliet*, given that the initial disturbance was the literal disturbance of the peace on the streets of Verona because the feud between the Capulets and Montagues broke out again, we know that we have a final resolution (apparently) of the end of the feud in the wake of the deaths of Romeo and Juliet. The families reconcile and promise to honour their children.

Two other elements of structure that you are likely to find in a drama are **conflict** and **suspense**. Conflict can arise almost anywhere – it might be conflict between the protagonist and the antagonist, it might be part of the complications that arise from the effort to implement the plan, or a major conflict might even provide the climax. The conflict might be internal to the protagonist as well; it does not have to be a conflict between two different characters. In *Romeo and Juliet*, the many conflicts are famous: the feud between the two families, the conflict between Tybalt and Romeo, the conflict between the prince and the families, the conflict between the servants and so on.

Suspense arises when the playwright keeps the audience waiting to see what will happen next, and, like conflict, it can occur at various places throughout a play. Every time a problem arises, whether it be the disturbance, an obstacle or a complication, and we don't know that the outcome is inevitable, we have suspense. Probably the greatest moment of suspense in *Romeo and Juliet* is the moment during which Romeo is observing Juliet's apparently-dead body and is about to kill himself. The audience knows that she is not dead, and that moment of **dramatic irony** provides suspense.

■ Departure from the basic structure

The elements of dramatic structure that are detailed in the previous section are what might be considered to be standard elements. The fun for a playwright and for the audience, however, is to begin with that basic structure and then manipulate it to create a certain effect. We have already seen some hints of variation from the basic plot structure in the brief examples from *Romeo and Juliet*.

One of the most common variations on that standard structure is the inclusion of subplots, each one with its own structure – balance, disturbance, protagonist and so on. Shakespeare's plays always feature at least one important subplot which offers a different version of the main plot. In *The Taming of the Shrew*, for example, the main plot features the problem of the marriageability of Katherine, the shrew, who battles with Petruchio even after they are married. But there is also a strong subplot that features her sister, Bianca, who appears to be a much better marriage prospect than Katherine, but who turns out to be a problem in her own right.

■ A detailed study of structure in Athol Fugard's *"Master Harold"...and the boys*

The following chart illustrates a detailed structural analysis of *"Master Harold"...and the boys*. On the chart, red text highlights the places where the dramatist has manipulated the traditional structure for his own benefit. It might be tempting to analyse the structure of a play by diligently trying to force it into the standard structure, but one of the beauties of art is that the artist has the power to take the standard and alter it for his or her own purposes. Astute readers know the basic structure and then show that they appreciate what the playwright has achieved by changing it.

Your job when studying plays is to consider how the standard structure has been manipulated *and to what purpose*. *"Master Harold"...and the boys* is a good example to look at in detail because it is surprisingly complex in terms of structure. In a short 90-minute play that features only three characters, Fugard has created a beautifully complex and revealing structure.

Play title: *"Master Harold"...and the boys*

Main story line (main plot): Hally's story

Element of drama	Your explanation: you are required both to identify elements and to justify your claims
Opening balance: What is the status quo at the time that we, as audience members, get access to the events of the fabula?	At the point at which the audience gains access to the fabula, Hally is relatively content. His family life is always bad – his father is an alcoholic, his mother is ineffectual, and no one has time for Hally. At the moment, however, Hally's father is in the hospital, so the usual uproar at home is gone. Hally has been left in relative peace for some undetermined amount of time.
Disturbance: has anything happened to force the characters to deal with an unexpected problem?	Sam tells Hally that his mother called from the hospital, where she has gone in order to pick up Hally's father and take him home.
Protagonist: who has the plan for dealing with the disturbance?	Hally: he is the one who implements a plan in response to the disturbance.
Plan: (Remember a plan does not have to be a good plan, nor does it have to be the result of careful, strategic thinking.) Identify the **goal** and the **strategy**.	Hally's plan is to deny the problem. His goal is to not have to deal with his father, so he must believe that his father is not coming home. His strategy is to argue with Sam and to claim that Sam must be mistaken. This is a terrible plan, in that it denies reality, and it is one that arises without thought or reason. It's a knee-jerk reaction.

Obstacle(s): What elements of the fabula, which already exist before the disturbance and before Hally formulates his plan, present obstacles to the success of the plan? (There may be more than one.) Note: Since you are considering the structure after knowing the whole play, you must identify all obstacles, not just those that are immediately obvious to the audience at the time the protagonist tries to implement his or her plan.	The important obstacle is the fact that Sam is correct; Hally's mother is, in fact, at the hospital collecting Hally's father to take him home. We know that Sam is telling the truth (Fugard counts on the audience's ability to judge character and to know that the petulant child is less reliable as a judge than a patient, kindly grown man), so we know that Hally's plan, such as it is, is doomed to failure. One might also consider Hally's failure to think rationally and to judge based on his knowledge of Sam's actual character as an obstacle.
Complication(s): What problems, which could potentially keep the plan from succeeding, arise as a result of the attempt to implement the plan? Note: Since you are considering the structure after knowing the whole play, you must identify all complications, not just any that are immediately obvious to the audience at the time the protagonist tries to implement his or her plan.	No complication arises out of Hally's arguing with Sam. Sam does not take offence. A complication which does occur arises not as a result of Hally's attempt to implement his plan, but rather out of events that are going on out of his control. The phone call from Hally's mother telling him that she is at the hospital and will be bringing his father home destroys Hally's plan completely, because he has to believe her. Reality does not match Hally's wishes, and he is forced to face that fact.
Conflict(s): What conflicts arise as a result of the protagonist's effort to implement his or her plan? Note: Since you are considering the structure after knowing the whole play, you must identify all conflicts, not just those that are immediately obvious to the audience at the time the protagonist tries to implement his or her plan.	Possibly we might see Hally's mercurial treatment of Sam and Willie as a consequence of the attempt to implement the plan. There is some conflict (mostly one-sided, as Hally is angry at Sam and Willie but they tend to appease him rather than fight back), but I would argue instead that his changing attitudes reflect his own internal state, and not the changing feelings of Sam or Willie. So in this case, some relatively minor conflicts arise out of the disturbance, which is Hally's unwillingness to face reality and to believe what he has been told, rather than directly out of his effort to implement his plan.
Conflicts, continued	The second phone call (again not a result of Hally's trying to implement his plan, but rather the result of his plan clashing with reality), however, causes a major (in the sense of important) conflict between Hally and his mother. As with the conflict between Hally and Sam and Willie, the conflict with his mother seems to be fairly one-sided; Hally gets worked up and angry, but the person with whom he is trying to fight is strangely (to him) unmoved by his emotion. Sam and Willie do not get mad and fight back to Hally (of course the social conditions under Aparthied forbid that), nor does Hally's mother respond by giving in to Hally's temper and giving him what he wants. Hally's sense of conflict, however, drives his future actions.
Crisis/Crises: What obstacles or complications occur which become crises for the protagonist? A crisis is something that must be dealt with immediately because the consequences of failing to act are so dire. A consequence can be a physical, environmental consequence, or it can be a mental, emotional consequence. Note: Anything you list as a crisis must also be on the list of either obstacles, complications or conflicts.	The phone call from Hally's mother definitely causes a crisis for Hally's plan because it puts paid to any idea that the plan, such as it was, could succeed. Hally must immediately abandon that plan and develop a new one if he is to achieve his ultimate goal of not having his father at home.
Climax: Which of the obstacles, complications or conflicts becomes the climax? The climax is the one problem which either is solved, resulting in a successful end to the problem caused by the initial disturbance, or is not solved, resulting in the failure to resolve the problem.	The phone call, in addition to causing a crisis, is the climax of the implementation of Plan A, because it determines, without possibility of a reversal, that the initial plan has failed.

Resolution: What is the final outcome? Think of the resolution as a new balance (which might not be good) which is now in place as the audience loses access to the fabula. What happened to the problem raised by the disturbance? Did the protagonist get what he or she wanted?	The resolution of the first plan, Plan A (denial of reality), is that the plan failed. The initial disturbance has not been eliminated; the problem remains, and now Hally's emotional state is ratcheted even further up because he cannot pretend the problem away. He immediately comes up with Plan B: convince his mother to keep his father in the hospital.
Suspense: Did suspense arise from any of the obstacles/complications/conflicts? (Consider that you may get an exam question about how a playwright generates suspense.)	No particular suspense, since part of what Fugard is doing is putting the audience in the position of knowing that Hally is in the wrong and will inevitably fail.

Element of drama	Your explanation. You are required both to identify elements and to justify your claims
For this play, a whole new structural chart is required, since we have a second plan developed to deal with a different (but very closely related) problem.	
Opening balance: What is the status quo at the time that we, as audience members, get access to the events of the fabula?	There is no opening balance for Plan B; Plan B arises from the crisis/climax of Plan A (the phone call in which Hally speaks to his mother directly for the first time), which might justly be considered to function as a new disturbance, since it requires a new plan.
Disturbance:	See 'opening balance' on page 87.
Protagonist:	Hally remains the protagonist; he has the plan to deal with the problem. Incidentally, it is really only a problem for him – in other words, no one else could possibly be the protagonist, because no one else perceives a problem.
Plan: (Remember, a plan does not have to be a good plan, nor does it have to be the result of careful, strategic thinking.) Identify the **goal** and the **strategy**.	Hally's plan is another knee-jerk reaction, conceived without thought of an emotional need to try to control his circumstances (here we begin to see a pattern which reveals a good deal about Hally's character). His goal is to keep his father from coming home so that his own life will be made easier (unquestionably true), and his strategy is to order his mother around and make her do what he, Hally, wants.
Obstacle(s): What elements of the fabula, which already exist before the disturbance and before Hally formulates his plan, present obstacles to the success of the plan? (There may be more than one.) Note: Since you are considering the structure after knowing the whole play, you must identify all obstacles, not just those that are immediately obvious to the audience at the time the protagonist tries to implement his or her plan.	As with the first plan, one obstacle is Hally's proclivity to deny reality. This problem is the most significant obstacle to the plan, because when he hangs up the phone, after giving his mother a variety of orders about how to keep his father in the hospital, Hally has managed to convince himself that there is a real chance that his plan will succeed and that his father will remain where he is. A second, very significant, obstacle is the fact that Hally's father has already been told that he is going home, and, since he is getting what he wants, he is not likely to change his mind. As we learn over the course of the play, neither of Hally's parents ever seems to consider Hally's needs in any serious way, so that, too, is an obstacle to Hally's plan. Another obstacle is the fact that Hally's mother is the parent and Hally is the child, and the child is unlikely to have any ability to successfully command the parent. We might also consider pragmatic obstacles such as the fact that in no society can one just stay in a hospital because one wishes to. (In this case, however, the fact that the patient wishes to go home is a bigger problem for Hally's plan than the societal barrier to using a hospital as a hotel.)

Complication(s): What problems, which can potentially keep the plan from succeeding, arise as a result of the attempt to implement the plan? Note: Since you are considering the structure after knowing the whole play, you must identify all complications, not just any that are immediately obvious to the audience at the time the protagonist tries to implement his or her plan.	No actual complication arises out of Hally's effort to implement his plan. He gives his orders, eventually hangs up the phone, and then hopes that his mother will do what he says. What we have, instead, is a repetition of the structure which developed as a result of Hally's first plan: he denies reality, eventually a phone call comes which reveals to him undeniably that his father is coming home, and he has to abandon the plan, which has failed.
Conflict(s): What conflicts arise as a result of the protagonist's effort to implement his or her plan? Note: Since you are considering the structure after knowing the whole play, you must identify all conflicts, not just those that are immediately obvious to the audience at the time the protagonist tries to implement his or her plan.	Here, too, we have a repetition of the structure that Plan A generated: Hally is internally conflicted because his fears and desires are at war with each other, and he takes that out on the people around him. Since others do not respond by returning his negativity, his frustration is not assuaged, but the external conflicts are very minor, and Sam, in his role as antagonist, tries to bring Hally out of his mood by focusing his attention on something better (the world without collisions).
Crisis/Crises: What obstacles or complications occur which become crises for the protagonist? A crisis is something that must be dealt with immediately because the consequences of failing to act are so dire. A consequence can be a physical, environmental consequence, or it can be a mental, emotional consequence. Note: Anything you list as a crisis must also be on the list of either obstacles, complications or conflicts.	The second phone call from Hally's mother informing Hally that his father is already at home causes a crisis for Hally's second plan because it drives home the understanding that, as with the first plan, this plan, such as it was, did not succeed – and, possibly worse, never could have. He is forced to realize that his hopes and ideas were foolish and futile. Hally, acting once more in character, immediately abandons his plan and develops a new one, having been forced to accept ultimate defeat, this time, with a new purpose.
Climax: Which of the obstacles, complications, or conflicts becomes the climax? The climax is the one problem which either is solved, resulting in a successful end to the problem caused by the initial disturbance, or is not solved, resulting in the failure to resolve the problem.	The phone call, in addition to causing a crisis, is the climax of the implementation of Plan B, because it reveals, without possibility of a reversal, that the plan has failed.
Resolution: What is the final outcome? Think of the resolution as a new balance (which might not be good) which is now in place as the audience loses access to the fabula. What happened to the problem raised by the disturbance? Did the protagonist get what he or she wanted?	The resolution of Plan B (command people to order the world as he wishes), like the first plan, is that it failed. The initial disturbance has not been eliminated; the problem remains – indeed it is worsened, since his father is actually at home, and Hally must now deal with that fact rather than with the potential for it – and now Hally's emotional state is ratcheted even further up because he cannot pretend the problem away. He immediately comes up with Plan C: get power in the world any way I can, and since I am white, my society grants me power to treat these two black men who are currently in my presence any way I wish. Goal: feel powerful, as a means of off-setting my current feeling of total helplessness and its resultant rage. Strategy: abuse two men who have been lifelong friends because I can.
Suspense: Did suspense arise from any of the obstacles/complications/conflicts? (Consider that you may get an exam question about how a playwright generates suspense.)	No particular suspense, since part of what Fugard is doing is putting the audience in the position of knowing that Hally is in the wrong and will inevitably fail.

Element of drama	Your explanation. You are required both to identify elements and to justify your claims
Extraordinarily, especially for such a short play, a third structural chart is required, since we have a third plan developed to deal with the failure of Hally's second plan.	
Opening balance: What is the status quo at the time that we, as audience members, get access to the events of the fabula?	Because the original disturbance has been resolved finally, there is now a sort of new 'balance' in Hally's world: the opening situation is that he feels weak and powerless, and his rage has got the better of him.
Disturbance:	The disturbance is effectively the climax and resolution to the second plan, so the opening balance, such as it is, is a result of the latest conflict. Nothing further has to happen to cause Hally to institute a new plan – attack Sam and Willie, and especially Sam.
Protagonist:	Hally remains the protagonist, as he is still the one implementing the plan.
Plan: (Remember a plan does not have to be a good plan, nor does it have to be the result of careful, strategic thinking.) Identify the **goal** and the **strategy**.	Goal: Gain power over someone or something – almost anything will do. Strategy: Attack Sam and Willie because, since they are black and Hally is white, they cannot fight back. He is therefore guaranteed (at least in his own mind, conditioned as he has been by Apartheid) to win and get the power he so desperately wants.
Obstacle(s): What elements of the fabula, which already exist before the disturbance and before Hally formulates his plan, present obstacles to the success of the plan? (There may be more than one.) Note: Since you are considering the structure after knowing the whole play, you must identify all obstacles, not just those that are immediately obvious to the audience at the time the protagonist tries to implement his or her plan.	Sam's graciousness, goodness and moral rightness is an obstacle to Hally achieving his plan. Sam is not actually going to sit back and take whatever Hally dishes out, not only because Sam does not want to be shamed, but also, and more importantly, because Sam cares what kind of man Hally grows up to be. Sam is not going to sit by and watch Hally descend into the pit of immorality and bigotry that Hally is at this moment choosing. Even Hally's own nature – or maybe his lifelong experience with Sam – is an obstacle, because Hally deep down knows, and must at some level acknowledge, that Sam is the best thing that has ever happened to him. Sam has been not just a friend but the father that Hally really did not have.
Complication(s): What problems, which can potentially keep the plan from succeeding, arise as a result of the attempt to implement the plan? Note: Since you are considering the structure after knowing the whole play, you must identify all complications, not just any that are immediately obvious to the audience at the time the protagonist tries to implement his or her plan.	Because Sam decided long ago to be responsible for trying to ensure that Hally did not grow into a bigot, he does take on the role Hally did not expect him to take on: the role of the antagonist. Instead of just giving in and saying 'Yes, sir, Master Harold', Sam pushes back against Hally's juvenile behaviour, thus denying Hally the satisfaction he thinks he wants.
Conflict(s): What conflicts arise as a result of the protagonist's effort to implement his or her plan? Note: Since you are considering the structure after knowing the whole play, you must identify all conflicts, not just those that are immediately obvious to the audience at the time the protagonist tries to implement his or her plan.	The conflict that arises is between Hally and Sam because Sam did not just cave in as Hally expected him to do. That conflict escalates rapidly because every time Sam refuses to give in to Hally's temper, Hally gets angrier and raises the stakes by treating Sam even worse.
Crisis/Crises: What obstacles or complications occur which become crises for the protagonist? A crisis is something that must be dealt with immediately because the consequences of failing to act are so dire. A consequence can be a physical, environmental consequence, or it can be a mental, emotional consequence. Note: Anything you list as a crisis must also be on the list of either obstacles, complications or conflicts.	The crisis comes at the height of this upward spiralling conflict when Sam drops his pants and Hally spits in Sam's face. At that moment, Sam has, for the first time, lost control of himself because Hally finally managed to behave in an ugly enough manner to cause Sam to lose his temper. (This is, ironically, the outcome Hally thought he wanted.)

Climax: Which of the obstacles, complications or conflicts becomes the climax? The climax is the one problem which either is solved, resulting in a successful end to the problem caused by the initial disturbance, or is not solved, resulting in the failure to resolve the problem.	Despite the extremity of the hatred and bigotry that Hally has spewed over the past few minutes, and despite that it was, at one point, bad enough to make Sam lose control of his normal ability to see the bigger picture of what is good for Hally, Sam is able, in an amazing act of magnanimity, to put Hally's nastiness aside. He accepts responsibility for his (Sam's) own failure to behave, as he puts it, 'like a man', and to offer Hally a chance to forgive and begin their relationship again. In a play with a true climax and resolution, one would expect that offer to be accepted or rejected definitively, in which case, the offer would in fact function as the climax. In this case, because the offer is neither accepted nor rejected (see resolution below), the offer has the nebulous function of 'would-be climax'.
Resolution: What is the final outcome? Think of the resolution as a new balance (which might not be good) which is now in place as the audience loses access to the fabula. What happened to the problem raised by the disturbance? Did the protagonist get what he or she wanted?	There is no resolution to the disturbance or to Hally's final plan. He did get what he thought he wanted – he caused Sam to call him 'Master Harold' and he gained power, of a sort, by making Sam behave as childishly as Hally himself was behaving. (Hally knows that this is a 'victory' over Sam because Sam doesn't ever stoop to that level of immaturity.) The problem is that having achieved what he wanted, Hally is also forced at last to recognize that he was at fault, that what he wanted and the actions he took were both completely unreasonable, cruel and even immoral. He has come face-to-face in a moment with the very difficult decision of what kind of a man he is going to be. Is he going to choose to be the kind of man Sam is, or is he going to choose to be the kind of man his father is? When he walks out of the shop at the end of the play, he says to Sam that he doesn't know whether he can come back tomorrow and try again. The audience is left hoping that Hally will do the right thing, but fearing that he will not.
Suspense: Did suspense arise from any of the obstacles/complications/conflicts? (Consider that you may get an exam question about how a playwright generates suspense.)	Because of the lack of resolution at the end of the play, we are left in a state of suspense: the audience is deliberately left to wonder what Hally will do. We know that this suspense is not ever going to be resolved.

■ Summary chart showing plot development in *"Master Harold"…and the boys*

Plot	Element	Present?	Description/Departure from normal
Plot #1	Opening balance	Yes	Father in hospital; congenial atmosphere in tea room.
	Disturbance	Yes	Sam tells Hally his mother is taking his father home.
	Plan	Yes	Knee-jerk reaction: denial.
	Obstacles	Yes	Reality.
	Complications	Yes	Departure from normal: complications arise from reality, not from Hally's plan.
	Conflict	Yes	Internal: Hally is conflicted, but others decline to take on a battle with him.
	Crisis	Yes	Phone call reveals that denial won't work.
	Climax	Yes	Phone call is the climax.
	Resolution	Yes	Plan has failed; new plan must be implemented. (Departure from normal.)
	Suspense	No	Dramatic irony: audience knows that the plan was doomed from the start.

Plot #2	Opening balance	No	Same problem carries over from original disturbance: Hally does not want his father to come home.
	Disturbance	Yes	Departure from normal: the disturbance was the phone call which was the crisis for Plan A.
	Plan	Yes	Bully mother into leaving father in hospital.
	Obstacles	Yes	Hally has no power over his mother; can't use hospital like a hotel. (Essentially same problem: denial of reality.)
	Complications	Yes	Departure from normal: complications arise from reality, not from Hally's plan.
	Conflict	Yes	Internal: Hally is conflicted, but others decline to take on a battle with him.
	Crisis	Yes	Next phone call: father is actually home.
	Climax	Yes	Phone call is the climax.
	Resolution	Yes	The original disturbance has now been resolved: the father is home and the protagonist's plan has failed utterly.
	Suspense	No	Dramatic irony: audience knows that the plan was doomed from the start.
Plot #3	Opening balance	Yes	Departure from normal: new opening balance is very short-lived because disturbance in a way precedes it.
	Disturbance	Yes	Departure from normal: the crisis/climax of Plan B is the disturbance which causes Hally to come up with Plan C.
	Obstacles	Yes	Nature of characters: Sam and Hally.
	Complications	Yes	Sam does not behave as Hally expected.
	Conflict	Yes	External: this time, Hally does get a fight because Sam takes on the role of antagonist, but with the intention of acting in Hally's interest.
	Crisis	Yes	Spitting in Sam's face.
	Climax	No	Departure from normal: technically no climax, because no resolution follows. There is an identifiable act which could have been a climax, had Hally behaved differently: Sam's offer of peace and reconciliation.
	Resolution	No	Departure from normal: Hally leaves without giving an indication of what he will do about Sam's offer.
	Suspense	Yes	Departure from normal: audience left to live with suspense.

Notice that this plot analysis shows that Fugard's structure not only departs from the simple traditional structure of drama by including three separate plans made by the same protagonist, but he also includes nine other departures from the norm within the structure of those three plans. This analysis gives you the plotlines for Hally's story and for Sam's story, but in this play we also get a separate subplot for Willie. If you are studying *"Master Harold"…and the boys*, you should make a point of analysing the structure of Willie's story.

■ Some examples of how other plays depart from normal dramatic structure

Note: This chart gives just one example for each play; in the sample we just developed in detail on the previous pages, we noted 11 departures from normal, so you should definitely not think that the items listed below represent a complete picture of how the plays' structures depart from the normal!

Play	One example of a departure from the basic dramatic structure
The Winter's Tale by William Shakespeare	The disturbance, Hermione's supposed adultery with Polixenes, is entirely in Leonte's mind. Good performances make sure not to provide any action between Polixenes and Hermione which might function as an actual disturbance and thereby justify Leontes' rapid descent into tyranny.

Long Day's Journey Into Night by Eugene O'Neill	The disturbance, Mary's relapse into drug taking, has occurred before the play begins, so that the apparent opening balance is just an illusion.
Fences by August Wilson	The crisis and climax of the original disturbance and plan come a long way before the end of the play when Troy has to tell Rose that he has made another woman pregnant. What, then, constitutes the rest of the play?
Waiting for Godot by Samuel Beckett	The plan, wait for Godot, has been formed long before the audience gains access to the fabula, and it never alters no matter what obstacles or complications come along. Therefore, there really cannot be anything called a crisis or climax or resolution. (Remember this is an absurdist play, and so Beckett should be expected to have upended the whole structure.)

ACTIVITY 3: ANALYSING WILLIAM SHAKESPEARE'S *THE COMEDY OF ERRORS*

Read the following two extracts from the opening of the play, and determine: the opening balance, the disturbance, who the protagonist is, and what his or her plan is for solving the problem caused by the disturbance. When you have finished, you can read the notes at the end of this book.

DUKE   For since the mortal and intestine jars
        'Twixt thy seditious countrymen and us,
        It hath in solemn synods been decreed,
        Both by the Syracusians and ourselves,
5   To admit no traffic to our adverse towns.
        Nay, more, if any born at Ephesus
        Be seen at Syracusian marts and fairs;
        Again, if any Syracusian born
        Come to the bay of Ephesus, he dies,
10   His goods confiscate to the Duke's dispose,
        Unless a thousand marks be levièd
        To quit the penalty and to ransom him.
        Thy substance, valued at the highest rate,
        Cannot amount unto a hundred marks;
15   Therefore by law thou art condemned to die.
    ...

EGEON   My youngest boy, and yet my eldest care,
        At eighteen years became inquisitive
        After his brother, and importuned me
20   That his attendant—so his case was like,
        Reft of his brother, but retained his name—
        Might bear him company in the quest of him,
        Whom whilst I labored of a love to see,
        I hazarded the loss of whom I loved.
25   Five summers have I spent in farthest Greece,
        Roaming clean through the bounds of Asia,
        And, coasting homeward, came to Ephesus,
        Hopeless to find, yet loath to leave unsought
        Or that or any place that harbors men.
30   But here must end the story of my life;
        And happy were I in my timely death
        Could all my travels warrant me they live.

DUKE   Hapless Egeon, whom the fates have marked
        To bear the extremity of dire mishap,
35   Now, trust me, were it not against our laws,
        Against my crown, my oath, my dignity,
        Which princes, would they, may not disannul,
        My soul should sue as advocate for thee.

		But though thou art adjudgèd to the death,
40		And passèd sentence may not be recalled
		But to our honor's great disparagement,
		Yet will I favor thee in what I can.
		Therefore, merchant, I'll limit thee this day
		To seek thy life by beneficial help.
45		Try all the friends thou hast in Ephesus;
		Beg thou, or borrow, to make up the sum,
		And live. If no, then thou art doomed to die.—
		Jailer, take him to thy custody.
	JAILER	I will, my lord.
50	EGEON	Hopeless and helpless doth Egeon wend,
		But to procrastinate his lifeless end.
		(Act 1 Scene 1)

Aristotle's unities

Another way to consider structure in drama originated with Aristotle in his *Poetics* in the fourth century BC. He described features of drama, but that description was revised and formalized as a set of rules by Italian critics in the 16th century. The rules, then, as they were finally formulated, required that plays adhere to these three unities:

- **Unity of action**: there should be only one main plot; all events in the play must contribute to that plot. Nothing extraneous is allowed.

- **Unity of place**: there should be only one place in which the action occurs. The stage was not expected to become different places one after the other.

- **Unity of time**: the action of the play should take no more than one 24-hour day. Extreme adherents suggested that in fact the action should take no longer than the play took to present.

KEY TERM

Dramatic time – in a play, describes the fact that regardless of when in history the play is set, the audience experiences the events as they happen, as if they have never happened before. Characters often discuss events from the past, but those events are rarely staged as actual flashbacks.

What is interesting for you, as a reader or viewer of plays, is to decide what the effect is of the way that the playwright chooses to use or manipulate those 'rules'. As you may have noticed, Athol Fugard, in *"Master Harold" ...and the boys*, adhered rigidly to the unity of time and place. The running time of the play is 90 minutes, so we live through those 90 minutes as the characters do (in **dramatic time**). This creates a powerful sense of immediacy, as well as a sort of shocking understanding of how quickly people's lives can change in significant ways. The action of the play takes place in 90 minutes of the characters' lives, and it takes place in one room: the tea shop. The effect of that choice in this play is that the characters are isolated from the society around them – an isolation that allows for interactions that would not be possible in public. In terms of the unity of action, however, Fugard has violated that rule by including a subplot in which Willie's experience reflects Hally's to some degree. You can also consider whether Fugard's use of the sequential plots (as described in the structural analysis, pages 87–92) constitutes a violation of the unity of action. The complexity of the plot and the compression of actions and emotions in a small space and a short period of time helps to emphasize the drama – the powerful effect of unchained emotion.

Other playwrights have, of course, made quite substantially different choices: Shakespeare violates all the unities wildly in *The Winter's Tale*. It takes place over a period of 16 years (and there is even a character who comes out and announces that he is time, turning the hourglass of sand and moving things along over a gap of 16 years), it takes place in two strikingly different countries and cultures, and there are, as there always are in Shakespeare plays, subplots that reflect aspects of the main plot.

Tracy Letts' *August: Osage County* takes place over several weeks, though largely in the same place. The time passes more quickly as the play goes on, so that the final act takes place only hours after the previous one. Eugene O'Neill's *Long Day's Journey Into Night,* as suggested by the title, takes place in one long day and into the night, but intertwines several subplots. August Wilson's *Fences* takes place over several years, with the longest gap taking place right near the end of the play. Lorraine Hansberry's *A Raisin in the Sun* takes place over a couple of days, but adheres to unity of place, and the family's being trapped in a very small apartment adds significantly to the events and emotional state of the characters.

The skill for you to develop, as a reader and viewer of plays, is to identify how the playwright has constructed time, place and action, and then to consider the effect of those choices on meaning.

Shakespeare and plays in verse

William Shakespeare is probably the most famous playwright to write plays in verse, but there have been many others: Greek tragedies, plays by Ben Jonson and Christopher Marlowe, and *Faust,* by Johann Wolfgang von Goethe. Plays in verse were particularly popular in the Jacobean and Elizabethan eras, but they died out pretty much completely in the 20th century. TS Eliot was possibly the last well-known playwright to write his plays in verse.

If a play is written in verse, you can study the metre of that verse just as you can study any other literary strategy. We mentioned the role of versification in poetry briefly in Chapter 2, and the more detailed analysis we will show you here can be used in the study not only of verse drama but also of any poem with a formal verse structure.

■ Common verse patterns in English

There are a variety of standard metrical forms which are used in works written in English. These patterns appear in units called **feet**. A **foot** is one unit of **metre**. The feet which are likely to occur in English verse consist of either two or three syllables each.

Each type of foot has a different pattern of stressed and unstressed syllables. In English, we are likely to find the following patterns:

Two-syllable feet	Three-syllable feet
1. Unstressed-stressed	5. Stressed-unstressed-unstressed
2. Stressed-unstressed	6. Unstressed-unstressed-stressed
3. Stressed-stressed	
4. Unstressed-unstressed	

You may have noticed that other patterns would be possible in the three-syllable feet, such as stressing the middle syllable or having two stressed syllables, but those patterns do not, as a rule, occur in works written in English, so we will not consider them here.

In order to show the stress pattern of a word or phrase, we use a standard notation in which U indicates an unstressed syllable and / indicates a stressed syllable. There are names for each of these patterns:

Pattern 1 as listed in the table on page 96 is called an **iamb**. This is the most common metrical pattern in English. Unfortunately, the word 'iamb' is not an iamb, so you will need to remember a different word to help you learn the pattern. The word 'behold' is an iamb, notated as follows:

U /
Behold

Pattern 2 is called a **trochee**. Helpfully, the word 'trochee' is also a trochee. The word 'hammer' is a good example of a trochee and would be notated as follows:

/ U
Hammer

Pattern 3 is called a **spondee**. The word 'spondee' is not a spondee (do you recognize it? It is a trochee!). The word 'shortcake' is a good example of spondee, notated as follows:

/   /
Shortcake

Pattern 4 is a very rare and special metre called a **pyrrhic foot**. You may know the word 'pyrrhic' from your history class in the context of discussing a 'pyrrhic victory'. A pyrrhic victory is an empty victory; one side won the battle but gained nothing from it. A pyrrhic foot is likewise one which is empty – it has no stresses. There aren't any multi-syllable words in English without any stresses, so you will need at least two words in order to discover a pyrrhic foot. Here is an example from the 50th verse of Tennyson's 'In Memoriam':

U U   /   /   U U   /   /
When the blood creeps, and the nerves prick

When you are looking at what you think might be a pyrrhic foot, you need to be sure that you are not actually looking at a three-syllable foot with two unstressed syllables either at the beginning or the end. In this case, we know that the metre is based on two-syllable feet because there are eight syllables in the line, not nine.

Pattern 5 is called a **dactyl**. The word 'dactyl' is not a dactyl (this should be a familiar pattern by now though!), it is a trochee. We know that the word 'dactyl' could not be a dactyl because a dactyl has three syllables not two. The word 'enterprise' is a dactyl:

/ U U
Enterprise

Pattern 6 is called an **anapest**. The word 'anapest', alas, is not an anapaest – it is a dactyl. The stress is on the last syllable and the other two are unstressed. The word 'understand' is an anapest:

U U   /
Understand

This chart sums up all the types of metrical feet you should look for in works written in English:

	Name	Adjective form	Number of syllables	Stress pattern	Example
1	Iamb	Iambic	2	U /	Behold
2	Trochee	Trochaic	2	/ U	Hammer
3	Spondee	Spondaic	2	/ /	Shortcake
4	Pyrrhic foot	Pyrrhic	2	U U	When the
5	Dactyl	Dactylic	3	/ U U	Enterprise
6	Anapest	Anapestic	3	U U /	Understand

When doing metrical analysis, you cannot expect each word to stand alone as a metrical foot, despite the simple examples we have given you. Instead, feet will very often consist of one syllable from one word and another syllable from another word, or even of two or three one-syllable words in a row. The most famous phrase from Hamlet's most famous soliloquy, for example, consists of iambs: 'To be or not to be' (Act 3 Scene 1, 64).

U / U / U /
To be or not to be

■ Names for the number of feet in each line

Each named metrical pattern has two parts: the first part names the specific pattern of stresses, which we have just learned, and the second part names the number of those patterns which are in a line. Those terms are easier to remember for most people than the names of the type of metre, because they use the Greek roots to indicate number:

Number of feet in the line	Name of the pattern of feet
1	Monometer
2	Dimeter
3	Trimeter
4	Tetrameter
5	Pentameter
6	Hexameter
7	Heptameter
8	Octameter

There are one or two other oddities you might come across, such as the Alexandrine, a 12-foot line, but those in the table are the most likely.

■ Names of metrical patterns in English poetry and verse plays

Now that you know both types of terms, the name of the metrical type and the number of feet in a line, you can combine them. Take the adjective form of the metre name and add it to the name of the number of feet:

Dactylic octameter = eight feet of dactyls. Since a dactyl is three syllables, that would be 24 syllables in the line.

Trochaic dimeter = two feet of trochees. Since a trochee is two syllables, that would be four syllables.

ACTIVITY 4: NAMING METRICAL PATTERNS

1   Give the proper name for each of the following patterns. The answers are at the end of the book.

  a   Lines of four anapests

  b   Lines of six iambs

  c   Lines of two dactyls

2   Give the description of each of the following metres and include the total number of syllables you would find in each line. The answers are at the end of the book.

  a   Dactylic heptameter

  b   Trochaic tetrameter

  c   Iambic trimeter

Iambic pentameter, lines that consist of five iambs (and, therefore, a total of ten syllables) is the most common verse pattern in English. Iambic pentameter is the verse form in which Shakespeare wrote. He sometimes switched to prose, especially for characters of low social status, but you will find that iambic pentameter predominates. Here is a short example from *A Midsummer Night's Dream*:

> Four days will quickly steep themselves in night;
> Four nights will quickly dream away the time;
> And then the moon, like to a silver bow
> New-bent in heaven, shall behold the night
> Of our solemnities.
> (Act 1 Scene 1, 7–11)

ACTIVITY 5: MARKING THE METRE

The above passage from *A Midsummer Night's Dream* is made up of just over four lines of perfect iambic pentameter. You will notice the last line being short – that is part of what is called a shared line; the next speaker picks it up and speaks the last four syllables.

Taking what you have learned so far, copy out the passage above and mark the syllables to show the iambic pentameter. The answer is at the end of the book.

Although that particular passage from *A Midsummer Night's Dream* is in perfect iambic pentameter, you will not find that every line from every Shakespearean play is. You cannot expect any playwright or poet to stick rigidly to the predominant metrical pattern, and it will be, in fact, in the variations where most of your analysis will occur, as we will investigate in the next sections.

Determining the predominant metrical pattern

■ Number of feet in a line

KEY TERM

Predominant metre – the metre that is used most often.

The first thing to be aware of is that the metres are not random; no poet or playwright alters the metrical pattern from one line to the next and back again. Each work that does rely on a metre will have a **predominant metre**. You can begin identifying that metre by counting the syllables in all the lines (if the text is short, as a poem usually is) or a good chunk of the lines, if you are working with a play. The number of syllables is a good indication of what the possible metres are: you can't have iambic or trochaic metre if the lines have an odd number of syllables, since odd numbers are not divisible by two, and iambs and trochees each have two syllables. Likewise, you can't have dactylic or anapestic metre if the lines are of four, eight or ten syllables, because dactyls and anapests are each three syllables, and neither four, eight nor ten is divisible by three.

Note, though, that if you have lines of six syllables, the job is a little harder, because you will need to consider whether you might have three iambs or trochees or two dactyls or anapests.

Keep in mind as you are counting that the metre will vary a bit – some lines will be longer or shorter, but most will have the same number of syllables. That predominant pattern is the one which we use as a basis for exploring interesting diversions from it.

■ Type of feet in a line

Once you have decided on whether you are looking for feet of two syllables or feet of three syllables, you have to decide which type of foot the writer has used. For that, you have to read the lines slowly, preferably out loud, and listen to where you pronounce the stressed syllables. Mark the stressed and unstressed syllables as you go.

TIPS FOR IDENTIFYING METRICAL PATTERN

✔ One important tip is that you need to pronounce the words as they are normally pronounced. Don't let anticipation of some metrical pattern cause you to force a pattern where none exists. Remember that words have a very specific pronunciation: sometimes words are pronounced differently in the noun form from the way they are pronounced in the verb form. The noun 'conduct', for instance, is not pronounced the same as 'conduct', when it is used as a verb:

> 'His conduct was reprehensible.'
> 'He did not conduct himself appropriately.'

✔ Words that are not nouns or verbs, such as 'when' or 'and' might be stressed in one context but not in another. Consider the difference in the stresses in the following two lines:

> 'I will wash the dishes when I feel like it.'
> 'When I decide to wash the dishes, I will.'

✔ Remember that you will not find either spondaic or pyrrhic feet forming the basis for the metre. No one in English speaks long series of either stressed or unstressed feet – such a pattern would be entirely unnatural. You will find the occasional spondaic (and even more rarely a pyrrhic) foot, but in general if you're looking for two-syllable feet, you're looking for iambs or trochees, and if you're looking for three-syllable feet, you're looking for anapests or dactyls.

✔ Sometimes, you might feel that a word must be stressed on a particular line because the character needs to emphasize it in order to make a point.

■ Looking for variations

As we have mentioned, it is usually the variations in metre that are the most interesting in terms of understanding the author's strategies. Here is an example from *Romeo and Juliet*. The prologue to Act 1 Scene 1 is in almost perfect iambic pentameter, but there are two very interesting deviations.

```
    U    /    U     / U/  U / U /
    Two households, both alike in dignity              10
    U  / U /U   /   U / U    /
    (In fair Verona, where we lay our scene),          10
     U /  U   /    /   U U  / U /
    From ancient grudge break to new mutiny,           10
    U   /U  /   U  /U  /   U /
    Where civil blood makes civil hands unclean.       10
    U   /   U /U   / U /   U  /
  5 From forth the fatal loins of these two foes       10
    U / U /   U   /U  / U   /
    A pair of star-crossed lovers take their life;     10
     U  /U  / U   /U /U   /
    Whose misadventured piteous overthrows             10
    U   / U   /   / U U / U   /
    Doth with their death bury their parents' strife.  10
```

The remainder of the prologue is all regular iambic pentameter, so we have not shown the metre here. The two variations are indicated in red. In line 3 the third foot is not an iamb, it is a trochee. The effect of that is to place stress on the word 'break', which is the heart of the problem in the play: the fight in Act 1 Scene 1 *breaks* the peace and sets all the conflict in the play in action. In line eight, Shakespeare has once again used a trochee for the expected iamb in the third foot. This time, the substitution focuses our attention on the word 'bury'. Since it is the death of the children and their burial in the tomb that causes the two families to bury the strife, 'bury' is a very important word. The variations in the metre in this prologue naturally draw our attention to two very important ideas which will shape the action of the play.

It is worth noting, too, that the prologue is a sonnet. You can review the structure of a sonnet in Chapter 2 (see pages 22–23). The fact that Shakespeare chose a well-known poetic form for the opening of his play suggests that we should pay particular attention to the elements of the poetry to help us understand what is to come in the rest of the play.

ACTIVITY 6: LOOKING FOR VARIATIONS

Read the following extract from the final speech from *A Midsummer Night's Dream* and discuss any variations you find from regular iambic pentameter. Speculate on why Shakespeare might have made those changes, to what listeners would have expected. There are notes on this passage at the end of this book.

> If we shadows have offended,
> Think but this and all is mended:
> That you have but slumbered here
> While these visions did appear.
> And this weak and idle theme,
> No more yielding but a dream,
> Gentles, do not reprehend.
> If you pardon, we will mend.
> (Act 5 Scene 1, 440–7)

■ Extra stresses

A spondee has one more stress in it than either the iamb or the trochee, so where you find a spondee, you are going to find some idea that is being stressed. It's easy to just say 'the playwright was trying to stress something', but you will do much better if you identify exactly what was being stressed and why. In one famous line from *The Winter's Tale*, for example, Shakespeare added a wealth of extra stresses – in fact, one can make an argument for the line having ten stressed syllables:

> / / / / / / / / /
> Good queen, my lord, good queen, I say 'good queen'
> (Act 2 Scene 3, 72)

One might make an argument that the 'my' and the 'I' ought not to be stressed; however, in the context of the scene, those two words are quite important. At this point in the play, Paulina, who speaks the line, is the only person in the court who is standing up to King Leontes, who is behaving extremely irrationally. The emphasis on the 'my' and 'I' show the importance of the voice of the one person – and a woman – who is not cowed by the power of someone whose behaviour is really quite mad. The fact that all ten syllables are stressed – a very unusual occurrence – shows the degree of passion with which Paulina is defending Hermione, the queen, from Leontes' unjust accusations. Shakespeare is showing us through excessive emphasis just how wrong Leontes' actions are.

This example, then, shows you two important things:

1 Sometimes authors vary expected metre in a quite spectacular way.

2 The metre is not always perfectly straightforward; you sometimes have to justify a particular reading of a line.

Final notes

Learning to do metrical analysis or scansion, can be a difficult process, so be prepared to practise. Realize, also, that you can make an argument for a metre that you feel is present, and so long as you are careful with the vocabulary and point very specifically to the precise words and phrases you are claiming play an important metrical role, you can make a successful argument. You can be wrong, of course; for example, if you try to argue that 'To be or not to be' is trochaic, you are going to be in trouble. If you completely mispronounce words – claiming, for example, that the word 'married' is an iamb (try pronouncing it that way: mare-EED), you will not impress an examiner. But as we saw with the example from *The Winter's Tale*, there is scope for interpretation based on how you feel that the words should be pronounced to greatest effect. If you begin with the assumption that a play in verse is likely to rely heavily on iambic pentameter, you can look for variations from there.

One final strategy that you should be aware of, particularly with regard to the use of metre in Shakespeare's plays, is that he often used verse for royalty and other characters of high social status and prose for lower-class characters such as the clowns or other peasants. You should consider what the contrast in the metrical styles suggests about the characters in the particular play you are reading. When he did use verse, Shakespeare wrote in what is called **blank verse**, which is an indeterminate number of lines of iambic pentameter. Blank verse does not rhyme; however, as with all other aspects of analysing verse, you should be alert for places where the playwright does decide to interject a rhyming couplet, or a series of rhyming couplets, or other types of rhymes, and then ask yourself what that rhyme adds to the effect of the verse.

> **KEY TERM**
>
> **Blank verse** – an indeterminate number of lines of iambic pentameter.

Conclusion

This chapter has shown you that in many respects the tools necessary for analysing a drama are very similar to the tools needed to analyse poetry and prose. Playwrights use nearly all the same literary elements to create their meaning: setting, character development, figurative language, allusion and so on. As it does in poetry, metre often contributes to meaning, and metre is particularly important in Shakespeare's work. When it comes to drama, however, the structure takes on a particular role which is not quite the same as the role structure plays in poetry or prose. If you learn, therefore, to analyse the structure of a drama, paying particular attention to the ways in which the playwright has manipulated the traditional base structure for his or her own purposes, you will be able to talk and write about plays in a sophisticated way.

Resources for additional study

The *Players of Shakespeare* series, from Cambridge University Press, comprises six books. They all consist of essays by actors from the Royal Shakespeare Company, in which they discuss their conceptions of roles they played at the Royal Shakespeare Theatre. The final book in the series focuses specifically on the history plays. These are excellent resources for anyone who wants insight into characters in Shakespeare's works.

In his *Dramatic Structure in the Contemporary American Theatre*, Robert Andreach focuses on tragedies and especially on trilogies to explore how failure in character development over time can form the basis of a tragedy.

In *The Thirty-Six Dramatic Situations: The 100-Year Anniversary Edition*, George Polti identifies what he considers to be the 36 basic stories that form the basis for drama. This can be useful in helping to identify underlying basic stories in the plays you read; however, we suggest that you be cautious in thinking that there are no new stories not covered here. The book is 100 years old, after all – modern life may very well have led to the creation of new base stories that Polti would not recognize! You could use the book as a tool, but do not consider it to be completely authoritative on this subject.

Works cited

Andreach, Robert J, *Dramatic Structure in the Contemporary American Theatre*, Terra Nova Books, 2018 (print).

Beckett, Samuel, *Waiting for Godot*, New York, NY: Grove Press, 2011 (print).

Figgis, Mike, *36 Dramatic Situations*, London: Faber & Faber Ltd, 2017 (print).

Foster, Thomas C, *How to Read Poetry like a Professor: a Quippy and Sonorous Guide to Verse*, HarperLuxe, an Imprint of HarperCollins Publishers, 2018 (print).

Fugard, Athol, *"Master Harold" … and the Boys*, Media Production Services Unit, Manitoba Education, 2012 (print).

Goethe, Johann Wolfgang von, *Faust*, Place of publication not identified, CreateSpace Independent Publishing Platform, 2014 (print).

Hansberry, Lorraine, *A Raisin in the Sun*, Robert Nemiroff, ed., Modern Library, 1995 (print).

Letts, Tracy, *August: Osage County*, New York: Theatre Communications Group, 2013 (print).

ONeill, Eugene Gladstone, *Long Days Journey into Night*, New Haven: Yale University Press, 2002 (print).

Paul, SL, 'Understanding Media', *Aristotle's Unities*, Blogger.com, Web, accessed 7 October 2018, **mediaelectron.blogspot.com/2008/10/aristotles-unities.html**

Shakespeare, William, *A Midsummer Night's Dream*, Barbara A. Mowat and Paul Werstine, eds., *Folger Digital Texts*, Folger Shakespeare Library, Web, accessed 8 October 2018, **www.folgerdigitaltexts.org/?chapter=5&play=MND&loc=p7**

Shakespeare, William, *Hamlet*, Barbara A Mowat and Paul Werstine, eds., *Folger Digital Texts*, Folger Shakespeare Library, Web, accessed 8 October 2018, **https://www.folgerdigitaltexts.org/?chapter=5&play=Ham&loc=p7**.

Shakespeare, William, *Romeo and Juliet*, Barbara A Mowat and Paul Werstine, eds., *Folger Digital Texts*, Folger Shakespeare Library, Web, accessed 3 October 2018, **www.folgerdigitaltexts.org/html/Rom.html#line-2.1.0**

Shakespeare, William, *Taming of the Shrew*, Barbara A Mowat and Paul Werstine, eds., *Folger Digital Texts*, Folger Shakespeare Library, Web, accessed 8 October 2018, **https://www.folgerdigitaltexts.org/?chapter=5&play=Shr&loc=p7**.

Shakespeare, William, *The Comedy of Errors*, Rebecca Niles and Michael Poston, eds., *Folger Digital Texts*, Folger Shakespeare Library, Web, accessed 8 October 2018, **www.folgerdigitaltexts.org/?chapter=5&play=Err&loc=p7&_ga=2.192697644.785110063.1541009857-253774902.1538429814**

Shakespeare, William, *The Winter's Tale*, Rebecca Niles and Michael Poston, eds., *Folger Digital Texts*, Folger Shakespeare Library, Web, accessed 2 October 2018, **www.folgerdigitaltexts.org/?chapter=5&play=WT&loc=p7**

Tennyson, Alfred, 'In Memoriam', *Lord Alfred Tennyson*, The Literature Network, Web, accessed 10 October 2018, **www.online-literature.com/tennyson/718/**

Wilson, August, *Fences*, NY, NY: Plume, 2016 (print).

Writing about literature

Types of writing

You will have to write about literature several times for your IB course assessments. If you are an HL student, you will have to write an essay of 1 200–1 500 words about one of the works you study. You will develop your own line of inquiry, but you will be recommended to use one of the central concepts in the course as the basis for your choice.

For the exams at the end of the course, you will have to write two papers: Paper 1 on unseen texts and Paper 2, a comparison and contrast essay on works you studied in your course. For Paper 1, you will get two unseen texts (from two different literary forms), each with a question which is not compulsory. Students at SL will choose one of the texts to write about; students at HL will write about both. Any of the four literary forms can appear (prose fiction, poetry, drama and non-fiction), so be prepared for all four forms. For Paper 2, you will get four questions of a general nature about literature, and you will choose one to answer. In your answer you will be expected to discuss two of the works you studied in your course. The restriction will be that you may not write about the works you used for your other components (the internal assessment and the HL essay).

For all three of these assignments, you will have to accomplish three things: directly address the question being asked, demonstrate that you have a sophisticated understanding of the work in your analysis and write your ideas in a logical, coherent and clear way. This chapter will provide you with some ways to develop your skills for these requirements.

Summary vs analysis

One of the most important things for you to master in order to write about literature is the difference between **summary** and **analysis**. While you need to provide a certain amount of summary to provide context for your analysis, the analysis must be the focus of your work.

A summary is a description of a text which consists of a retelling of the story. In a summary, there is little to no sense of your voice as a critic; you are merely regurgitating an author's ideas.

An analysis, on the other hand, is an investigation into the elements of a literary work. In an analysis, you are performing the role of literary critic and examining aspects of the work in close detail in order to reach a conclusion. An analysis has to include a carefully chosen and limited summary, along with quotations, to set the context for your analysis, and to support your thesis or line of argument, but the main focus must be an interpretation of how the aspects of the text you have chosen to write about contribute to the work as a whole.

If you are familiar with Bloom's Taxonomy, you will know that summary sits at the bottom level of the pyramid as *remember*. Analysis involves the higher-order thinking skills that are found at the top of the pyramid: *understand, apply, analyse, evaluate* and *create*.

You will not be able to demonstrate beyond a superficial level of understanding if you merely summarize a text. In order to demonstrate *appreciation* for a text you need to dig deeper and really consider the effects of the tools that the writer has used.

■ Example: *The Whistling Season* by Ivan Doig

Read the following extract and then examine the responses below. Notice the difference between the summary and the analysis. Consider what characterizes each response.

> This jilted old house and all that it holds, even empty. If I have learned
> anything in a lifetime spent overseeing schools, it is that childhood
> is the one story that stands by itself in every soul. As surely as a compass
> needle knows north, that is what draws me to these remindful rooms as if the
> 5 answer I need by the end of this day is written in the dust that carpets them.
>
> The wrinkled calendar on the parlor wall stops me in my tracks. It of
> course has not changed since my last time here. Nineteen fifty-two. Five years,
> so quickly passed, since the Marias Coulee school board begged the vacant old
> place from me for a month while they repaired the roof of their teacherage
> 10 and I had to come out from the department in Helena to go over matters with
> them. What I am startled to see is that the leaf showing on the calendar –
> October – somehow stays right across all the years: that 1909 evening of
> *Paul, get out your good pen and paper,* the lonely teacher's tacking up of
> something to relieve these bare walls so long after that, and my visit now
> 15 under such a changed sky of history.
>
> The slyness of calendars should not surprise me, I suppose. Passing the
> newly painted one-room school, our school, this morning as I drove out in my
> state government car, all at once I was again at that juncture of time when
> Damon and Toby and I, each in our turn, first began to be aware that we were
> 20 not quite of our own making, and yet did not seem to be simply rewarmed 'tovers
> of our elders, either. How could I, who back there at barely thirteen, realized
> that I must struggle awake every morning of my life before anyone else in the
> house to wrest myself from the grip of my tenacious dreams, be the offspring of
> a man who slept solidly as a railroad tie? And Damon, fists-up Damon, how
> 25 could he derive from our peaceable mother? Ready or not, we were being
> introduced to ourselves, sometimes in a fashion as hard to follow as our father's
> reading finger. Almost any day in the way stations of childhood we passed back
> and forth between, prairie homestead and country school, was apt to turn into a
> fresh puzzle piece of life. Something I find true even yet. (4–5)

Summary

The narrator returns to his childhood home, which has been empty for a number of years, and he describes what he sees there. He notices that the calendar is set to October 1952, five years before. He reminisces about how he felt when he was a child, and he ponders the way in which children find out about who they are as people, different from their parents.

Analysis

The calendar in this passage serves as a symbol for time and the way in which our sense of time and change is the result of the way in which we remember events and find connections among them. In this case, the narrator shows how the calendar, which is set to October 1952 (lines 7 and 12), causes him to remember an important October day from 1909 (line 12). Since the time in which he is speaking is October 1957 (lines 7 and 8), he uses the alignment of these three Octobers to signify a connection between them.

We know that the narrator has a decision to make on this day (lines 4 and 5), and we see that he himself sees the calendar page with its reference to October as a sign that the answers he needs today will be found in his memories of the past. We don't know from this passage what decision it is that Paul has to make; however, we can surmise, because the narrator chose to speak of memories from the past which have to do with figuring out who we are as people, that whatever the decision is, it is a very important one that has implications for who Paul will become.

Finally, the narrator gives us the image of travelling back and forth between homestead and school, and we see that in his mind, that journey has become a metaphor for grappling with life's difficulties. He tells us that any such journey, 'was apt to turn into a fresh puzzle piece of life'. In the present day, Paul has made a journey here from Helena (line 10), and by using the reference to the significance of his childhood journeys he connects the present to the past and elevates the significance of his present-day journey. We are alerted to wait for the revelation that whatever decision he has to make is a big one with widespread and/or lasting ramifications.

Note that the summary is quite a bit shorter than the original (409 words in the extract and 67 words in the summary), but that it includes mention of all the major events/ elements of the passage. This would be too much summary to use in an essay focused on a particular topic relative to the passage. Note also that the analysis, although it is much longer than the summary (326 words) does not include everything that could have been said about what this passage means or what it says. The writer of the analysis had to choose important elements, and so chose to focus on the symbol of the calendar and how it stood for the connection of events from past and present. You will never have time to write about everything you notice in a passage or work. Finally, notice the verbs used in the summary: 'returns', 'describes', 'notices', 'reminisces' and 'ponders'. These are all actions that the narrator takes. This is typical of a summary: when summarizing, you describe what the narrator and/or characters *do* in the passage. That is very different from what you will do in the analysis.

Here are some of the verbs from the analysis: 'serves as a symbol'; 'shows how the calendar … causes …'; 'uses the alignment … to signify …'; 'narrator chose to speak of …' And so on. All of these verbs describe what the narrator is doing in terms of shaping his telling of the story. Summary focuses on actions in the dramatic moment; analysis focuses on the construction of stories.

■ Dramatic situation vs narrative situation

In any text with a speaker or narrator (that is, any text except a drama), the reader must deal with two different situations:

- the **dramatic situation**, the situation in which the actions of the story occur
- the **narrative situation**, the situation in which the narrator tells the story.

Sometimes there is a big difference between the two. Think of the extract from *The Good Soldier*, by Ford Madox Ford, in Chapter 3 (pages 60–61). That uses a first-person narrator, and during the novel the narrator actually describes his writing situation for us. He tells the reader that he begins writing the novel 12 years after the earliest events that he describes, he writes for six months, and then he picks up the tale again three years later.

Sometimes, as with the passage from *The Whistling Season*, there is very little time between the events happening and the telling of them. Here we see a scene in which the narrator is standing in the house, talking as he observes the space around him. There is almost no difference at all between the narrative situation and the dramatic situation. Towards the end of the passage, however, he thinks back to events that occurred many years before – 48 years earlier, to be exact. When he does that, there is, of course, a long distance between the dramatic situation (the events that happened when he and his brothers were children) and the telling, which happens on one day in 1957.

Summary is the description of the events of the dramatic situation. Analysis is the reader's observation of how the narrator is telling the story, the identification of the various elements of that story-telling process, and the explanation of how those elements create meaning.

> **KEY TERMS**
>
> **Dramatic situation** – the situation in which the actions of the story occur.
>
> **Narrative situation** – the situation in which the narrator tells the story.

■ Author vs narrator

One decision you will always have to make when writing about literature is whether you are writing about what the *author* does or what the *narrator* or *speaker* does. This decision always poses an interesting problem because, of course, the author creates the narrator, so it is fair to say that everything the narrator does is something that the author made him or her do.

In making your decision, then, you will need to carefully consider where you want to focus your attention. Here are some important considerations:

IDENTIFYING THE VOICE

✔ If you have a third-person narrator, it is not particularly interesting to consider what the narrator is doing, because the narrator is not a character in the story, and so his or her actions and attitudes do not influence the story. In that case, focus on what the author is doing to create the effects that you notice.

✔ If, on the other hand, you have a first-person narrator who is a character in the story, then you have someone whose actions and attitudes do influence the story, and it is definitely important to consider how.

✔ If, furthermore, you have a **reliable first-person narrator** (refer back to Chapter 3, page 57 for the difference between a reliable narrator and an unreliable one), then you don't have to worry too much about how the narrator's efforts to tell the story differ from the author's, and you can safely choose to discuss either the author's strategies or the narrator's.

✔ If, however, you have an **unreliable first-person narrator**, then you definitely need to show that you understand that fact. You will need to demonstrate that you understand what the narrator is up to, how the narrator's strategies effectively misrepresent reality and to what extent. In a full-length essay, eventually you would also want to address the question of *why* the author created such a narrator. You would need to show, in other words, how the author's values, attitudes and understanding of the world differ from those of the narrator.

In the analysis of the passage from *The Whistling Season*, the writer doing the analysis focused on the narrator's strategies. That decision was correct for that passage because the narrator is not only constructing the story but is also the main character in that story. The story is about a decision that the narrator has to make, and so showing that you understand how the telling of the story relates to the decision also shows that you understand how he is creating meaning.

■ Assessing the effectiveness of the sample analysis

Imagine that this was the prompt for the analysis of *The Whistling Season*: *Choose at least one important literary strategy from the passage. Identify it and explain its significance.*

At the beginning of the chapter we considered three requirements you should meet when writing about literature: directly answer the question being asked, demonstrate a sophisticated understanding of the work and write your ideas and arguments in a logical, coherent and clear way. If we consider those requirements against the analysis, it fulfils all three. First, it directly answers the question as it was asked: the writer chose the literary strategy of symbol, identified where it was in the passage, and then explained that the function of the symbol was to show us the narrator's view that past and present events are connected. The rest of the analysis demonstrates how the narrator connected past and present in his own mind and finished by showing us the significance of that: it sets up an expectation of something that is still to come.

Second, it is analysis, not summary. It locates significant elements (symbol, use of time, connection between past and present) rather than simply retelling the story.

Third, it is well-written. Later in this chapter, we will examine some features of clear, strong writing.

■ Including an appropriate amount of summary

Finally, we considered earlier that you will need to provide a certain amount of summary in order to set context for your analysis. When you are writing literary papers, you must presume that you are writing for an educated audience, in this case an audience familiar with reading and analysing literature, but that your reader might not be familiar with this particular work of literature. You must, therefore, provide whatever summary is relevant to the focus of your analysis, so that your reader will understand enough about what is happening to follow your argument, but no more.

Here is a bit of summary that would be appropriate for the extract from *The Whistling Season* as introduction to the analysis provided:

In this passage, the narrator, Paul, is revisiting his childhood home, and he notices a calendar hanging on the wall.

That should be enough for a reader to then be able to understand the rest of the analysis. Note how this summary is tailored specifically to what is said in the analysis, and that it is a good bit shorter than the summary that was given earlier (20 words as opposed to 67), which was intended to be a summary of the entire extract from the novel.

ACTIVITY 1: *AN UNNECESSARY WOMAN* BY RABIH ALAMEDDINE

Read the extract from *An Unnecessary Woman* and write a summary of the whole extract and an analytical paragraph. Assume that you have been given the following guiding question: *What can we learn about the narrator from this passage, and what strategies does the author use in order to reveal the narrator's nature?* You are welcome to ignore that guiding question, as you will be on your Paper 1; however, the comments at the end of the book have been written on the assumption that the practice analysis does address that question. Finally, imagine that you are using this passage in an essay and need to write just enough summary to provide context, as we did for *The Whistling Season* above. Write that short summary here.

> Usually vanity isn't one of my concerns, doesn't disconcert me much. However, I'd overheard the three witches discussing the unrelenting whiteness of my hair. Joumana, my upstairs neighbor, had suggested that if I used a shampoo like Bel Argent, the white would be less flat. There you have it.
>
> 5 As I understand it, and I might be wrong as usual, you and I tend to lose short wavelength cones as we age, so we're less able to distinguish the color blue. That's why many people of a certain age have a bluish tint to their hair. Without the tint, they see their hair as pale yellow, or possibly salmon. One hairstylist described on the radio how he finally convinced this old woman that her hair was much too blue. But his client still refused to change the color. It was much more
> 10 important that she see her hair as natural than the rest of the world do so.
>
> I'd probably get along better with the client.
>
> I too am an old woman, but I have yet to lose many short wavelength cones. I can distinguish the color blue a bit too clearly right now.
>
> Allow me to offer a mild defense for being distracted. At the end of the year, before I begin
> 15 a new project, I read the translation I've completed. I do minor final corrections, set the pages in order, and place them in the box. This is a part of the ritual, which includes imbibing two glasses of red wine. I'll also admit that the last reading allows me to pat myself on the back, to congratulate myself on completing the project. This year, I translated the superb novel *Austerlistz*, my second translation of W. G. Sebald. I was reading it today, and for some reason, probably the
> 20 protagonist's unrequired despair, I couldn't stop thinking of Hannah. I couldn't, as if the novel, or my Arabic translation of it, was an inductor into Hannah's world. (2–3)

Full summary
Summary appropriate for analysis

Analysis

Short summary

Writing specifically about poetry

When writing about poetry, the same three obligations will apply: address the prompt as assigned, analyse rather than summarize, and write clearly and well. There are, however, a few things to consider that are particular to poetry.

▪ Understanding the literal

Although you must not focus on summary to the exclusion or reduction of analysis, you also must not ignore the literal and try to jump straight to the figurative. This is an important instruction for writing about prose or drama as well; however, students are more likely to make this mistake with poetry than with any other genre. There is a strong temptation to leap straight to abstractions, but the literal must always work in any poem, and you must demonstrate that you understand the poem at both levels.

▪ Example: 'Birth of the Owl Butterflies' by Ruth Sharman

> They hung in our kitchen for days:
> a row of brown lanterns that threw no light,
> merely darkened with their growing load.
> Pinned to a shelf among the knick-knacks
> 5 and the cookery books;
> ripening in the radiator's heat:
> six Central American *Caligo* chrysalids,
> five thousand miles from their mountain home.
>
> My father had brought them here,
> 10 carefully packed in cotton wool,
> to hatch, set, identify, and display:
> these unpromising dingy shells plumped up

> like curled leaves, on each a silver spur,
> a tiny gleam or drop of dew
> 15 Nature had added as a finishing touch
> to perfect mimicry.
>
> For weeks the wizened fruit had been maturing.
> Now, one by one, the pods exploded,
> crackling in the quiet kitchen,
> 20 and a furry missile emerged—quickly,
> as if desperate to break free—
> unhinged its awkward legs,
> hauling behind it, like a frilly party dress,
> the rumpled mass of its soft wings.
>
> 25 It clung unsteadily to the cloven pod,
> while slow wings billowed with the blood
> that pumped them full.
> The dark velvet began to glow
> with a thousand tiny striations,
> 30 and there, in each corner,
> boldly ringed in black and gold,
> two fierce owl-eyes widened.
>
> Uneasy minutes, these, before *Caligo*
> can flex its nine-inch wings and fly.
> 35 They drooped still, gathering strength,
> limp flags loosely flowing.
> When two butterflies hatched too close,
> and clashed, each scrabbling for a footing,
> one fell and its wings flopped
> 40 fatly on the kitchen floor.
>
> I pictured them shattering later
> on taps and cupboard corners;
> but my father gauged his moment well,
> allowed a first few timid forays,
> 45 then swooped down gentle-fingered
> with his glass jar for the kill.
> The monstrous wings all but filled it,
> beat vigorously, fluttered, and were still.

On first reading, we can already see that this is a poem that has something to do with life and death. Since it's about butterflies, we might be very tempted to leap to issues of freedom – because flight is a classic symbol of freedom. It's also easy, with this poem, to pick up on the image of missiles and of the unsteady legs and 'monstrous wings' (line 47) and then get carried away with an idea that the butterflies are intended to represent monsters or evil. We have to resist the temptation, however, to dive into a discussion of death and freedom and evil without reference to the literal level of the text, because to do so misses the entire point of the poem.

If you read the poem carefully, with an eye to understanding the literal, you will see that what is happening is that the narrator's father has brought six chrysalids from South

America to his home, thousands of miles away. He has then pinned the chrysalids to a shelf in the kitchen to await their hatching. When they do finally hatch, they are ungainly, wet and clumsy, as are all freshly hatched butterflies. The wings have to spread and dry before butterflies can fly. (Possibly you didn't know that detail; however, you should be able to figure it out from the poem. You can imagine that a butterfly with 'five-inch wings', line 34, which have been folded up tightly into a chrysalid needs time for the wings to spread.)

So far, the story is pretty clear. We have, however, to be careful not to get caught out by the final stanza, because what is literally happening there is that the narrator is *imagining* what is likely to happen to the butterflies in the future – the smashing of the butterflies against the fixtures in the kitchen does not actually happen. What does happen is that the father catches the butterflies, holding them gently so as not to destroy the wings, and then he puts them in a kill jar. What lepidopterists – people who study butterflies – do is to put butterflies in jars with a weak formulation of cyanide gas which kills the butterflies rapidly before they have time to beat their wings apart inside the jar. You can't tell that from the poem, but even if you don't know that, you can tell that this jar has something in it that will kill the butterflies rapidly, because they die immediately, as depicted in the last line: they fill the jar, the wings beat, flutter and stop. The shortness of the phrases matches the shortness of the time that passes while the butterflies die.

If you understand the literal level of the story this narrator is telling about her father's collection of the butterflies, you realize that it is about man's relationship to nature and a tension between letting the butterflies live in their natural habitat in South America and the desire to preserve them with pristine wings so that their beauty can be saved and appreciated by people who would never otherwise see them. The poem, in other words, explores a fundamental question about humankind's desire for learning and preservation and display of beautiful things, and a potentially moral question about how far it is acceptable for us to commandeer natural creatures and objects for our own purposes. That focus is vastly different from the grand questions of evil, monsters, death and lack of freedom that we gravitated to when we tried to deal with the figurative level of the poem first. Only the last of those items on the list is truly relevant – at least in the sense that we were tempted to think about early on.

■ Summary vs analysis in poetry

When you are writing about poetry, you have the same obligation to write analysis rather than summary that you have when writing about prose. Writing an appropriate summary of a poem can pose particular difficulties, however, as we just saw with the effort to make sure you understand the literal level of poems that you study.

Once you do understand the literal, of course, you still have to choose which bits of summary are relevant to your paper. In 'Birth of the Owl Butterflies', for example, we would not begin a paper with that whole lengthy recounting of the events at the literal level. We would have to give only a little context and then, as we develop the analysis, provide any additional summary needed. We might begin with just this much summary:

In 'Birth of the Owl Butterflies', the speaker recounts an experience she had when her father brought six butterfly chrysalids home from South America to hatch them and then kill them in order to preserve and display their magnificent wings.

That would be sufficient to start off the essay. We will examine in detail an essay about this poem a little later in the chapter. For now, we want to be sure we understand the difference between summary and analysis in poetry.

■ Example: 'One Art' by Elizabeth Bishop

Read the following extract 'One Art' by Elizabeth Bishop (Bishop 110) and then examine the responses that follow it. Notice the difference between the summary and the analysis. Consider what characterizes each response.

> The art of losing isn't hard to master;
> so many things seem filled with the intent
> to be lost that their loss is no disaster.
>
> Lose something every day. Accept the fluster
> 5 of lost door keys, the hour badly spent.
> The art of losing isn't hard to master.
>
> Then practice losing farther, losing faster:
> places, and names, and where it was you meant
> to travel. None of these will bring disaster.
>
> 10 I lost my mother's watch. And look! my last, or
> next-to-last, of three loved houses went.
> The art of losing isn't hard to master.
>
> I lost two cities, lovely ones. And, vaster,
> some realms I owned, two rivers, a continent.
> 15 I miss them, but it wasn't a disaster.
>
> – Even losing you (the joking voice, a gesture
> I love) I shan't have lied. It's evident
> the art of losing's not too hard to master
> though it may look like (*Write* it!) like disaster.

Summary

In this poem, the speaker appears to be lecturing to a listening audience about how easy it is to lose things. She begins by listing small objects or insignificant losses such as keys and a wasted hour, and then she moves on to making claims about how easy it is to lose things that most people would think are more significant: a watch with sentimental value. Then she takes a leap into the fantastic, claiming that she has lost houses, cities, realms, rivers and a continent. Clearly these claims cannot be literal. In the final stanza, she tries to claim that the loss of 'you', someone she loved, is also easy, but she betrays herself by losing the thread of her argument. She gets distracted by memories of the person's voice and gestures, then she has to resort to reiterating her claims most emphatically.

Analysis

'One Art' is essentially a villanelle; however, Bishop has altered the form in some significant ways. Lines 1 and 3 do not repeat exactly as we expect in a villanelle. Line 1 repeats properly until the very end of the poem, when it has been altered to 'not too hard to master'. Line 3, however, never repeats exactly. The word 'disaster' does end each of the appropriate lines, but nothing else is the same. Finally, the end rhymes are not perfect rhymes; Bishop has given us a number of slant rhymes such as 'fluster' and 'master' in stanza 2, 'last or' and 'master' in stanza four, and 'gesture' and 'master' in stanza 6.

If we consider that Bishop also created an unreliable narrator, we can understand why the villanelle form is not quite correctly rendered.

We know that the speaker is unreliable because of the last stanza. We see in lines 16–17 that she loses control over the argument she has been so carefully building, that no matter how important something is, it can be lost quite easily. The 'you' is evidently the most valuable thing the speaker has to lose, since he comes even after the loss of rivers and realms and continents. But rather than being able to brush that loss off lightly, as she does with all the others she mentions, the speaker gets side-tracked into a memory of his voice and gestures. She can't sustain the light-hearted, flippant tone; she slides into nostalgia. She tries to get herself back on track by fiercely defending her earlier position – that 'I shan't have lied' is most emphatic. She is determined that her claim that losing the 'you' is easy shall be true. But by the end of the poem, when she has to force herself to write the word 'disaster', which, because of the form of the poem must come next, we see that she realizes that her argument is futile. She has been trying to convince herself, and she has failed.

The speaker tried, through the first five stanzas, to tell one story, but in the last stanza, she herself has to recognize that she was fooling herself. This use of the unreliable narrator is quite interesting; the speaker is unreliable through the first part of the poem and becomes reliable at the end.

The effect of the shift in the narrator's relationship to truth also reveals to us why the villanelle form is imperfect. The speaker cannot control the form because her falseness is showing through. Every time she gets to a line about 'disaster', it loses its required form. That failure of form reflects the failure of intention.

So, the speaker's use of the villanelle form failed because the speaker couldn't pull it off. The poet, on the other hand, knew exactly what she was doing. She did not fail to write a perfectly formed villanelle because she could not; she wrote a villanelle whose form reveals to the reader important aspects of the speaker's character.

Summary vs analysis in the sample passage

As we saw with the summary of the prose passage at the beginning of the chapter, the summary here focuses on the speaker in the context of her role as a character in the dramatic situation. It does not investigate the means by which the speaker tells her story; instead, it focuses on the speaker's actions.

Dramatic situation vs narrative situation

In this poem, we have an interesting relationship between the dramatic situation and the narrative situation. The dramatic situation consists of a speaker talking about past events in her life. Some of those events appear to be invented. From the perspective of the speaker, then, she is talking about her past. The poet, however, is showing her readers the present: the moment of actual speaking. Because we see that the narrator is not telling the truth about events as she speaks, we are able to discover that the claims she makes about losing are false, and that the loss of the 'you' is, after all, quite painful.

Author vs narrator

The analysis in this particular example addressed the difference between author and speaker directly. Here we have an unreliable narrator and, as we noted previously, when we have an unreliable narrator, it is always important to investigate the question of *why* the author chose to create such a narrator. In this poem, the unreliability of the narrator reveals the author's ideas about loss, and we particularly see that, even if we lie to ourselves, the loss of a loved one inevitably brings suffering.

ACTIVITY 2: 'THE THOUGHT FOX' BY TED HUGHES

Read the poem 'The Thought Fox' by Ted Hughes (2) and write an analytical paragraph. Finally, write the short summary that you would need to include in order to give context to your analysis. Be sure that your summary focuses on the literal level – on what happens in the dramatic level of the poem, as opposed to the narrative level, just as you did for the prose passages previously. When you are done, you can read the comments on this activity which are at the end of the book.

I imagine this midnight moment's forest:
Something else is alive
Beside the clock's loneliness
And this blank page where my fingers move.

5 Through the window I see no star:
Something more near
Though deeper within darkness
Is entering the loneliness:

Cold, delicately as the dark snow
10 A fox's nose touches twig, leaf;
Two eyes serve a movement, that now
And again now, and now, and now

Sets neat prints into the snow
Between trees, and warily a lame
15 Shadow lags by stump and in hollow
Of a body that is bold to come

Across clearings, an eye,
A widening deepening greenness,
Brilliantly, concentratedly,
20 Coming about its own business

Till, with a sudden sharp hot stink of fox
It enters the dark hole of the head.
The window is starless still; the clock ticks,
The page is printed.

Full summary

Summary appropriate for analysis

Analysis

Short summary

How do you decide which aspects of the text to focus on?

Regardless of which assessment you are writing for, you will have to decide which very few aspects of a work of literature you will focus on in your paper. You will never have time to focus on everything interesting or important from any work – not even from a very short poem. A choice to give a superficial overview of many different aspects of a text will always be a much weaker choice than choosing to examine a few aspects of the text deeply and thoroughly. Depth, in other words, is always going to be more successful than breadth in terms of gaining marks.

■ Focus on what the question directs you to

The decision about what to write about is easiest when the assignment or prompt directs you to focus on certain features. Here, for instance are some questions from the 2018 IB English HL exam:

Some characters in plays remain static: they don't change. With reference to at least two plays you have studied, compare how static characters are used and to what effect.

As we said from the beginning of the chapter, your most important responsibility is to answer the question as asked. When the questions in Paper 2 direct you to specific literary strategies or elements of text, then you absolutely must write about those. This question requires students to focus on static characters. The decision was made for them by the examiners who set the question. Your job in this case is to choose works with static characters in them to write about.

Many poets seem to employ deliberate ambiguity. Comparing the work of at least two poets you have studied, consider how ambiguity adds to the reader's experience of the poems.

Similarly to the first question, this question takes the problem of choice away from the writer. If you were writing this paper, you would be required to focus on the use of ambiguity in poems that you read. Notice that in choosing the question you are going to respond to, you must understand the vocabulary. If you don't know what a static character is or what ambiguity is and how a poet uses it, then these first two questions would be poor choices for you.

In the works of at least two authors you have studied, consider and compare the techniques used to make their fictional worlds believable.

This question is slightly different in relation to your choice of what to write about because it is more general than either of the first two. The question directs you to focus on how authors make their fictional worlds believable, and that goal could be accomplished through a wide variety of strategies. You really have to make two choices here: a choice of texts which are highly believable, or in which there are at least elements of the very believable, and you would then choose the strategies in those texts that the authors used to create that sense of believability. The range of possibilities is potentially endless, but your choice will be circumscribed by the texts themselves. If the author used extremely detailed description, you would write about that. If another author used real-world settings or carefully drawn characters or accurately depicted reference to historical events, you would focus on those. You might need to write about multiple strategies from a single text, as well.

■ Focus on elements that are important to creating meaning

Some writing tasks, such as the paper that HL students will be required to write, are much broader. You will have to choose the work or works you wish to write about, which aspect of those works you will discuss, and the elements of the texts which are relevant to those choices. In such an instance, then, how will you decide?

First, you will need to ensure that whatever you choose is a literary element that you can connect both to the topic you chose and to the meaning of the work you are writing about.

Knowing that you have to focus on analysis, you know that you have to break down the literary work into the component parts, but also that you have to connect those parts to meaning. A paper which merely identifies the presence of a number of literary strategies will not earn high marks. Such a paper only does half the job. Don't, in other words, just point out that there is a metaphor in the first stanza of a poem or in a particular paragraph in a novel; identify the metaphor and then explain how it helps you understand the meaning of the text. In the analysis of 'One Art' earlier in this chapter, you saw how the writer identified the villanelle form and the presence of an unreliable narrator, and then went on to connect both of those features to the idea that loss is, despite what the narrator claims, inevitably very painful.

That last step is crucial to writing a good paper, so if you know that a strategy is present, but you cannot explain what it contributes to the meaning of the work, do not choose that strategy.

■ Show off your skill as a reader

Knowing that you have to choose literary features which contribute to meaning does not narrow down your choice very much. All the literary elements you can identify from any given work contribute to meaning. One important consideration to help you narrow down the choice is that you want to show yourself to be as sophisticated a reader as you possibly can. Some strategies are more complex than others by their nature, both because they are harder to recognize and because they are harder to explain in a meaningful way. Metre, structure, symbolism and narrative perspective are all strategies which, if you can discuss them intelligently, will show you to be a sophisticated reader.

■ Metre

As we saw in Chapter 4, metre is a complicated strategy for several reasons: the technical terminology involved, the potentially wide variety of metres that might be present and because it is when it varies from the expected norm that metre really gets interesting. When you write about metre, make sure that you use the terminology precisely and correctly. In addition, be sure that you demonstrate that you know exactly where and how the metre is varied, and, as mentioned in the previous section, be sure you connect the metrical patterns and/or variations to meaning.

This table shows an example of how you could do this for Shakespeare's Sonnet 116.

Strategy	Identification	Explanation of how the variation in metre relates to meaning
Replacement of iamb with trochee.	Line 2: Last two feet of the line. The first foot in the pair (the fourth foot of the line) is a trochee instead of an iamb; the final foot in the line is an iamb.	This replacement emphasizes an example of antithesis: 'Love is not love' — the trochee means that both times 'love' is said, it is stressed. 'Not love' is the opposite of 'love', so the antithesis is underlined by the variation in metre. That antithesis is central to the sonnet, since it means to define real love as being unshakeable and unalterable. In the case of this phrase, the alteration in metre swings immediately back to an iamb, so that normality is restored. Even though the phrase ends with 'not love', what we get, metrically speaking, is normal rhythm (the rhythm of the heartbeat) representing true love after all. Just as the line says: the initial alteration in metre cannot substantively alter love.

■ Structure

It's quite easy to identify formal structures in poems, such as those you learned about in Chapter 2; however, analysing the *function* of those structures is much more difficult. Identifying important structural elements in novels, short stories or poems that don't have a recognized poetic structure is much harder. Refer to Chapter 3 (page 67) for a review of how to identify structure in prose fiction.

Discovering the structure of a poem which has no identifiable structural elements is similar to the problem of discovering the structure of a work of prose. You have to consider how the poet or speaker has constructed the poem in terms of a developing story, a developing argument, or the creation of another type of effect.

■ Example: 'Farewell Wild Woman (I)' by Lorna Goodison

> I seemed to have put distance
> between me and the wild woman
> she being certified bad company.
> Always inviting me to drink
> 5 bloody wine from clay cups
> and succumb to false promise
> in the yes of slim dark men.
> Sometimes though when I'm
> closing the house down early
> 10 and feeling virtuous for living
> one more day without falling too low
> I think I see her behind the hibiscus
> in dresses competing with their red,
> and she's spinning a key hung on a
> 15 cat's eye ring
> and inviting me to go low riding.

Here we have a poem with only one stanza and no consistent metre. But we can look at what the speaker is doing as she structures her thinking. In the first two lines, she makes a claim about distancing herself from a bad influence. In lines 3–7, she describes the behaviours that make the wild woman a bad influence. In lines 8–16, she offers a counterclaim, acknowledging that despite her attempt to distance herself, she sees the wild woman hanging about the edges of her life, tempting her to fall. In this interpretation, we can see a structure of three sections: claim, justification and counterclaim. We might argue that since half the poem is devoted to the counterclaim, the structure helps us see that the woman's determination to avoid the wild woman is a precarious one.

You could write about the structure of this poem using those three sections as a structural breakdown. Notice, though, that there is not a cut and dried correct answer: you could make an argument for a different structure. The critical requirement is for you to justify the claims you make about how the text is structured – and, ultimately, how that structure contributes to meaning.

■ Symbols

The analysis of symbols is a more sophisticated skill than the analysis of metaphors and similes because symbols are less fixed in their meaning and require more imaginative and rational work on the part of the reader. Generally speaking, the comparison is stated in the text for both metaphors and similes. For symbols, however, that overt comparison is often not present. When you think of the green light in *The Great Gatsby*, for example, we are never told that the green light stands for Daisy Buchanan. Readers have to work that out for themselves. That green light, furthermore, can certainly be seen to stand for more than just Daisy: you can argue that it stands for Gatsby's desire, as an encouragement to him to keep pursuing the dream, for wealth, for rebirth, and possibly for other things. In writing about that symbol, it would be up to you to explain which of those (or all of them) function in the text. That need requires more sophistication of you as a reader and writer than metaphors and similes generally do.

When writing about symbols, metaphors or similes, make sure that you identify both parts of the figure. For metaphors and similes, the two parts have names: **tenor** and **vehicle**. The vehicle is the object to which the main thing is being compared, while the tenor is the thing that the writer wants the audience to see in a new way. Your job is to figure out which characteristics of the vehicle enlighten us about the nature of the tenor. So, when Shakespeare has Romeo say:

> But soft, what light through yonder window breaks?
> It is the East, and Juliet is the sun.
> (Act 2 Scene 2, 2–3)

> ### KEY TERMS
>
> **Tenor** – in relation to a metaphor, the tenor is the thing or object that the author wants the reader to understand better.
>
> **Vehicle** – in relation to a metaphor, the vehicle is the thing or object that the author is comparing the subject to.

Juliet is the tenor and the sun is the vehicle. To interpret the metaphor effectively, we must consider which features of the sun apply to Juliet. We might consider that to Romeo, the relevant features are the fact that the sun is bright, it brings happiness and a sense of well-being, and, as he mentions, it rises in the east, bringing a new day. Juliet is, for Romeo, the joy of a new day. Conversely, we might also consider that the sun is a source of life, an enormous ball of fire, and if we were to get too close to the sun, it would burn us to death. Having read the play, we know that that is what happens to Romeo following his relationship with Juliet, so we can see that Shakespeare was foreshadowing something that Romeo couldn't yet know.

We do not use the terminology of tenor and vehicle with symbols; however, the concept is the same. You must consider what the symbol is, and which of its characteristics shed light on the object or idea for which it stands. For further analysis on how rhythm is used in this extract, please see page 20.

■ Narrative perspective

You can review Chapter 3 for the discussion of understanding the narrative perspective in prose. The speaker of a poem is not usually called a narrator, because the speaker is not always narrating an actual story, but all the same important concepts regarding narrators apply to speakers. Speakers of poems can be reliable or unreliable, they can be characters in the dramatic situation or observers and so on. If you can identify the narrative perspective of a text and explain how that perspective influences the meaning of the text, you are working at a very sophisticated level of textual interpretation.

IDENTIFYING NARRATIVE PERSPECTIVE

To make a basic interpretation of the narrative perspective, ask yourself these questions:

✔ Who is the speaker or narrator? What can you tell about the speaker as a person? If there is a third-person narrator or speaker, you cannot answer this question.

✔ When is the speaker or narrator talking relative to the events of the dramatic situation? Is it immediately afterwards? Years later? Before the events are even finished?

✔ How is the speaker or narrator speaking? Is there any indication of the speaker's emotional state or circumstance that might interfere with his or her objectivity?

✔ What is the speaker or narrator's relationship to the events about which he or she is speaking? Do they directly affect him or her?

When writing about the narrative perspective, you would not list off those questions and answers; you would, instead, synthesize your answers into a statement describing the narrative perspective.

Let's revisit the passage from *The Whistling Season* by Ivan Doig from earlier in this chapter (page 105) and consider the narrator, using these questions:

Question	Answer
Who is the narrator?	Paul, a state school official, is a man who is visiting his childhood home in order to try to make an important decision. We know that he must be at least 60 years old, as he was apparently a young teen in 1909, and it is now 1957.
When is the narrator speaking?	The narrator is speaking as he is visiting the house. He is in the house and talking about what he sees. He is also talking about events that happened five years ago, as well as events that happened 48 years ago.
How is the narrator speaking?	The narrator is quite calm and reflective. He is remembering the past without any extreme emotion. Although he has an important decision to make, he does not seem so stressed about it that he cannot think, remember or observe accurately.
What is the narrator's relationship to the events about which he is speaking?	Paul is speaking of events in which he was directly involved. The story is evidently memoir. The present events also involve Paul directly – the onus is on him to make a decision that is obviously quite difficult.
Description of narrative perspective:	The narrative perspective of this passage from *The Whistling Season* is from a man named Paul, a state school official who must make an important decision about the schools in his state. He has returned to his childhood home, and although the events about which he speaks concern him directly, his demeanour is calm and balanced. He comes across as quite a reliable source of information about what is happening.

Being able to show your understanding of how the narrative perspective and the reliability of the narrator contributes to the meaning of the text is a sophisticated skill, and these questions are a useful prompt to understanding what kind of narrator or speaker you are reading. When deciding whether to write about the narrator, you will have to determine the degree to which that perspective influences our ability to determine the truth about events. Unreliable narrators or speakers are generally more important as literary tools than reliable narrators are. Very often, their stories or poems are about those narrators as flawed human beings as much as they are about whatever content those narrators think they are delivering.

ACTIVITY 3: 'FAREWELL WILD WOMAN (I)' BY LORNA GOODISON

We reviewed this poem on page 117 in terms of its structure; now examine it in terms of narrative perspective by answering the questions below the poem 'Farewell Wild Woman (I)' By Lorna Goodison (116). At the end, write a statement describing the narrative perspective of the poem. When you are finished, you can read the notes at the end of the book.

> I seemed to have put distance
> between me and the wild woman
> she being certified bad company.
> Always inviting me to drink
> 5 bloody wine from clay cups
> and succumb to false promise
> in the yes of slim dark men.
> Sometimes though when I'm
> closing the house down early
> 10 and feeling virtuous for living
> one more day without falling too low
> I think I see her behind the hibiscus
> in dresses competing with their red,
> and she's spinning a key hung on a
> 15 cat's eye ring
> and inviting me to go low riding.

1 Who is the speaker? What can you tell about the speaker as a person?

2 When is the speaker talking relative to the events of the dramatic situation? Is it immediately afterwards? Years later? Before the events are even finished?

3 How is the speaker speaking? Is there any indication of the speaker's emotional state or circumstance that might interfere with her objectivity?

4 What is the speaker's relationship to the events about which she is speaking? Do they directly affect her?

■ An important consideration

There is one big caveat, however, to the idea that you ought, if you can, use one of these more sophisticated literary elements: if there is a 'less sophisticated' literary strategy in a particular work that is absolutely central to its meaning, then you undoubtedly must write about it.

John Donne, for example, in his poem 'A Valediction: Forbidding Mourning', used an extended metaphor of a mathematical compass to describe the connection between a husband and his wife, even if they were many hundreds of miles apart. The fixed point of the compass forms the centre of the relationship, and Donne portrays the idea that the leg of the compass will lean so that the angle between the two parts of the compass can increase, but never break apart. If you were to write about that poem and not discuss that metaphor, you would fail to demonstrate that you have a good understanding of that poem.

Likewise, Shakespeare's Sonnet 130 ('My mistress' eyes are nothing like the sun') uses that simile in the opening line to kick off a series of comparisons which ultimately prove to be ironic. You cannot demonstrate that you understand that sonnet without showing that you know how the similes and metaphors work. Part of your decision-making process then, when deciding what to write about, must be the determination of which literary strategies play the most important role in that particular work.

Finally, diction is generally not a very good choice – at least not if you cannot focus the concept further. 'Diction' just means word choice, and all the words of any text have been chosen. If you can, you should characterize the diction in some way. In almost every case, you can take the word or words you were tempted to call diction and re-categorize them as something else. Many words in English are already metaphors – think of the verb 'fall' used to describe someone losing status, or as a noun, as in the biblical 'fall from grace'. Another example is the adjective 'crowning', as in a 'crowning achievement'. In neither case is the action literal; no one physically falls and no one is literally crowned. Because English is so richly riddled with metaphor, you can often discuss the metaphorical use of language instead of simple diction.

If you can label a category such as 'technical jargon', 'financial terminology' or 'religious references', you will be showing a more refined understanding of the choice of words, and you will make it easier for yourself to be able to analyse the function of those words in creating meaning.

Final notes about choice

Your choice of what to write about depends on three important factors that you must take into consideration:

- the specific task assigned
- the most important elements which contribute to meaning
- your ability to show off your skills as a reader.

These three factors are listed in the order of their importance. All three are important, however, so you cannot approach the task of writing about literature with the idea that if you do the most important one you will have a good paper. You must do all three.

Organization

Once you know what to write about, you are left with the problem of how to organize your paper. You have two aspects of organization to deal with: the organization of the essay as a whole and the organization of each body paragraph, which is where the actual analysis appears.

You are probably used to organizing an essay by writing an introduction with a thesis statement, followed by the body of the paper, and finishing with the conclusion. Each of those sections requires a particular set of skills, outlined here.

Introductions

You have probably often heard that the introduction should grab the reader's attention. That might be true, but that is not the sole function of an introduction. An introduction must set up the argument that follows, so it has to be integrally related to the rest of the paper. Something that grabs the reader's attention but does not contribute in a significant way to the argument is a waste of words.

There follow six examples of introductory paragraphs for literary analysis essays. All six are written for the same thesis statement describing an interpretation of Eavan Boland's poem 'It's a Woman's World'. As you read the introductions, consider these points:

- None of these paragraphs make statements of anything that the reader is likely to already know.

- The sixth example, 'Ask a rhetorical question', is included only because it is a technique that writers have often been taught and is a warning of what *not* to do!

- These five types of introductions are useful devices, but in writing an effective essay, the writer has the responsibility of selecting whatever type of introduction will most effectively create the intended effect – even if that means writing an introduction which is not one of these types.

- Confident writers will be able to use these techniques in innovative ways, combine them or ignore them altogether.

- There is no rule for writing good introductory paragraphs. Good writing is any writing that gets the job done.

- The job is to mean what you say and say what you mean.

■ Type 1: Use a quotation

I walked beside the evening sea
And dreamed a dream that could not be;
The waves that plunged along the shore
Said only: 'Dreamer, dream no more!'

In these lines from 'Ebb and Flow', George William Curtis compares the relentlessness of the sea wearing away at the shore with the hopelessness of trying to hold on to an unattainable dream. Eavan Boland confronts the same subject in her poem, 'It's a Woman's World', in which she examines the question of whether time, like Curtis' ocean, has the power to erode a person's capacity to dream and to achieve that dream. Boland gives us snapshots of women at various points in history apparently caught in thankless, spiritless roles, and then prompts us to look beyond the surface grinding of the waves to see if there might not be a teeming life. The conclusion that she draws is opposite to Curtis': a woman's role in the world is complex, and her apparent domestic docility does not, in fact, undermine her capacity to dream and accomplish her dreams.

Note that this sample combines the use of a quotation with setting up an argument only to knock it down (see also Type 4). A quotation can be used just as effectively when it conveys an idea that is in accordance with the ensuing argument of the thesis.

■ Type 2: Begin with an anecdote

In 'Pride and Prejudice', Jane Austen created a protagonist in Elizabeth Bennet who struggles to find the balance between acting the role assigned to her by her culture effectively and finding for herself the personal satisfaction that comes from intellectual stimulation. Lizzy, born to moderate wealth, is trained from childhood to be the perfect wife and mother, to keep her husband's house, to play music and embroider, and to serve as the gracious hostess to all who enter her home. For Lizzy's sister Jane, her friend Charlotte and some of the other women in the book, the fulfillment of that role – or at least the chance to fulfill it – is sufficient motivation for living. In Elizabeth, however, a greater need burns, and she alone among the women of her acquaintance dares to turn down proposals of marriage from men who could provide her with the home and social standing in which to perform that role. Elizabeth, rather than hastening to marriage, holds out for a man who will be an emotional and intellectual partner, so that although she will, indeed, perform the social role assigned to her, she will do so in the context of a marriage of equal partners. It is this kind of domestic power that Eavan Boland seems to be advocating in her poetry, and notably in 'It's a Woman's World', in which she seems to suggest that a woman's role in the world is complex, and her apparent domestic docility does not, in fact, undermine her capacity to dream and accomplish her dreams.

Note that this example uses a literary anecdote; the anecdote can come from history, personal experience, literature or even current events. Any story that illustrates the idea to come in the thesis, and, subsequently, in the essay, will work.

■ Type 3: Give pertinent background information

Eavan Boland is a controversial figure among modern poets and particularly among Irish poets. Writing in a cultural context in which her field has long been predominately ruled by men who felt the artist's imperative was to battle the political status quo, she has been criticized most often for two things. First, for daring to deal with such seemingly insignificant issues as the everyday tasks of the woman in the home, rather than the vast moral struggle that has encompassed Irish history for the past several hundred years. And secondly, among those who accept her content as an appropriate subject for poetry, she has been further castigated for failing to take a position that is radically feminist. Boland's poetry is neither dogmatic nor blatant. Her work refuses to take the position that women should break out of the home and staunchly never budge. Instead, it often suggests, as 'It's a Woman's World' does, that a woman's role in the world is complex, and her apparent domestic docility does not, in fact, undermine her capacity to dream and accomplish her dreams.

Note that the trick here is to provide background information that is necessary (or at least helpful) for understanding the argument about to come, but that is not intuitively obvious to the most casual of readers. Remember that your audience for a literary analysis paper is the unknown educated reader, but not one who knows the work or its context in detail.

■ Type 4: Set up a counter argument

The traditional view that a woman's place is in the home carries with it an implication that usually goes unacknowledged: that those confined to roles in the home are in some way limited creatures. Presumably, under this view, women who have been constrained to the job of keeping house and raising children have been constrained because they lack the strength, intelligence, creativity and/ or character required for other jobs. If that is so, then the logical conclusion is that women in those roles necessarily lack the ability to break out of them, and they cannot, therefore, maintain a dream long or well enough to achieve it. Eavan Boland, however, in her poem, 'It's a Woman's World', provides an effective counter-argument to that position and demonstrates instead that a woman's role in the world is complex, and her apparent domestic docility does not, in fact, undermine her capacity to dream and accomplish her dreams.

Note that with this type of introduction, the balance of the paper deals with proving the thesis, and the initial argument presented in the introduction is generally not alluded to again – certainly not in any detail.

■ Type 5: Begin with a generality and move to the specific

One of the tasks every person faces in the process of growing towards a state of self-realization is deciding whether he or she is going to be concerned with how they are perceived by others. A classic example of this is the centuries-old debate about the woman's place. During the twentieth century, the feminist movement has claimed to fight for a vastly changed role for women in society, and feminists claim credit for opening up opportunities for women that didn't previously exist. This has sometimes led to women feeling guilty for wanting to take on traditional roles, as they are worried that others will think them weak. Eavan Boland takes a slightly different view in her poem, 'It's a Woman's World', in which she shows that a woman's role in the world is complex, and her apparent domestic docility does not, in fact, undermine her capacity to dream and accomplish her dreams.

Note that the generality posed should be thought-provoking. Do not make generalities that are statements of the obvious: 'Throughout history, poets have written about love' may be a generality, but it is an insult to the reader's intelligence. The example above is marginally acceptable, but really it is quite difficult to come up with a generality that is both general and subtle.

■ Type 6: Ask a rhetorical question

What is the proper place for a woman in today's world? This is the question that Irish poet Eavan Boland takes up in much of her poetry. Her portrayal of the woman's role throughout history is often ambiguous; sometimes the women in her poems seem downtrodden and powerless, but in some poems a strange strength underlies the seeming helplessness. One such poem is 'It's a Woman's World', which, right from the title, seems to suggest that a woman's role in the world is complex, and her apparent domestic docility does not, in fact, undermine her capacity to dream and accomplish her dreams.

Type 6 is a popular but ultimately ineffective method of writing an introduction. If you read the sample paragraph above carefully, you will see that the rhetorical question first and foremost adds nothing to the paragraph. The author could just as easily reword the second sentence and start there. The rhetorical question, furthermore, is very difficult to manage in print. The reason a question is rhetorical is that there is presumably only one possible answer to it. So there are three problems:

1 If there is only one possible answer, then the question really is not providing necessary information that the reader doesn't already know.

2 There really are very few questions for which there is only one possible answer (in the example above, for example, which is typical of what inexperienced writers try with rhetorical questions, there are many possible answers).

3 When there really isn't only one possible answer, the effect on the reader is that, by the nature of the medium, the reader must take in the question as if it were a direct question asked to him or her as an individual. That gives the reader the chance to answer the question for him or herself, and if the answer the reader provides doesn't match the answer the author had in mind, the reader is already thinking something in opposition to your ideas right from the very beginning.

There is, therefore, really only one way to use a rhetorical question effectively, and it is extremely hard to achieve: a rhetorical question works in an argument paper when it has been so masterfully set up that there truly is only one possible answer to the question *given the context in which it is posed*, and that it sneaks up on the reader so the answer, although the only possible answer in the context, comes as a surprise to the reader. The effective rhetorical question makes the reader do the work of drawing the only possible conclusion, and makes him or her do it right on the spot, so that the idea the question forces on the reader is new. If you can achieve that, then by all means, use a rhetorical question in your essay. If you can't, then avoid it. Rather than functioning as a 'Eureka' moment, that rhetorical question will function as a signpost to the reader that you are an inexperienced writer using a trick you have been shown but which you don't really understand.

Generally, it is always going to be wiser not to use questions in your essays; confine yourself to beautifully crafted and confident statements.

■ Thesis statements

The thesis statement for your paper should be the last sentence of the introduction. It is possible to write a good essay with a more general statement at the beginning of the paper so long as you build your argument to the thesis in the final paragraph. That structure can be quite difficult to manage, however, especially during a timed writing, so in most instances you will be wiser to begin with your thesis. You will see an example of the more sophisticated structure later in this chapter.

Here are some tips for writing a good thesis:

TIPS FOR WRITING THESIS STATEMENTS

1 Write a statement that offers your interpretation of what the author's meaning is. That means your thesis must make a claim about something the author believes, values, thinks or cares about.

2 The thesis must contain an idea which transcends the facts of the work. A sentence about the characters in a novel is not a thesis; the characters in the novel reveal something about human experience. Your thesis must state that broader idea.

3 The thesis must be a complete sentence.

4 The thesis should not contain a list of strategies. The analysis of the strategies belongs in your body paragraphs (see the following section) and should not begin in your introduction. The temptation to list some strategies can be strong but resist it. The list of strategies detracts from the idea around which you are organizing your paper.

5 Avoid the three-part thesis. Many students are taught to formulate thesis statements which contain three claims. An example of this type would be: 'In *The Great Gatsby,* Jay Gatsby is obsessed with Daisy, deluded about what he can accomplish, and fails to achieve his goals'. Notice that this statement already violates the second point above, because it is about what a character is like rather than about human experience in general. Notice also that if you wrote a paper on the basis of this thesis, it would end up being three separate little sections, independent of each other and not really a unified essay at all. If you manage to write a thesis that has three parts, all of which are appropriately formatted as statements of ideas about human experience, you will simply have too much to do in your relatively short paper.

6 Be specific! Claiming that the author 'makes a point' about something is not a thesis. A general statement of topic is not a thesis.

ACTIVITY 4: THESIS STATEMENTS

Read each of the following proposed thesis statements and identify which of the numbered tips above it does *not* comply with. Note that a statement might violate more than one of the recommendations! If the statement doesn't violate any, then it is a viable thesis. You can find the answers in the notes at the end of the book.

1 In *The Great Gatsby,* Fitzgerald shows how obsessed Gatsby is with Daisy.

2 In *The Great Gatsby,* Fitzgerald reveals that we can be driven to desire something which is not attainable, that failure to recognize what is possible leads to tragedy, and that wealth often goes along with a failure of morality.

3 In *The Great Gatsby,* Fitzgerald demonstrates the sometimes powerful correlation between wealth and lack of morality.

4   In *The Great Gatsby,* Fitzgerald uses metaphors, symbolic function of setting and flashbacks to make his point.

5   In *The Great Gatsby,* Fitzgerald writes about love.

6   Fitzgerald's *The Great Gatsby* shows that love, revenge, tragedy and resentment.

■ Analysis paragraphs

The body of your essay is where the analysis belongs. Analysis paragraphs have a very simple structure, with three parts, called **claim**, **evidence** and **warrant**. That structure is often abbreviated to **C-E-W**. The claim is the statement of what you intend to demonstrate in the paragraph, and it must tie directly back to the topic of the paper and your thesis statement. The evidence is the easiest part: the evidence is the stuff from the text, either quoted or paraphrased, which demonstrates the accuracy of your claim. The warrant, comprising most of the paragraph, is the explanation you give of how the evidence proves the claim. If you look back at the chart with the explanation of metre from Shakespeare's Sonnet 116 (page 116), the first column is the claim, the second column is the evidence and the third column is the warrant. You could take that material out of the chart and turn it into an effective analysis paragraph.

You must write a warrant for each bit of evidence you include, and you must not list several pieces of evidence and then try to tack the warrant on the end. The most common mistake that beginning writers make when writing about literature is to leave off the warrant, or to include a warrant that is not detailed enough. You cannot make assumptions; you must spell out your whole line of thinking.

ACTIVITY 5: SAMPLE ANALYSIS PARAGRAPH

Read the following paragraph from an essay comparing narrative perspective in several poems. This paragraph focuses on one poem: 'Domestic Interior', by Eavan Boland. Identify the claim, all the pieces of evidence and all the warrants. You might want to make a copy of the paragraph and then use three different colour highlighters to mark the various parts. When you have finished studying the structure of the analysis paragraph, you can read the notes at the end of the book.

The narrator of 'Domestic Interior' is a woman who comments on the Van Eyck painting as she views it. In the end, she contrasts the vision of domestic life that she sees in the painting with what is presumably her own personal experience with domestic life and shows the vision in the painting to be the lesser. What Boland's speaker objects to is that the woman has been portrayed solely as a vessel to ensure the continuance of the man's genes, rather than as a person who will have an individual experience of marriage. The painting depicts a woman heavily pregnant on her wedding day. This image reflects the contemporary cultural practice of ensuring that the woman is fertile before a man wastes his chances by marrying poorly. Portraying this bride in this state on this day reduces her worth to the ability to procreate. That the narrator of the poem disapproves of this depiction is shown through death imagery: the effect of the wedding ring is described through the invented verb 'ambering', a word which prefigures the image, later in the poem, of the woman being trapped in the varnish of the painting. Boland's narrator also describes the woman as being 'interred' in her joy. The marriage, as portrayed in this painting, and as interpreted by this narrator, amounts to the death of the woman. By contrast, the last two stanzas of the poem talk about a different way of life, one in which women make a space for themselves that is warm and domestic. The poem thus ends with the assertion that there is a way of life in which the things women deal with – pots and kettles, the implements of the kitchen – 'grow important'. In this portrayal of a woman's life, time moves on, the child is born, the woman has her own space in the house and her own experience quite apart from being a prize captured by the man. This vision of a woman's life is not in the painting; it is presumably drawn from the narrator's own experience.

Conclusions

Conclusions are notoriously difficult to write, but that reputation is somewhat misleading. When one has written a strong, logical, coherent argument, the conclusion is often inevitable. In such a case, the conclusion is the paragraph which must be written to finish the job the essay set out to do. If, however, you find yourself in the position of not knowing quite what to do to finish your paper, you can try one of the following methods.

TIPS FOR WRITING CONCLUSIONS

- ✔ Include a brief summary of the paper's main points.
- ✔ Ask a provocative question.
- ✔ Use a quotation.
- ✔ Evoke a vivid image.
- ✔ Call for some sort of action.
- ✔ End with a warning.
- ✔ Universalize (compare to other situations).
- ✔ Suggest results or consequences.

The most important characteristic of an effective conclusion is that it develops organically out of the paper. Think of a mathematical proof or a formal argument: you lay out the premises and then the conclusion is the inevitable implication of the fact that all those premises are true. The same must be true of your essay: in the body, you lay out the observations you have drawn about the work of literature, and the best conclusion will be one which must inevitably follow from the basis you laid down.

Overall organization

The important thing to remember when you are planning your essay is that you are building an argument. Each of your analysis paragraphs is one premise in your argument, and the conclusion is that which must be true now that you have demonstrated all the premises. You need to order the paragraphs in such a way that your reader follows your line of thinking: first, one must realize this, then this, then this and so on. If you have organized your essay well, the reader must read each paragraph in order to understand the paragraph that follows it.

The most common error that beginning writers make is to write separate paragraphs, all of which relate to the thesis and/or the topic of the paper, but which do not relate to each other. Your best tool for ensuring the interrelation of your paragraphs is the transitions between them. The transitions must provide an overt connection between the ideas in one paragraph to the ideas in the one that follows it.

Under no circumstance should you be aiming to write a five-paragraph essay. The five-paragraph essay is a beginner's structure; it's like having training wheels on your bicycle. By the time you reach your Diploma Programme course of study, you should be moving beyond those structures. Possibly, you might end up with an essay that happens to have five paragraphs, but you are much more likely to end up with an essay with more paragraphs – especially in the case of a comparison/contrast essay, as you will see later in the chapter.

■ Writing about unseen texts

In Exam Paper 1, you will have to write about a text (or two texts at HL) that you have not seen before. You will be working under timed conditions, so you will have to both study the text and plan and write the essay in the time allotted. You should assign about half of your time to the studying of the text and the planning of your paper and half the time to writing. If you are an HL student writing about two texts on Paper 1, you need to plan your time carefully. Allot half the overall time to each text, and then half of that for planning and half for writing.

You will have questions that you can use to help guide you in your reading. The following tips will help you approach the task of writing about unseen texts effectively:

TIPS FOR WRITING ABOUT UNSEEN TEXTS

✔ Plan your time carefully.

✔ Read the text thoroughly and at least twice. Consider the vocabulary carefully. Do you know all the words? If there are numerous words you don't know, especially in a poem, then you should not choose that text.

✔ Read the questions and consider the text with them in mind.

✔ Choose the literary elements you want to write about. You will probably not have time to write about more than two, so make sure you choose the two most important ones in terms of helping you understand the meaning of the text. If there are several equally important elements, then choose the most sophisticated ones you can find.

✔ Write the thesis statement before you write the introduction. In a timed writing, you do not need an elaborate introduction. If you are stuck for what to write as an introduction, leave some extra lines to add a paragraph later, write the thesis, and go from there. You can go back and write the introduction at the end if you have time.

■ Sample essay

The following essay was written under timed conditions. You will see from the comments that it has some flaws, particularly in the organization of the analysis paragraphs. It is, nevertheless, a very fine essay and would earn high marks. You may wish to review the poem (see pages 109–110) before you read the essay.

The writer used an anecdote to introduce the essay, one of the six types of introductions discussed. Note that the anecdote is true, and that it relates directly to the content of the poem. Do not try to invent an anecdote to fit a paper; if you don't have a true anecdote, use a different introduction.

If you come back and look at this again after you read the essay and the conclusion, you will see that the idea of immortality and preservation of beauty are key ideas in the overall interpretation of the poem. This is the connection that makes the anecdote integral to the essay and not just a cutesy add-on to try and interest the reader.

This statement is not a true theme. It connects the anecdote directly to the poem via a contrast ('less ambiguous vision'), and it generalizes what the events of the poem are about. You can get away with this only if you later (in the conclusion) offer a real theme statement that gets at what the poem means. If you struggle with keeping an essay coherent, then you should not try this method; use the traditional thesis at the start.

This is not the best transition sentence ever. This essay would, in fact, lose a few points on organization because the paragraphs are not rigorously structured as claim-evidence-warrant. There is no claim here in terms of meaning.

Evidence directly from the text with the location identified – by line number, not by stanza number or other method which would make the examiner hunt.

Here is the strategy that the writer is analysing. It is present, but not in the claim (hence the problem with organization). The writer actually names two strategies: imagery and irony.

The warrant, however, is effective. It begins with 'The image of the cotton wool ...' and goes to the end of the paragraph. It constitutes well over half the paragraph, and it does take us to meaning: the irony reveals the idea of man interfering with natural processes. (The attitude toward that idea will be developed in ensuing paragraphs.)

The title of the poem by Ruth Sharman is 'Birth of the Owl Butterflies', but it might just as well be called 'Death of the Owl Butterflies', as death is where the poem, in fact, takes us. As the daughter of an entomologist, I read this poem against a background of similar memories, and my first reaction was to read the story with the regret of the little girl I once was to see such beautiful creatures dead and pinned, but I also read the story with the remembered fascination of the paradox: sad as it made me to know that museum butterflies would never fly again, the pinned specimens also generated a certain satisfaction that came from knowing that the butterflies would be forever preserved in their freshly-hatched, pristine, and most beautiful state, never subject to the inevitable bashing, breaking and dulling fate of the butterfly fending for itself in a world much more solid than it. Pinning conferred on museum butterflies a kind of immortality they could never have attained by living out their normal lives. The narrator of the poem, however, offers a less ambiguous vision of the short life of six Owl Butterflies, and gives us the story of ill-fated creatures whose potential power fades before it ever had a chance to flex its wings.

Any chance that these six Owl Butterflies ever had of living out a normal butterfly life died when the narrator's father plucked the not-yet-butterflies from their natural home in the mountains of Central America. Human purposes over-rode nature's purposes, and the chrysalids were 'packed in cotton wool' (10) to be used by the father who would hatch them, set them (put them on pins), identify them and display them (11). The image of the cotton wool is telling: we use cotton wool to protect something valuable, to preserve it from harm. Ironically, then, the cotton wool itself becomes a source of harm, because in packing them so carefully away, the narrator's father was encasing them in a human-made chrysalis from which they would not be able to escape back to their mountain homes. Man in devising a purpose for the un-metamorphosed butterflies, appropriated them for his purpose, diverting them from whatever purpose nature might have had for them. By the time they could emerge from the cotton wool, they would already have metamorphosed from natural things to objects made, in a way, by man.

Sharman's narrator first encounters the chrysalids after they have been freed from the cotton

This paragraph is organized better than the previous one. Though the claim itself is not in the first sentence, it is in the second one. The first sentence is a transition which connects the claim of this paragraph to the idea set up in the previous one.

Specific evidence from the text.

Warrant explaining the significance of the symbol of the cookbooks and, by extension, of the kitchen.

More evidence from the text.

Another detailed warrant explaining the significance of the pin. Notice that in this paragraph, although the writer does not use a lot of words from the poem as evidence, she analyses the few she does choose in great detail. This shows sensitivity to language.

Here again, the claim is at the beginning of the paragraph, but it could probably be better worded: 'in terms of hell' could be explained as a metaphor, for example.

Evidence.

Warrant all the way to here explaining the significance of the heat from the radiator and why the paper's author thinks that that heat refers to hell. She could additionally have mentioned that this is a symbolic function of setting.

More textual evidence, followed by warrant tying that word to the idea of hell.

More textual evidence.

The warrant here begins with the use of the word 'home' and goes to the end of the paragraph. This is the part of the paragraph that explains the claim the writer made at the beginning, that the setting is ironic. Note the elegant phrasing in the very last phrase: 'unholy exchange' ties in the idea of hell without having to use the same word again.

This is a much more direct statement of technique: description that focuses on mimicry.

This time the writer uses a much lengthier excerpt from the poem as evidence.

wool, but entrapped in a different, equally alien, equally human-made, environment. The kitchen serves as a strikingly ironic setting – a sort of anti-sympathetic place – for the chrysalids. The kitchen, with its cookery books (5), symbolizing the meals that routinely bind the family of humans together in a natural communion, offers no such haven for butterflies who could partake neither of human meals nor of human succour. The chrysalids are 'pinned', furthermore, to the shelf (4). Not only does the image of being pinned to a shelf contrast sharply with the lost image of the chrysalis woven delicately to its natural plant, but the sharp silver image of the pin also pre-figures the pin that will set these butterflies for display, and suggests, in so doing, an insect crucifixion.

Indeed, these creatures have been sacrificed: not in service of redeeming man's sins, but rather, in service of furthering his knowledge, and Sharman portrays that sacrifice in terms of hell. The heat of the radiator (6), which provides comfort for the human inhabitants, hastens the chrysalids toward an unnatural birth – out of both time and place – and premature death. If hell is a place both alien and inhospitable, then this heated kitchen might be seen as a particular kind of hell for the butterflies. Indeed: the narrator describes the empty chrysalis, after the first butterfly hatches, as 'cloven' (25), a word which may mean, simply, something split in two, but which also offers a time-honoured reference to the devil. The narrator tells us that these chrysalids are 'five thousand miles from their mountain home' (8); the use of the word 'home' refers to the butterflies' literal place in the world, but it also recalls to us the homey setting of the kitchen for the humans. That home, however, is alien territory for the butterflies to be. The afterlife that these butterflies will experience will preserve them, unnaturally, for all posterity. These creatures will not, as in the normal course of events, return to dust, and so the setting tells us that the distance reflected in that unholy exchange of homes is not merely literal.

Sharman heightens the sense of displacement by describing the chrysalids and by pinpointing the mimicry which has evolved as their protection. She tells us that the chrysalids are '... like curled leaves' (13) and that each one is tipped with '... a silver spur,/a tiny gleam or drop of dew,/Nature had added as a finishing touch/to perfect mimicry' (13-16). There is no place for a dew-tipped leaf in a kitchen, and in this environment, the chrysalids, far from blending safely in, stand, strikingly, out. The idea of mimicry itself heightens the irony: the dew drop, which is not actually a dew drop, but, rather, only looks like one, suggests an impending rebirth. In the course of nature, the rebirth would have been literal, and while the literal will still occur in this alien kitchen, the caterpillar will still be reborn as the butterfly, the rebirth will also be metaphorical, and the metaphorical transformation will only mimic the real thing. Here, in the human home, rather than the caterpillar one, the butterfly will be born into a whole new world for which it is ill-equipped, unprepared, and over-matched.

The butterflies, not knowing that they are already lost, emerge from their chrysalises fighting: '... the pods exploded' (18) and the butterflies themselves are missiles (20). For a brief moment, the battle is the same battle that would occur in the Central American mountain-top, because the first battle is the battle for wings. One imagines that the butterfly, who used to be a caterpillar, has to make, in the first few minutes of its life, the transition into something wholly other. The legs, longer and thinner than the caterpillar's short, stubby, much more plentiful ones, are 'awkward' and 'unhinged' (22), and the wings, described here as 'a frilly party dress' (23), are dead weight, as useless, in their current state, as an actual party dress would be. The effort to spread the wings and gain control over them is the same effort that every Owl Butterfly expends in the moments after its birth. Here, though, the beautiful image of '... slow wings billowed with the blood/that pumped them full' (26–27) makes us understand the life that is flowing through the wings and which ends with the opening of the eponymous owl-eye spots on the underside of the hindwings. That ending, however, has a twist: the 'fierce owl eyes widened' (32), we are left to imagine, not merely as a matter of course, but also in surprise at finding themselves born into a place so vastly removed from the one they left. The owl eyes are not, of course, actually eyes: they are an evolutionary adaptation, another form of mimicry intended to protect the butterfly from predators, and so readers of the poem are left to understand that it is the narrator who infuses into this moment the sense of tragic irony.

The battle continues into the last stanza, but we know, as the butterflies do not, that it is already lost. There is no place for the butterflies to go,

---

The rest of the paragraph is warrant – note again that the warrant takes up at least half the paragraph – and ties the description of the butterflies to the irony that has been established, now, as an ongoing concern in the essay (and throughout the poem).

No claim here – this oversight solidifies the deduction the essay will get for organization. It won't be a huge deduction, and the writer of the paper might have got away with the first error if she hadn't made another one here.

Here we get the indication of which strategy is being analysed here. The evidence is functional and the point is clear; it is just not presented in a fully controlled analytical paragraph.

This is an excellent image, and the analysis of it would have benefited from the use of the term.

The discussion is redeemed somewhat by this sentence, because the use of the word 'imagine' builds on the idea of an image and makes the point about why that particular image is important to a reader's understanding of the text.

By the end of the warrant, the point about how the technique is working is clear.

This is a claim, but it is not a claim about strategy; it is a claim about interpretation. The poem does not use the word 'battle'; that is an interpretation this writer made.

This is an example of a simple reference to the significance of diction. Since it is one word (and one example) in a lengthy essay which deals with many other, more sophisticated, strategies, this use is not a problem.

This paragraph is also less well organized than it might be. Notice that the evidence goes all the way to the end. In fact, the warrant is in the next paragraph, and, since the paragraph was getting to be a bit lengthy, this decision might not be too bad.

This is the phrase that tells the reader that the writer is now analysing the evidence she brought up in the preceding paragraph: 'grief' connects directly to 'funeral bell' in the preceding sentence.

The strategy here is narrative perspective; it is implied however, rather than actually named. Naming it would have been better.

This is all interpretation, however, and explains the significance of the narrator's observation.

This opening is another claim that is interpretive, rather than focusing on strategy. The paper's author is, in fact, interpreting symbols, and it would have been a good idea to make sure that that term got used prominently!

This conclusion, however, makes up for a lot of sins, since it makes a highly original, and interesting, observation that most readers would miss: the leap from the literal fixing of the butterflies on their pins in a museum to their figurative fixing in the words of the poem is one of those observations that says to the examiner that this reader was really engaged with the text. The final sentence of the essay turns out to be the thesis, and it is, surprisingly, about poetry, rather than about butterflies.

when they take their 'first few timid forays' (44), because the kitchen is not their element. Even those few tentative flights were not an exercise of will or power, but something which was 'allowed' (44) by their killer, the narrator's father, who wanted, no doubt, to know that the wings were fully fixed before he froze them into one permanent moment. He swoops (45) down on the butterflies, as much predator as any bird in the wild would be, and, despite the vigorous beating of the now fully-formed wings (49), the butterflies can fly nowhere. The thrice-repeated rhyme (the only place in the poem with such clear repetition of sound) of 'kill', (46) 'fill(ed)' (47), and, in the last word of the poem, 'still' (48) ring with the finality of the funeral bell.

Before we can decide that grief is what is called for, however, Sharman gives us one final thought to ponder: the image of the glass gas-chamber jar is chilling, but the sad reality, for these six Owl Butterflies, is that the glass tomb is the best that they could get, under the circumstances. The narrator imagines for us the future that would have met them had they not been re-fitted into a wing-enclosing pod: 'I pictured them shattering later/on taps and cupboard corners' (41–42). These creatures have been so far removed from their natural habitat that there was no hope of survival. The jungle of the manmade fixtures poses easily as many dangers as the outdoor one could have offered, and at least in the glass jar, the remarkable wings are preserved from damage, and the butterflies go to their death whole, things of beauty and wonder, instead of broken to pieces.

And so in the end, the Owl Butterflies are returned to chrysalids, this time not of their own making. Their story does not end there, however, as in writing that story, Sharman gives them one more chrysalis, of an altogether different nature. 'Birth of the Owl Butterflies' consists of six octets, one, one imagines, perhaps whimsically, for each of the six Owl Butterflies that hatched and died in that kitchen far from their rightful place in the world. The poem, like the glass killing jar, allows us a look in from the outside at the very brief life of these 'monstrous' and beautiful creatures, but the poem can do what the jar, and the museum display to which the dead specimens were no doubt taken, cannot: the poem-jar gives us the whole life story of the butterflies, and not just the fixed, and rather cold, Linnaean image of Caligo, generic. In recording the birth and death – and all the short life in between – the poem and poet give us a Caligo that science cannot: equally permanent, equally fixed, and yet repeatedly alive, so that those fierce owl-eyes widen anew for each reader. The poem, I conclude, confers its own brand of immortality and redeems, to some degree, the cotton wool and the glass jar.

■ Comparison/Contrast

Exam Paper 2 will require you to write a comparison/contrast essay. The two ways to organize a comparison/contrast essay are called **block-by-block** and **point-by-point**. A block-by-block organizational structure is much less sophisticated than a point-by-point structure. If you are very short on time, you can use the block-by-block method, but even during the exam, you will show yourself to be a more sophisticated writer if you use the point-by-point method, so you should do so if you can. If you are not writing under timed circumstances, you should not resort to block-by-block for any reason.

The block-by-block structure looks just like it sounds: you would write all your analysis of one work and then all your analysis of the other work. The problem with this structure is that it tends to turn into two miniature essays which don't really connect to each other, so that you end up with two essays which answer the question, but which do not show that you can really compare and contrast. Block-by-block structure looks like this:

- Introduction

- Block one: all analysis of one text

- Block two: all analysis of the second text

- Conclusion

A point-by-point organization forces you to do the actual comparison/contrast work, because you must choose specific points to discuss about each work. Once you have chosen the main points of your argument, you bring them up one at a time and you analyse how each one is used in both texts before you move on to the next point of argument. Point-by-point structure looks like this:

- Introduction

- Point one: text one

- Point one: text two – *this paragraph needs to contain an overt reference back to the previous paragraph, stating whether this text handles the technique in the same way as the first text or differently.*

- Point two: text one

- Point two: text two – *this paragraph needs to contain an overt reference back to the previous paragraph, stating whether this text handles the technique in the same way as the first text or differently.*

- (Add more alternating points as needed)

- Conclusion

You write two paragraphs for each point, one for each work, for however many points you are going to write about. You probably should not be trying for more than three different points in a Paper 2 essay, given the limitations you are under. Too many points mean superficial treatment of one or more of them. You can write an excellent essay with deep analysis of two different points of comparison and/or contrast. If your points are not extremely complicated, however, you should aim to make at least three points of connection between the two works.

The following sample essay is a good model of how to use this structure. The points around which the student has structured his analysis are:

1 historical attitudes towards gender

2 the contrast of historical attitudes and structures with modernity.

This essay was also written under the pressure of time, and you will see that it is not perfect in terms of achieving all the goals laid out in this chapter; however, it is still very fine work. You do not have to be perfect. Strive to achieve all the objectives; however, you should realize you can still earn very high marks if you have a few relatively minor errors.

The student has written a solid comparison/contrast essay in which he connects the two works to each other with each point that he makes, so we, as readers, get a clear sense of how the two works are alike and different in their handling of the topic that was assigned for the paper.

> *Writers often import or adapt historical material in writing their works. In at least two works you have studied, explore what or how this material contributes to the works.*
>
> 'The Awakening' by Kate Chopin and 'The Great Gatsby' by F Scott Fitzgerald were published less than 30 years apart. Despite, however, their relative proximity in date of publication, they propose radically different portraits of contemporary America. Both Chopin and Fitzgerald use their texts to harshly critique the social attitudes and morals of the time, be they too rigid or too loose. They each effectively examine the historical attitudes in play shaping contemporary society and morality. 'The Awakening' takes place in 'turn of the century' Louisiana, a predominantly catholic and conservative state and emblematic of a fading social order in which women acted as the property of their husbands. 'The Great Gatsby' has come to define the so called 'Jazz age' of the 'Roaring' 1920s, marked by economic prosperity, unrestrained consumerism and rapidly crumbling post-war social morals. Here, the society in question appears to be lurching forward to the future whereas 'The Awakening's Louisiana seems to cling to the past. This essay will explore, with reference to gender roles and social structure, how Chopin and Fitzgerald use historical material (namely preserved attitudes) as a foil for the more modernist and progressive forces shaping each story.
>
> Gender is a compelling element of both texts. While Edna in 'The Awakening' promotes a highly progressive vision of womanhood and female autonomy, her counterpart Daisy, in 'The Great Gatsby' appears to reject the 'looser' morals of the society around her to cling onto a perhaps more historical notion of devoted loyalty to husband and child. The primary conflict within Chopin's 'The Awakening' is Edna's struggle to liberate herself from the oppressive gender expectations placed upon her. These expectations and limits are stressed by the bird imagery running throughout. Birds, traditional symbols of freedom through flight, are kept in cages for human pleasure. Like the birds, Edna feels entrapped within a context of unchanging social attitudes. Her independence and movements are limited and she, like Madame Lebrun's

parrot, is unable to effectively communicate. In the New Orleans social world in which the novel is set, femininity is severely dictated and governed. A woman is expected to act as a loving daughter, wife and mother, with no recognition of her own sexuality. The women surrounding Edna (such as Mme Ratignolle) appear to embrace their outlined social role: 'They were women who idolised their children, worshipped their husbands, and esteemed it a holy privilege to effect themselves as individuals and grow wings as ministering angels'. These 'angels' use their wings to protect and administer care rather than fly. Edna comes to understand that her husband considers her 'a valuable piece of personal property'. These rigid social attitudes can be considered historical in that they are preserved from the past without discernible change. Edna, in contrast, develops a heightened awareness of her status in the world and attempts to reject it to 'free her soul from responsibility'. She abandons her husband and two sons and personally instigates affairs (one sexual with Alcee, and one emotional with Robert). In this, her modern ideas about womanhood clash with the historical attitudes towards womanhood of the society to which she belongs.

'The Great Gatsby' also considers gender politics (though to a lesser extent) in its portrait of the roaring twenties. While the women here are perhaps 'freer' than those featured in 'The Awakening', they are still bound by social constraints that the male characters are able to avoid. The primary female characters: Daisy, Jordan and Myrtle, are all to some extent defined by their relationships to the male characters in the story. This can be observed by the casual fashion by which Nick refers to Tom and Daisy: 'I drove over there to have dinner with the Tom Buchanans', Tom's identity encompasses his wife. At Gatsby's party, Nick observes the 'men and girls' (using the term girls rather than women). These details can be appreciated as remnant of historical attitudes and practices governing society despite the widespread modernisation of many other societal elements. 1920s New York appears somewhat accepting of sexual liberalism (the difference can be visualized when women attend Gatsby's parties sporting revealing outfits). Tom openly engages in a sexual affair with his mistress Myrtle, without remarkable retribution or consequence. Daisy also lacks serious hesitation before rehabilitating her romantic relationship with Jay Gatsby. However, despite her affair, Daisy retains a historically inspired attitude towards female duty. She eventually decides to remain in a marital union with Tom rather than leave him for Jay. In this, she rejects the progressive attitude that Edna pushed for and embraced. She hopes that her daughter be 'a fool — that's the best thing a girl can be in this world, a beautiful little fool'. Daisy thus promotes a patriarchal vision of the female ideal as ditzy and beautiful, oblivious of social entrapment and 'gilded cages'.

In addition to gender, the two texts also foil preserved historical structures and attitudes with modernity when it comes to societal structure and materialism. 'The Awakening's New Orleans possesses a deeply entrenched class system reminiscent of historical divides that Edna appears to snub when she rejects huge wealth to live alone in a cottage: 'There was with her a feeling of having descended in the social scale, with a corresponding sense of having risen in the spiritual'. Edna thus rejects the security of her position at the top of the historic class structure just as she rejects its oppressive nature, she identifies an inverse relationship between social rank and liberation/independence. This proves her character to be unfazed by social materialism and thus socially progressive. She recognizes that her value is not linked to wealth or status. Chopin employs the motif of houses to emphasize this rebuke of historically valued wealth and class. Edna stays in multiple houses in the course of the story (in the Grand Isle cottages, the large family home in New Orleans and finally her 'pigeon house'). Each of these homes can be seen as a marker of her emotional awakening as well as her shifting social status. The most significant shift takes place when Edna moves from her family's large New Orleans home to a much smaller cottage. This move can be seen as an attempted liberation from the plethora of Leonce's material objects with which Edna ultimately equates herself. In this move, Edna's progressivist ideas come into play and historical priorities are dismissed.

'The Great Gatsby' also approaches class and material success from a lens of conflict between history and modernity, as seen in the clash between 'Old Money' and 'New Money', personified by Tom Buchanan and Jay Gatsby. Fitzgerald stresses the division of the classes through setting and imagery. House locations in 'West Egg' and 'East Egg' respectively signify 'New and Old Money'. Similarly to Chopin, Fitzgerald uses the motif of houses as markers of social order. The rapid modernisation and economic boom driving the east coast New York's rampant consumerism divides the wealthy class into the historical 'old money' families with fortunes built up over hundreds of years alongside influential social connections with the newly developing 'new money' class who made their money in the 1920s boom and thus compensate for their lack of historical social status with lavish exhibitions of wealth. Gatsby's 'new money' is a key component of his identity and his insecurities and this class rivalry of the wealthy is a key underlying theme in the struggle over Daisy. Materialism also plays a major role in 'The Great Gatsby'. While Edna is repelled by the concept of being a man's possession and is dismissive of the wealth and materialism, Daisy finds wealth alluring and attractive. She ultimately envisions herself as a possession of Tom's. She conflates her attraction to Gatsby with attraction to his newfound wealth and status, this conflation is best observed when she breaks down at the sight of Gatsby's luxurious and extensive collection of English shirts as well as through the superfluous and continuous luxury imagery. Daisy embraces the historical concept of selecting a partner for material gain and security. She ultimately envisions herself as a possession of Tom's.

'The Awakening' and 'The Great Gatsby', while they promote fundamentally disparate portrayals of America, are each decisively influenced by the societal context and culture in which their stories take place. Chopin and Fitzgerald, each in their treatment of context, consider the clash of historical material with the more modernist progression of either the protagonist or society itself. These contrasting attitudes and perceptions succeed in constructing a more nuanced vision of the characters as well as the macro societal shifts and evolution at large, thus enabling the reader to fully appreciate each story and each character's actions.

Ten tips for improving your writing style

1 Make sure that whatever subject you choose for your sentences can do the verb that you attach to it. Beginning writers very often associate active verbs to non-sentient subjects, which results in false statements. For example: the sentence 'Poetry understands that symbols can have flexible meanings', is not a true statement. Poetry cannot understand anything; readers can understand and poets can understand. Ensure that as many of your sentences as possible have people as subjects – the author, the narrator or speaker, the characters in the text, and the readers should be the focus of your analysis, not abstractions.

2 Related to number one is the problem of passive voice and overuse of 'be' verbs. No form of the verb 'to be' is an action; 'to be' is just to exist. The 'be' verbs are: is, am, are, was, were, be, being and been. A paper filled with lots of instances of things existing is a very flat paper. Passive verbs nearly always use some form of the verb 'to be' as well, and you can see, just from the name, that nothing happens when you use the passive voice. Note the difference between the following two sentences:

   a The metaphor of the green light is used to show how Gatsby is in love with Daisy who is, to his mind, far away from him.

   b Fitzgerald uses the metaphor of the green light to embody Gatsby's obsession with Daisy, whom he sees as a distant, but highly desirable, objective.

   The second version is a much more powerful sentence. The verbs actually reveal a more sophisticated understanding both of how the author uses the metaphor and of Gatsby's feeling for Daisy. Once you finish your first draft, go back and eliminate every 'be' verb that you can.

3 Make sure that you are precise in identifying subjects of sentences. 'This', 'that', 'these', and 'those' are not nouns; they are demonstrative pronouns. Every time you write one of those words, you must include the noun to which it refers. Many beginning writers tend to fill their sentences with statements like 'This shows what the poet meant'. Such a sentence does not demonstrate your understanding of the text at all. You need to write something much more specific such as: 'This contradiction creates a juxtaposition that we would not ordinarily expect, and so reveals the author's intention to startle the reader with a new insight'.

4 Rely on nouns and verbs to carry your meaning; eliminate adjectives and adverbs as much as possible. Sometimes you will absolutely need an adjective so as, for example, to differentiate two objects, but most adjectives end up being nothing but fluff. Read the following sample paragraph and notice how little is added to the actual analysis by the adjectives and adverbs.

This is the excellent and interesting opening paragraph of Jane Austen's most famous novel 'Pride and Prejudice', a novel about whether it is even really possible for most normal individuals to transcend rigid and unfair social expectations and make a highly successful marriage on their own personal and private terms. These first fascinating sentences are widely, famously renowned for their extremely clever wit, but they also slightly suggest a surprisingly wide range of interesting, deep philosophical possibilities, and perhaps it is that, as much as the engaging humour, which appeals. These two short sentences, only 71 words, reflect deep ideas not only about extreme wealth and successful marriage, but also about free will, individual selfhood, and the deep meaning or pointless meaningless of life.

If you read carefully, you will see that the words highlighted in yellow are mostly redundant, or they pile on extra words that add nothing to the point that the paragraph makes. Now read the revised version from which the excess words have been eliminated.

This is the opening paragraph of Jane Austen's 'Pride and Prejudice', a novel about whether it is possible for individuals to transcend social expectations and make a successful marriage on their own terms. These first sentences are renowned for their wit, but they also suggest a range of philosophical possibilities, and perhaps it is that, as much as the humour, which appeals. These two sentences, only 71 words, reflect ideas not only about wealth and marriage, but also about free will, selfhood, and the meaning or meaningless of life.

This version is much cleaner. All the words are necessary for the point to be made. Look, particularly, at the use of the phrase 'free will': if you leave out the adjective 'free' there, the meaning changes significantly. 'Free' here is a necessary adjective. Remove all the clutter from your writing that you possibly can. Examiners will certainly know if you are trying to pad your word count with essentially useless words.

5   Use the word 'it' as seldom as possible. Never use 'it' without a clear antecedent, unless it is in an idiom, such as 'it is raining'. If you cannot identify the antecedent for 'it', neither can the examiner. 'It' all by itself has no meaning, and if your paper gets filled up with lots of instances of 'it' without antecedents, you will find that the essay has little substance. The more specific and concrete you can be in your statements the better.

6   Equally problematic, though for different reasons, is the reliance on the pronoun 'you'. In spoken English, especially colloquial English, people often use 'you' to mean something like 'everyone' or 'anyone'. In writing, however, 'you' is direct address to the reader. When we have said 'you' in this book, we have meant, specifically, you – the person reading the book. We are offering you, individually, advice. If you try to use 'you' in analytical writing, however, you will end up telling your reader (often an IB examiner) what he or she thinks or feels or does. If you do that, you run the risk of offending the reader by ascribing them a feeling he or she does not have, or you make untrue statements. Be sure that your pronouns properly identify the actual person who thinks, feels or acts the way that your sentence claims that he or she does.

7   Work hard on writing actual transitions, rather than relying on shortcuts such as 'to begin', or 'next', or 'similarly'. One-word transitions are shortcuts which let the writer off the hard work of being clear about how two sentences or two paragraphs relate to each other in a meaningful way. Consider the difference between these two pairs of sentences:

■   **Version 1: Last sentence of paragraph:** Not only does the image of being pinned to a shelf contrast sharply with the lost image of the chrysalis woven delicately to its natural plant, but the sharp silver image of the pin also pre-figures the pin that will set these butterflies for display, and suggests, in so doing, an insect crucifixion.

■   **First sentence of next paragraph:** Next, these creatures have been killed so that man can increase his knowledge, and Sharman portrays that idea in terms of hell.

Notice that in this version, the overly simplistic 'transition' between the two paragraphs means that the reader is left to try to figure out how the ideas in the two sentences relate to each other. The author of the essay has not done a good – or even sufficient – job of making the logic clear.

- **Version 2: Last sentence of paragraph:** Not only does the image of being pinned to a shelf contrast sharply with the lost image of the chrysalis woven delicately to its natural plant, but the sharp silver image of the pin also pre-figures the pin that will set these butterflies for display, and suggests, in so doing, an insect crucifixion.

- **First sentence of next paragraph:** Indeed, these creatures have been sacrificed: not in service of redeeming man's sins, but rather, in service of furthering his knowledge, and Sharman portrays that sacrifice in terms of hell.

Note that in this version, the words in blue in the second sentence make clear, specific connections to the words in blue in the preceding sentence, so that the reader is clearly guided through the developing idea.

8 Use punctuation correctly. Semi-colons must be used to join two independent clauses (complete sentences) or between items on a list. Commas are possibly the most frequently misused punctuation mark. Here are three rules for using commas that cover most (though definitely not all) situations in which you need to use commas. If you follow these three rules, you will use commas correctly almost all the time.

- Use a comma when you are joining two independent clauses (sentences) with a coordinating conjunction (and, or, or but). Example: 'I wrote my English paper, and then I went running.'

- Do use a comma after introductory elements. Example: 'Yesterday, when I went to the store, I bought milk.'

- Do use two commas when you are using a non-restrictive element. That is, you use commas to set off a descriptive phrase that applies to all the objects in question. Example: 'The band members, who wore raincoats, did not get wet.' This sentence means that none of the band members got wet, because all of them were wearing raincoats. If you leave the commas out, you suggest that some of the band members were wearing raincoats and some were not, and only those who were not wearing the raincoats got wet. The commas change the meaning of the sentence entirely.

Improved use of commas in almost all situations will make your writing much clearer. You can develop a more sophisticated understanding of other situations in which commas might be used as you become a more sophisticated writer.

9 Eliminate pretentious vocabulary and say what you mean in a straightforward way. There is no need to use 'utilize' when 'use' will do. 'Implement' has a particular meaning; 'implement' is not an effective synonym for 'use'. Use 'implement' when you actually mean that someone has conceived a new way of doing something and is putting it into practice for the first time. When you rely too much on pretentious vocabulary, you run the risk of actually saying something that is not true (because you don't really understand the nuances of the words you are using) and/or of making yourself look, to an examiner, like someone trying to show off, rather than someone who makes a real effort to write precisely and accurately.

10 Write simple, direct sentences. When you have finished writing your paper, read it out loud – or recruit someone to read it out loud to you. You will hear problems that you did not read, especially problems of long, convoluted sentences which change direction mid-stream so that the subjects you started with don't go with the verbs you ended up with.

Conclusion

You will have to write about literature quite often over the course of your IB English programme. You will have to write about different types of works, and you will have to address a variety of different questions about literature. This chapter has offered you quite a lot of advice about how to handle many aspects of that complex task. Try not to expect too much of yourself too soon. You will need to practise each skill over time in order to develop your ability. The ability to write is not an inborn skill: writers become better with practice. So practise, practise, practise! It is also well worth remembering that good writers are good readers. People who expose themselves to lots of good writing gradually internalise a great understanding of how effective language works. So along with practising your writing, read, read, read!

Additional resources

An excellent book for helping you write more clearly and succinctly is William Zinsser's *On Writing Well*. Finally, you may also want to check out some good practical advice on how to write conclusions from the writing center at Harvard University: **https://writingcenter.fas. harvard.edu/pages/ending-essay-conclusions** (see QR code).

Works cited

Alameddine, Rabih, *An Unnecessary Woman*, Grove Press, 2013 (print).

Austen, Jane, *Pride and Prejudice*, Clare West, ed., Oxford, Oxford University Press, 2008 (print).

Bishop, Elizabeth, 'One Art', *Poems*, New York, Farrar, Straus and Giroux, 2011 (print).

Boland, Eavan, 'Domestic Interior', John Jordan, ed., Poetry Ireland Review 2 18, Web accessed 1 November 2018, **https://www.poetryireland.ie/publications/poetry-ireland-review/ online-archive/view/domestic-interior**

Boland, Eavan, 'It's a Woman's World', *Night Feed*, Manchester: Carcanet, 1994 (print).

Chopin, Kate, *The Awakening*, New York: Dover Publication, 1993 (print).

Curtis, George William, 'Ebb and Flow', Bartleby.com, Web, accessed 1 November 2018, **www. bartleby.com/400/poem/1610.html**

Doig, Ivan, *The Whistling Season*, Harcourt, 2006 (print).

Fitzgerald, F Scott, *The Great Gatsby*, Scribner, 1995 (print).

Goodison, Lorna, 'Farewell Wild Woman (I)', *Selected Poems*, University of Michigan Press: Ann Arbor, 1992, (page 116) (print).

Ford, Ford Madox, *Good Soldier: A Tale of Passion*, Bantam, 1991 (print).

Hughes, Ted, 'The Thought Fox', *New Selected Poems, 1957–1994.* Faber and Faber, 1995 (print).

International Baccalaureate Organization. *English A: Literature – Higher Level – Paper 2.* International Baccalaureate Organization, 2018.

International Baccalaureate Organization, *Language A Literature Guide: First Assessment 2021*, Cardiff, Wales: International Baccalaureate Organization, 2019 (print).

Shakespeare, William, *Romeo and Juliet*, Rebecca Niles and Michael Poston, eds., *Folger Digital Texts*, Folger Shakespeare Library, Web, accessed 28 October 2018, **www.folgerdigitaltexts. org/?chapter=5&play=Rom&loc=line-2.2.1**

Shakespeare, William, Sonnet 116, Michael Poston and Rebecca Niles, eds., *Folger Digital Texts*, Folger Shakespeare Library, Web, accessed 8 October 2018, **https://www.folgerdigitaltexts. org/?chapter=5&play=Son&loc=Son-116**.

Sharman, Ruth, 'Birth of the Owl Butterflies', Web, accessed 25 October 2018, **ruthsharman. com/the-birth-of-the-owl-butterflies/**

Zinsser, William, *On Writing Well*, Harper Paperbacks, 2013 (print).

Notes on the activities

As previously noted, literary analysis is not a science. Interpretation is largely about developing a personal response to the text rather than arriving at a definitive answer, and therefore each interpretation may be slightly different. As long as your interpretation is supported by the language of the text, that's okay. The notes provided here should not be viewed as conclusive; they are merely included to provide you with some possibilities of analysis and interpretation. There is always room for varying interpretations in any literary work; your interpretations are bounded only by the facts of the text – the words that are actually used. If you feel that you missed more than you should have, don't worry! As with developing any other skill, your skill as an astute reader of poetry, prose and drama will improve with practice.

Chapter 2: Approaches to poetry

■ Activities 1–4

Possible responses to the first few activities will vary in nature based on your personal experience with poetry up to now, but you should have recognized some of the conventions of poetry (Activity 2) outlined throughout the chapter. For Activity 3, you may have recognized in the prose poems poetic elements such as imagery, figurative language and sound devices (such as internal rhyme and assonance); elements of prose include paragraphs and (in the Gomez example) a narrative situation.

■ Activity 5: Exploring rhythm

Blake's 'London' is a poem written in four regular stanzas of four lines each, with a regular (you might say predictable) ABAB rhyme scheme. This measured, repetitive rhythm (almost suggestive of hoof beats) reflects the speaker's monotonous, death-like march through the city of London as he observes the misery (woe) and unhappiness around him.

■ Activity 6: Identifying form

A 'We Wear the Mask' by Paul Laurence Dunbar is a **rondeau**. Dunbar's choice of form, which has a song-like rhythm, strikes an ironic contrast with the seriousness of the subject matter.

B 'Anne Hathaway' by Carol Ann Duffy is a **sonnet**. It is taken from her collection entitled *The World's Wife*. In the poem, Duffy adopts the persona of Shakespeare's wife, Anne Hathaway. She uses the sonnet form to describe Hathaway's love for her husband. By using this form, characteristic of Shakespeare, to assume the voice of his wife, Duffy is highlighting her collection's theme of female empowerment.

C 'Do Not Go Gentle Into That Good Night' by Dylan Thomas is a **villanelle** and is perhaps one of the most famous examples of the form. The repetition reinforces the speaker's attitude of defiance in the face of death.

D 'Incident' by Natasha Trethewy is a **pantoum**. The repetitive, cyclical pattern of the form complements the subject matter; this is an old story passed down through generations.

E 'O Captain! My Captain' by Walt Whitman is an **elegy**. Written in the traditional form, the poem uses extended metaphor to pay homage to President Abraham Lincoln.

F 'The Painter' by John Ashbery is a **sestina**. The sestina is an interesting choice for this subject. The form itself is highly controlled, perhaps reflective of a painter and his craft. However, this particular painter struggles to gain control of his creativity.

G 'To Autumn' by John Keats is an **ode**. Keats is well known for his odes. In this poem, Keats praises the season of autumn, which he personifies as a woman. The romantic language, characterized by rich imagery and euphony (especially the first line), is particularly appropriate for this type of poem.

■ Activity 7: Examining tone

1 As in Plath's 'Daddy', the speaker in 'I Go Back to May 1937' has a distinct tone. You might have characterized it as resentful, bitter, defiant or defeatist. Despite the title's suggestion otherwise, the speaker knows that she cannot undo her parents' marriage. The imagery Olds uses to describe the background of the photograph (for example, 'like bent / plates of blood', 'the wrought-iron gate['s] … sword-tips aglow') is particularly striking, with violent connotations, adding to the resentful tone. The 'pitiful beautiful untouched body' that Olds uses to refer to both the mother and the father hints at a feeling of foreboding. The violent image towards the end of the poem, where the speaker describes banging together the images of the mother and father, 'like chips of flint', reflects the anger and bitterness that the speaker feels.

2 Answers will vary. If you identified a bitter tone, you might feel tense or uncomfortable as the reader, as if you are being confronted by the speaker.

3 The repetition in the poem reinforces the speaker's feeling of helplessness and the bitter and resentful tone that she projects. We see this first in the following lines, which establish a brief narrative to the situation and build a sense of tension which leads to the inevitable outcome: 'they are about the graduate, they are about to get married, / they are kids, they are dumb, all they know is they are / innocent, they would never hurt anybody' (lines 10–12). Olds uses the future tense to foreshadow events to come; this series of statements read like accusations: 'you are going to do things / you cannot imagine you would ever do … you are going to want to die' (lines 15–19).

■ Activity 8: Exploring diction

You might have noticed some of the following in Heaney's poem. If not, go back to the poem and see if you can identify the aspects highlighted here.

■ Contrasting connotations of the words in the title. Before reading the poem, you may have assumed that the 'death' referred to in the title was a literal death. After reading the poem, it becomes clear that it is a metaphorical death. The contrast between 'death' and 'naturalist' reflects the duality of tone present in the rest of the poem.

■ Childish language in the first stanza (for example, onomatopoeia, words like 'daddy' and 'mammy'), reflecting the speaker's innocent perspective: a sense of fascination with the natural world.

■ Words with a negative connotation in the second stanza (for example, 'invaded', 'grenades', 'vengeance'), reflecting the shift in tone from wonder to scepticism and even disgust.

■ Cacophonous language (for example, the harsh fricatives in 'flax-dam festered', 'thick slobber', 'clotted water'), which further emphasizes the speaker's disgust for the frogs.

You can listen to Heaney read some of his poems on YouTube. His Irish brogue adds a particularly pleasing quality of sound to the reading experience.

■ Activity 9: Reflecting on imagery

1 Answers will vary. You may have been struck by the image of the 'Blue-lipped' child 'dressed in water's long green silk' being pulled from the lake. Or you may have been struck by the 'heroine, her red head bowed, / her wartime cotton frock soaked'. Both of these are emotive images.

2 Answers will again vary here. In response to the use of the word 'bleating', it adds to the child's vulnerability and suggests dependence on a mother figure (note that there is no reference to the child's mother, only the speaker's; the child's father is referred to in the last line).

3 The contrast of red and blue reflects the contrast between life and death that we see in this poem. For example, the 'blue-lipped child' becomes 'rosy' in the speaker's mother's arms. Red is also associated with the 'heroine' who saves the child. Another contrast is the image of the child being 'thrashed for almost drowning'; we associate drowning with helplessness and vulnerability, but the act of being thrashed is violent and unexpected.

4 The tactile imagery in the poem ('water's long green silk', 'wartime cotton frock') gives us something concrete to visualize, for the reader to figuratively grab hold of. This contrasts with the concept of memory, which is often fleeting. The penultimate stanza, beginning 'Was I there?' is far more abstract; the images of 'satiny mud' blooming in cloudiness and the 'treading, heavy webs of swans' suggest that the act of remembrance is fragile and hazy.

■ Activity 10: Analysing metaphor

1 From the title, we know that water is considered a blessing within the world of the poem. Other metaphors that you are likely to have identified include the following:

- 'the voice of a kindly god': This comparison to a deity emphasizes the water's power and importance.

- 'silver': The water is likened to a precious metal, something to be valued.

- 'liquid sun': This oxymoron is an interesting choice. At the beginning of the poem, the sun is indirectly described as punishing through the image of the skin cracking like a pod under its heat. However, now it is suggested that the sun actually quenches a thirst.

2 Other examples of figurative language include:

- Simile: 'The skin cracks like a pod' (line 1).

- Hyperbole: 'There is never enough water' (line 2).

- Personification: 'roar of tongues' (line 11) and 'the blessing sings / over their small bones' (lines 22–3).

- Synecdoche: The 'roar of tongues' is also an example of synecdoche because it is used in place of 'people' or even 'voices'.

- Metaphor: 'From the huts, / a congregation …' (lines 11–12). The villagers are compared to a congregation of worshipers.

▪ Activity 11: Considering sound

1 There are many examples of sibilance throughout the poem, most notably in the second and third stanzas. The repetition of the letter 's' is suggestive of the hissing of a snake. Contrasted with the images of hospitality presented in these stanzas, the sound suggests a sinister motive within the rival; the speaker indicates as much in the line 'But what squirms beneath her surface I can tell' (line 17).

2 The rhyme in this poem is subtle if you read it silently off the page, but if you read it aloud it becomes more obvious. The playful quality of rhyme contrasts with the tense and uncertain atmosphere suggested in the imagery. In the same way, the rhyme lightens the atmosphere, suggesting a more comical view of the rivalry presented.

Some additional sound devices worth noting in this poem are:

- the use of the word 'gilt' in line 2. You may be familiar with this word or have worked out its meaning by using context clues. 'Gilt' is a thin layer of gold leaf or gold paint, used for decoration; this is a fitting image for a poem about a woman who is concerned with appearances. You may have missed the *sound* of the word if you were just reading it off the page, so read it aloud to yourself. Notice that when saying the word aloud, it sounds like 'guilt'. This may be a coincidence, but it wouldn't be surprising if Lochhead intended for this word to carry a double meaning.

- the use of alliteration. We have already addressed sibilance, which is a specific type of alliteration, but another interesting example of alliteration is in line 20: 'fight, fight foul …' The fricatives in these monosyllabic words sound like jabs; the rival is prepared to fight for the affections of her son.

▪ Activity 12: Exploring theme

1 Answers will vary, but some possible themes include the fragility of life, the importance of carrying on family traditions, and the connection between human and natural forces.

2 Again, answers will vary. You might have picked up on some of the following:

- The sequoia in the title is the poem's central image. The speaker directly addresses the tree, which he is planting in memory of his first-born son. However, unlike the child, the 'native giant' will live for many more generations.

- Stanza 1 conveys a gloomy and oppressive atmosphere, comparable with the speaker's mood. This is achieved through the imagery of the rain blackening the horizon (line 3), the 'cold winds' (line 3), and the dull grey sky (line 4).

- Stanza 2 includes images of fruit trees which contrast with the sequoia, which does not bear fruit.

- The images used to convey the loss of the infant are startling and emotive: the delicate features ('a lock of hair', 'a piece of an infant's birth cord') reflect the fragility of life.

3 The poem has a formal, orderly structure: five stanzas of equal length, each stanza almost cyclical in its presentation of imagery (starting with a beginning, or birth, and ending with a literal or metaphorical death). As a whole, the poem begins with an image of the speaker working with his brothers to plant the tree and ends

with a similar image of the tree still standing after the infant's unborn brothers and other family members have all gone. This structure reinforces the idea of longevity versus transience.

Chapter 3: Approaches to prose

■ Activity 1: Analysing 'Why I Live at the P.O.'

You might have picked up on the narrator's tone in this opening passage. She is aggrieved about the return of her sister, towards whom she has been nursing a grudge. The narrator claims that her sister stole her boyfriend by telling a lie. Maybe this is true; however, the lie she claims her sister told is rather odd. We have to start wondering whether the narrator's version of the facts is true. When she goes on to call her sister 'spoiled', we can start noticing the resentment in her tone. Once we know the narrator has such strong feelings, we can be on the lookout for other signs of her likely unreliability. That unreliability will develop over the course of the whole story; however, we get one more confirmation that Sister is not to be trusted right in this passage, when she calls the Add-a-Pearl necklace 'gorgeous'. She tells us that her sister 'threw it away' (probably lost it?) when it had only two pearls on it. A long piece of string with two pearls is hardly believable as a 'gorgeous object'. Sister is looking for anything she can hold against her sister. We can look forward to the rest of the story revealing the narrator as being self-centred and arrogant, and probably, given the degree of her hyperbole, also quite funny.

■ Activity 2: Example from *The Night Circus*

This narrator has very specific information about the situation he is describing, which suggests that he himself was there and experienced the events he is talking about. He knows about the scarf, the chilly breeze, the ticket booth and the smell of caramel. So, on the one hand, the narrator seems to be talking about himself. The situation he describes, however, would be experienced by every person who waited outside the gates for the circus to open, so it makes sense to consider that in this case the narrator is using the 'you' as a generic term meaning 'anyone'. There is no evidence in this passage to suggest that the narrator is trying to distance himself from the events of the story, so, at least at this point, it seems that the use of the second person here is to draw the audience into the situation, as if they were experiencing it themselves.

■ Activity 3: Analysing 'My Sister's Marriage'

The narrator here is a first-person narrator. She is telling her own story – it involves her, her sister and her father. In such a situation, the possibility that the narrator might be biased has to be considered, and we have evidence in this passage that the narrator does not have a balanced and objective viewpoint. The accusation she makes to her listeners (real or imaginary – we can't tell from this passage) that they cannot possibly understand her situation and that they will naturally misinterpret it comes off as defensive. As soon as a narrator is defensive, we should be alerted to the probability that the narrator has a strong motivation to see the situation their way and to convince others that their vision is correct. That is not an objective or unbiased viewpoint. The insistence, in the final lines, that no one should hate Olive is another clue that the narrator is not telling the truth – whenever someone has to insist on something so strongly (the repetition here is a clue), we have to ask ourselves whether the person she is trying to convince is really herself. We have here a narrator under strong emotional stress who has a powerful need to convince others, and possibly herself most of all, that what she has done is fair and just. We should be expecting to find out, as the story progresses, that it is not.

■ Activity 4: Analysing a passage from *A Christmas Carol*

1   We know very little about Scrooge's physical appearance. Lines 4–5 tell us that he has a pointed noise, a shrivelled check, blue lips, red eyes, a stiff gait and the remnants of white hair ('A frosty rime'). That's it. If we tried to draw a portrait of Scrooge from this description, we would not be able to do so with any degree of accuracy.

2   We do know, however, that he is a cold, unfriendly and ungenerous person. He is compared to flint, that the cold that has frozen his features is a cold within him, and that he caused the area around him to feel cold. This does not seem like a person we would want to have to be around, and we would not expect to be able to get any favours from this man.

3   In terms of his motivations, we are told that 'no falling snow was more intent upon its purpose' than Scrooge, and that 'no pelting rain [is] less open to entreaty'. We know from this that Scrooge is determined to have things his way. He is purposefully ungenerous and, since even holidays do not draw any generosity from him, we can surmise that he wants to have as little to do with anyone else as he possibly can. We are told directly that he is a 'squeezing, wrenching, grasping, scraping, clutching covetous, old sinner', so we know that one of his most powerful motivations is to hang onto his money and spend as little as possible. *A Christmas Carol* is a story familiar to most people, and if you know the story, you know that the inferences we have drawn from this description hold up over the rest of the story and, indeed, form the reason for the visits of the three ghosts which change Scrooge's life and outlook permanently.

■ Activity 5: Analysing a passage from *Wuthering Heights*

The functions of setting are:

■   Mood: the description of the place as stormy, cold, and stunted suggests a somber mood. From this passage, we don't know anything about the mood of the characters, but we might keep a lookout for any indication that one or more is unhappy.

■   Characterization: since the description is of Mr Heathcliff's house, we should definitely consider what it suggests about his character. We have the words 'tumult,' 'exposed,' 'stormy' and 'stunted,' all of which suggest a place of isolation and trouble. We are also told that the north wind blows with 'bracing ventilation' (suggesting it is quite cold), and we are told that the wind blows 'at all times.' Those images suggest that Heathcliff himself is always a cold and wearing kind of person. The fir and thorn trees are described as 'stunted' and 'craving' the sun, which suggests that Heathcliff is a person who keeps those around him from thriving.

■   Symbolic: the scene described is one in which a stormy coldness predominates. The primary symbolism would seem to be the symbolism of Heathcliff's character. This scene suggests that he is a hard, lonely, isolated man who is hard to approach, and around which life does not flourish. We also have the symbolism of the building itself, which is described as strong, with 'narrow windows' which are set 'deeply in the wall'. Windows are typically symbols of freedom, but in this building, the chances of freedom would seem to be quite slim (literally 'narrow'), and difficult to attain. The 'large jutting stones' defend the house from outsiders. The fortress of the house suggests that Heathcliff is barricaded away from life and light and happiness. Although this is the very first page of the book, we will find out later that these images suit Heathcliff's life and character very well.

- Sympathetic: There is no change in either the setting or the character's emotional state in this passage, so there can be no sympathetic function.

- Supernatural: The strength of the house and the perpetual storminess of the weather may turn out to perform a supernatural function in that they keep people out. We would have to read more of the novel to see how viable such an interpretation is, but the seeds are there, and so we should be on the lookout.

- Actant: the setting here does not act as a character.

■ Activity 6: Analysing a passage from 'The Story of an Hour'

1 Some of the literary elements that you might have discovered in the passage are:

- The open window: windows, in contrast to walls, often signify gateways to new opportunities or a way to escape – especially if the window is open, as it is here.

- The mention of 'new spring life': spring is a classic symbol of rebirth; the earth comes alive again after the death-like effects of winter.

- The 'delicious breath of rain': rain can mean a lot of different things, such as sadness, or despair, but one thing it can mean is rebirth, or cleansing. In this case, because the rain is 'delicious', and because it is the 'breath' of rain, the suggestion is of life and cleansing.

- Singing: in the absence of any description of precisely what is being sung, we must consider singing in the context of the surrounding passage. Music in a happy world is spiritually uplifting.

- Sparrows (birds): Birds are very often signs of freedom – because they can fly and thus escape the earth.

- Blue sky showing through clouds: a fairly obvious symbol of the sun coming out; like spring out of winter, sun out of a storm is a sign of new beginnings.

2 What can we conclude from these observations? The striking thing is that all of these symbolic features appear as Mrs Mallard is reacting to the news of her husband's death. Chopin has really challenged her readers' expectations here: we do not expect someone whose husband has just died to be experiencing feelings of joy at sudden freedom and happiness at the prospect to a new life beginning. In this context, then, we have to think that Mrs Mallard's marriage was unhappy and oppressive. Chopin is making a point about what people do not know about others' marriages.

■ Activity 7: Literary elements in 'Crimes Against Dog'

Some elements you might have noticed from this brief passage are the historical allusion to slavery and the comparison of the situation of the dogs, which are kept for forced breeding, and human slaves, which were also bred for the convenience of their owner, and their offspring sold. Walker points out that the dogs were black and brown, which was certainly actually true; she didn't make the detail up, but she chose to point it out because it heightens the image of the enslaved race. The tone in that section is a little unnerving, since the comparison of a dog in captivity to a slave might seem to be flippant and maybe even disrespectful, but Walker is showing how, during slavery, humans were treated as dogs. We could say that she uses that comparison to unnerve her readers and make them think more closely about the treatment of both humans and animals. Towards the end of the passage, she lightens the tone by suggesting that the father dog might want a cigar. That is an allusion to an old tradition of the father of a human baby handing out cigars to all his friends when his child was born. The tradition is mostly (or completely) gone now, so the reader would have to recognize the historical fact in order to appreciate the allusion. The image of the dog smoking a cigar is more humorous than the images earlier in the passage, which helps us understand that Walker is not condemning the dog breeder for breeding dogs. A final element you might notice is the title of the essay, which is quite pertinent in this particular passage, as she has been talking about our inhumane treatment of animals which are used for our own convenience. The title is also a play on the familiar phrase: 'Crimes against God'. We might want to look out, as we read the whole essay, for actions which might be considered to be sins. The title might be functioning to foreshadow some of what Walker will be talking about.

■ Activity 8: Analysing a short story by Richard Powers

1 The narrator is a third-person narrator who may or may not be omniscient. In this sentence, the narrator only reports facts, not what is inside the minds of any characters. We have no reason to think that this narrator has any bias; since he reports only facts, and since the relationship between the facts is logical, we must presume, on the basis of this small amount of text, that the narrator is reliable.

2 The characters are implied – they are the people who perfected the lie-detector eyeglasses, the people who wore them, and the people who lived in the civilization that collapsed.

3 We can infer that the characters cared about the truth, since they developed and then wore lie-detector eyeglasses. Ironically, however, we must also conclude that some of the characters care about saving face or hiding things they've done, because for civilization to have collapsed once its citizens had the power to determine who was lying, there must have been many liars.

4 We know, therefore, what actions the characters took: some characters used the eyeglasses, and some characters told lies anyway.

5 The basic plot is spelled out literally: the events were the development of the lie-detector eyeglasses and the subsequent collapse of civilization.

6 The story is structured around an implied cause/effect relationship: we are told that first one thing happened and then another, but the implication is that the second thing happened *because* the first thing happened. The important idea in the story lies in this implied relationship.

7 We cannot tell anything about setting other than the fact that it took place inside of a civilization.

8 Eyeglasses are a standard symbol for the ability to see – the ability to gain knowledge. In this case, the eyeglasses are proposed as literally conferring the ability to see something which is not physical and not, in the ordinary course of events, visible to the human eye. Irony is also used: what the story suggests about human nature is that people lie, even when they know they will be caught.

Ironically, a tool that would be intended to improve moral behaviour led to the downfall of society. Symbolism and irony are the two major relevant literary strategies in this very short story.

Chapter 4: Approaches to drama

■ Activity 1: Stage directions from *A Raisin in the Sun*

Some important ideas you might notice from these stage directions are:

- Beneatha as described here has been differentiated from the rest of her family in a couple of ways. Her speech patterns are particularly identified as being the result of education and of a regional dialect which is different from the rest of the family. This suggests that Beneatha is in some way an anomaly, and we might expect her to value things differently and/or to behave differently from the others.

- The description also makes a point of mentioning that her 'thick hair stands wildly about her head'. That is a good point to attend to; later in the play you will come to a scene in which her hair is discussed a great deal, and it becomes a symbol of an effort to blend in to a dominant culture. You don't know that at the time you read this stage direction, of course, but it is always a good idea to attend to any detail which the playwright makes a significant effort to point out.

■ Activity 2: Literary elements in *A Raisin in the Sun*

The passage contains several literary elements, including:

- The mention of winter and ice. These are typical symbols of death. In this case, Rufus does not die, but he is badly injured, and Beneatha thought he was going to die. The near-death in this case is the result of urban children trying to adapt their environments into something that would occur naturally in the country. The idea of death, then, makes a statement about the disadvantages of living in a completely urban area.

- The injury itself is a symbol of something broken that is larger than Rufus' actual broken bones. In this case, one can see the environment as being broken and leading to suffering by the people who live there.

- The flashback to Rufus' accident which is used to explain Beneatha's fascination with medicine and the seeming miracles that doctors can do.

- The mention of God which is used as a comparison to the power of doctors. The comparison of what doctors can do to the creative power of God reveals to us the degree of Beneatha's admiration of medicine as a field of endeavour. One might argue that she is using a form of hyperbole to make her point, but the comparison can also be seen as nearly literal: the doctors put back together someone who Beneatha thought was dead; to her, it was a sort of resurrection.

■ Activity 3: Analysing *The Comedy of Errors*

Obviously it is difficult to ascertain many details from a short excerpt of the opening scene; however, there are some structural components we can recognize. The Duke gives us the opening balance when he describes the long-standing law of the land that any person born at Syracuse must pay a fine of 1000 marks or be executed. The disturbance has been that Egeon, a Syracusian, has come to Ephesus, has been unable to pay the fine, and so has been sentenced to die. This has all happened before the beginning of the play, so we can already see that Shakespeare has modified the expected structure by having the play open after the disturbance. We also can find a rather unusual protagonist with a plan for resolving the problem: the problem is that Egeon must die, and the person with a plan to deal with that is the Duke himself, who, though he cannot violate the law, offers a chance for saving Egeon's life: he gives Egeon a day to seek help from anyone he knows who might pay the fine on his behalf. The central suspense for the play is, therefore, established: we will be waiting throughout the play to see if someone will come to Egeon's aid.

■ Activity 4: Naming metrical patterns

1 a Anapestic tetrameter
  b Iambic hexameter
  c Dactylic dimeter

2 a Seven dactyls – 21 syllables
  b Four trochees – 8 syllables
  c Three iambs – 6 syllables

You should be aware that although we can make a fun exercise of putting together lots of various types of feet with different numbers of feet per line, they are not equally important for studying metre in drama (or in poetry either, for that matter). English is predominantly iambic in nature, and so iambic is the most common metre you will find as the basis for dramatic metre. You won't find spondees as the main metre in any work of literature – that many stresses would just be unnatural and jarring. Nor will you find a metrical style which is primarily pyhrric. Iambs are more likely than trochees just because we are more comfortable hearing stresses at the ends of lines; lines which end on unstressed syllables – especially two unstressed syllables, as with dactyls – seem unfinished (Foster 41).

If you think about line length, you will realize that no one would be likely to write a play (or even a poem) with only one foot (monometer) or even two (dimeter). In fact, hexameter, pentameter, heptameter and octameter are the most common line lengths in English. There is a form called the Alexandrine, which is a 12-syllable iambic line, but you are most likely to encounter that in poetry, not in plays.

■ Activity 5: Marking the metre

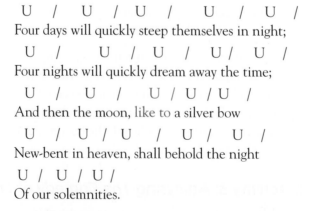

One might argue that the red foot in line 3 could be read as a trochee instead of an iamb; if you made an argument for that and explained your reasoning, your analysis would be acceptable.

■ Activity 6: Looking for variations

This passage consists almost entirely of iambs; however, it is not iambic pentameter. The first two lines have four iambs (8 syllables), and the remaining lines have three and a half iambs (7 syllables) each. It also consists entirely of rhymed couplets, so the speech is much more formal in structure than the speech of most of the play – and of plays in general. The effect is to create a very sing-songy rhythm (read it aloud and you will hear the bounce in the metre), and so the interesting question here is why would Shakespeare do this at the end of the play? The play is, of course, a comedy, and it is a particularly wild and farcical one. The speaker of this final speech is Puck (a character from whom the word 'puckish' has derived), a whimsical and playful character. The effect is perhaps a little ironic: although Puck is claiming, in the speech, to wish to make amends to the audience for any offense that the play might have conferred, the fact that the speech is like a game, or nursery rhyme, suggests that it is not really serious. Shakespeare leaves the audience wondering whether the happy ending that they have just witnessed is really what it appeared to be. (This trick is not untypical of Shakespeare – very often his very last scene has a little element which undermines what has gone before, just to raise a question in the minds of the theatre-goers.)

Chapter 5: Writing about literature

■ Activity 1: *An Unnecessary Woman*

In terms of summary, you might note that in this passage, we find out that the narrator overheard her neighbours talking about her, which led her to dye her hair using a particular product, and her hair is now too blue. She also talks about ageing eyes and the fact that elderly people can't see blue very well, and so they tend to have their hair bluer than others who see them would like it. She tells a story about a woman who, although finally convinced that her hair was very blue declined to have it changed. She cared only about what she thought – not what others thought, which the narrator likes. The narrator mentions that she finished a translation of a novel by WG Sebald into Arabic and undertook a celebratory ritual of reading it, putting it in a box, and having two glasses of wine. A short summary might only note that in this passage, the narrator thinks about how growing old changes one's perceptions of oneself and those around her.

In terms of analysis, you could choose to talk about narrative perspective, tone and the somewhat mysterious references to translating books and to a woman named Hannah, who was evidently important to the narrator. The narrative perspective is that of an elderly woman who translates novels, who is somewhat taken aback by finding her hair is blue, but who is philosophical about it. She does not appear to react overly emotionally. Her tone is self-deprecating and humorous. The perspective and the tone function in this passage to introduce us to the narrator and her personality. From reading the passage, you should understand that she is quite intelligent, skilled with languages, somewhat disdainful of her neighbours (whom she calls 'witches'), funny and capable of deep feeling. The author is establishing the narrator as a reliable observer and a likeable character. The references to translation and to Hannah, which are not explained, but rather presented as if we already know what the narrator is talking about serve to foreshadow events that we will learn more about later, and so they establish some suspense. We know that this passage occurs very near the beginning of the novel, so we can see that the author is building empathy for the character and curiosity about what else we will learn about her life.

■ Activity 2: 'The Thought Fox'

In terms of summary, you should note that the whole story of the fox in the woods in the winter is imagined. At the beginning of the poem, the speaker, who is evidently a writer, is sitting with a blank piece of paper, and he imagines a scene in which a fox creeps about in the woods, smelling things, watching around him, leaves footprints, casts a shadow, and darts out. The poet writes something.

The analysis in this case is much easier to do than the summary, because the imagined fox is clearly an extended metaphor for the process of getting an idea in order to write a poem. You could analyse all the parts of the metaphor, comparing the actions of the fox to the way thoughts occur in a head. You could also analyse the imagery of the poem, the use of time, and the surprising use of the phrase 'stink of fox'. All of these are strategies that Hughes uses to create the sensation of what it's like to be a writer and have an idea develop in one's mind.

■ Activity 3: 'Farewell Wild Woman (I)'

The narrator is first-person, and she is evidently a woman of an age to go out in the evenings and drink and associate with men. She feels bad about some of her past behaviours, and she has determined that she will no longer engage in them; she is speaking after she made a decision to change her life, but while she is still having trouble keeping to her resolution. She has actually personified that part of her personality into a 'wild woman'. Although she has banned the wild woman from her life, she finds that even when she is shut up in her house, presumably safe, the wild woman is waiting for her outside and tempting her to relapse into those wild ways. The narrator is self-aware and so reliable, and she seems to recognize that she has not secured herself as she wants to.

■ Activity 4: Thesis statements

Statement	Numbers of the objectives that this statement violates
1. In *The Great Gatsby*, Fitzgerald shows how obsessed Gatsby is with Daisy.	1 & 2
2. In *The Great Gatsby*, Fitzgerald reveals that we can be driven to desire something which is not attainable, that failure to recognize what is possible leads to tragedy, and that wealth often goes along with a failure of morality.	1, 2 & 5
3. In *The Great Gatsby*, Fitzgerald demonstrates the sometimes powerful correlation between wealth and lack of morality.	This is an effective thesis statement.
4. In *The Great Gatsby*, Fitzgerald uses metaphors, symbolic function of setting and flashbacks to make his point.	1, 4 & 6
5. In *The Great Gatsby*, Fitzgerald writes about love.	1 & 6
6. Fitzgerald's *Great Gatsby* shows that love, revenge, tragedy and resentment.	3

■ Activity 5: Sample analysis paragraph

This is the claim that needs to be proven in this paragraph. A complicated claim, such as this one, will need several subsets of evidence and warrants. In order to demonstrate everything that has been claimed in this sentence, the writer needs to demonstrate (1) the vision of domestic life in the painting, as seen by the narrator, (2) the vision of the narrator's domestic life, (3) the contrast between the two, and (4) the negative judgement of the portrayal of a woman's life as shown by the painting. Notice, too, that still will not tie this whole example to the thesis; to do that, the writer then has to explain her belief that the poet (Boland) is using this negative view of the painting, to show that the power of the artwork is in the hands of the audience (who is, in this case, the narrator).

This is the first sub-claim; it sets up the argument for part 1 (see note above).

This part of the paragraph is going to give the evidence and warrant to address parts 2 and 3 (see note above).

There are several pieces of evidence offered in the latter part of this paragraph in support of the one claim. The evidence is not all quoted, as the essay was written under timed conditions without access to the text. The writer did put the one phrase he or she remembered exactly in quotation marks. Notice that each piece of evidence is followed by a small warrant, which explains why that fact from the poem carries a negative connotation. Notice also that the nature of the task in Paper 2, which requires comparison and contrast among works, precludes the kind of detailed textual analysis necessary for Paper 1. Your job is not to analyse the poem in great detail, but rather to pick out those bits of the poem that are pertinent to your overall argument. In this case, that overall argument is that the use of narrative perspective reveals a particular attitude about art. What you say about the poem, however, must be accurate. You will show, by your choice of facts from the poem and your use of those facts to make a point, how well you actually know and understand the poem.

The narrator of 'Domestic Interior' is a woman who comments on the Van Eyck painting as she views it. In the end, she contrasts the vision of domestic life that she sees in the painting with what is presumably her own personal experience with domestic life and shows the vision in the painting to be the lesser. What Boland's speaker objects to is that the woman has been portrayed solely as a vessel to ensure the continuance of the man's genes, rather than as a person who will have an individual experience of marriage. The painting depicts a woman heavily pregnant on her wedding day. This image reflects the contemporary cultural practice of ensuring that the woman is fertile before a man wastes his chances by marrying poorly. Portraying this bride in this state on this day reduces her worth to the ability to procreate. That the narrator of the poem disapproves of this depiction is shown through death imagery: the effect of the wedding ring is described through the invented verb 'ambering', a word which prefigures the image, later in the poem, of the woman being trapped in the varnish of the painting. Boland's narrator also describes the woman as being 'interred' in her joy. The marriage, as portrayed in this painting, and as interpreted by this narrator, amounts to the death of the woman. By contrast, the last two stanzas of the poem talk about a different way of life, one in which women make a space for themselves that is warm and domestic. The poem thus ends with the assertion that there is a way of life in which the things women deal with — pots and kettles, the implements of the kitchen — 'grow important'. In this portrayal of a woman's life, time moves on, the child is born, the woman has her own space in the house and her own experience quite apart from being a prize captured by the man. This vision of a woman's life is not in the painting; it is presumably drawn from the narrator's own experience.

Claim

Evidence

Warrant

Glossary

Actant (setting): when a setting acts as a character.

Alliteration: the repetition of initial consonant sounds.

Allusion: a reference in literature to another piece of literature, art, music or history.

Analysis: the identification and evaluation of the way in which literary strategies are used to create meaning.

Anapest: two unstressed syllables followed by a stressed syllable.

Antagonist: a character who is working consciously to stop the protagonist from implementing his or her plan.

Anthropomorphism: the attribution of human characteristics or behaviour to an animal.

Assonance: the repetition of vowel sounds within words.

Blank verse: an indeterminate number of lines of iambic pentameter.

Cacophony: a harsh or unpleasant sound.

Caesura: pause within a line of poetry, often created by punctuation such as a comma, semi-colon or dash.

Characterization: the setting around a character can help the reader to understand the nature of that character.

Climax: in drama, the final complication that determines whether the plan is going to be successful or not.

Colloquialism: the use of informal or everyday language.

Complication: in drama, something that arises as a result of the protagonist's effort to implement the plan, and which interferes with the ability to employ the plan effectively.

Conceit: a type of metaphor that compares two different things in a surprising and inventive way.

Conflict: a struggle between two opposing forces.

Connotation: the ideas provoked beyond the literal meaning.

Consonance: the repetition of consonant sounds within words.

Dactyl: a stressed syllable followed by two unstressed syllables.

Denotation: the literal, dictionary definition of a word.

Diction: the words chosen in a text.

Disturbance: in a play, something that occurs to upset the balance and force the character(s) to deal with an unexpected problem.

Dramatic irony: when the audience knows something that the characters in the play do not.

Dramatic situation: the situation in which the actions of the story occur.

Dramatic time: in a play, describes the fact that regardless of when in history the play is set, the audience experiences the events as they happen, as if they have never happened before. Characters often discuss events from the past, but those events are rarely staged as actual flashbacks.

Elegy: a poem written in response to the death of a person.

Enjambment: when an idea or device carries on from one line or stanza to the next.

Entropy: a state of disorder.

Envoi: a short concluding stanza to a sestina.

Euphony: a sound that is pleasant to the ear.

Fabula: a fictional world created by the writer.

Figurative language: language that uses figures of speech, such as metaphors or symbols, to embellish meaning beyond the literal.

First-person narration: the narrator is presented as an actual character who has access to the events either as a participant or as an interested observer. The first-person narrator is not omniscient and so can be fallible.

Foot: one unit of metre.

Form: a type of text, closely relating to structure. In poetry, we can think of form as a specific type of poem, shaped into a pattern through structural devices such as line and stanza length, rhythmic features (including metre and rhyme) and repetition.

Free indirect speech: a narrative trick whereby the narrator is expressing a character's thoughts without quotation marks, so that we hear the thoughts not as reported by an onlooker or listener, but in their unedited form, as the characters themselves experience them.

Free verse: an open form of poetry that has no formal or recognized structure.

Freytag's pyramid: a way of looking at plot that includes an introduction, rising action, climax, falling action and resolution.

Functions of setting: the role that a setting plays in conveying meaning.

Hyperbole: exaggeration to make a situation seem more dramatic or humorous.

Iamb: the most common metrical pattern in English: an unstressed syllable, followed by a stressed syllable.

Iambic pentameter: a line of verse with five metrical feet, each consisting of one short (or unstressed) syllable followed by one long (or stressed) syllable. Shakespeare often wrote in iambic pentameter.

Imagery: a technique employed to convey emotion using language that appeals to the senses.

In medias res: the structural technique of beginning a story in the middle of the action and then going back to the beginning later.

Irony: using words or phrases to convey an intended meaning different to the literal meaning or in contrast to the expected meaning.

Jargon: words that are used in a specific context that may be difficult to understand, often involving technical terminology.

Lexical sets: a group of words that are related to each other in meaning, for example: leaf, green, trunk, bark and branch would all be part of the same lexical set in relation to the word 'tree'.

Line: the smallest unit of structure within a poem. Lines are typically grouped into stanzas.

Literary analysis: the systematic examination of a text or aspect(s) of a text – a consideration of how the individual parts contribute to the whole.

Metaphor: a comparison between two things.

Metonymy: a figure of speech in which the name of an object or concept is replaced with a word which is closely related to the original.

Metre: the arrangement and number of stressed and unstressed syllables in a line of a poem or a verse.

Mood: the feeling that is evoked in the reader (or audience) as a result of the tone that is set.

Narrative situation: the situation in which the narrator tells the story.

Obstacle: in drama, something that already exists in the fictional situation, which interferes with the protagonist's ability to implement his or her plan.

Octet: the first eight lines of a sonnet.

Ode: a lyrical poem, usually without a regular metre, in praise of a particular subject.

Omniscient (narrator): a narrator capable of knowing not only the actions characters undertake, but also their thoughts, feelings and motivations.

Onomatopoeia: a word which sounds like the noise that it makes. For example: bang, crash, plop, zoom.

Pantoum: a poem originating in Malaysia; composed of quatrains, with the second and fourth lines of each quatrain repeated as the first and third lines of the next. The second and fourth lines of the final stanza repeat the first and third lines of the first stanza.

Persona: the voice or person chosen by the author to tell the narrative.

Personification: giving human characteristics to inanimate objects.

Playwright: the writer of the play.

Plot: a series of events that are linked causally.

Plot snake: a series of rising and falling actions with a resolution.

Predominant metre: the metre that is used most often.

Prose poem: poetic writing in prose form.

Protagonist: in drama, the character who has the plan for dealing with the disturbance.

Pyrrhic foot: a very rare type of metre which has no stresses.

Quatrain: a stanza of four lines.

Quest: a journey which results in significant change.

Reliable narrator: a narrator whose version of the story can be relied upon because he or she is not confused, deluded or wrong.

Repetition: the repeated use of a word, phrase or image to draw attention to it.

Resolution: in drama, the outcome that brings a new balance.

Rhyme: the repetition of two or more similar sounds, often occurring at the ends of a line in poetry.

Rhythm: achieved through a combination of structural elements, which gives a poem its sound.

Rondeau: a form of medieval and Renaissance French poetry, characterized by a repeated refrain. The poem usually consists of 10 to 13 lines, with two rhymes, and follows the pattern AB aAab AB, with the capital letters representing the repeated refrains and the lowercase letters representing extra lines.

Second-person narration: a narrator who addresses his or her story directly to an audience using 'you' where the 'you' has had the experiences being described. Second-person narration has a first-person narrator behind it.

Semantic fields: a collection of words or phrases that are related to each other in meaning and connotation, for example: safety, welcome, support, shelter, structure and warmth would all be part of the same semantic field in relation to the word 'home'.

Sestet: the last six lines of a sonnet.

Sestina: a 39-line poem that follows a strict pattern of repetition of the initial six end-words of the first stanza throughout the remaining five six-line stanzas. It ends with a three-line envoi which includes all six words.

Setting: the place where events of the story happen.

Sibilance: the repetition of 's' sounds.

Simile: a comparison of two things using like or as.

Sonnet: a 14-line poem, usually based on the subject or theme of love. There are two main types of sonnets: the Italian (or Petrarchan) and the English (or Shakespearean).

Spondee: two stressed syllables.

Stage directions: in drama, instructions for actors on how to move or speak their lines.

Stanza: a group of lines in a poem.

Stream of consciousness: where the narrator says whatever comes into his or her head as he or she thinks it.

Structure: the way in which a text or poem is organized (it is not the same thing as layout or form).

Summary: the description of the events of the dramatic situation.

Supernatural: setting that functions either to aid or to hinder a character's actions, but without exhibiting any will—it helps or hinders simply by existing.

Suspense: a feeling from the audience when waiting for an outcome.

Symbol: a comparison between something the author wants the reader to think about and another element, often discussed as a subset of the category of metaphor.

Symbolic: setting which functions as a symbol.

Sympathetic: setting that functions as a reflection of a change in the character's mood.

Synecdoche: the naming of a part for the whole or the whole for the part.

Syntax: the arrangement of words and phrases in a sentence.

Tenor: in relation to a metaphor, the tenor is the thing or object that the author wants the reader to understand better.

Terza rima/ottava rima: a poem that is arranged in triplets (three-line stanzas), usually written in iambic pentameter and following the rhyme scheme aba bcb cdc, and so on.

Theme: an overarching idea or concept.

Tone: the attitude of the writer or speaker towards his or her subject.

Trochee: a stressed syllable followed by an unstressed syllable.

Unreliable narrator: a narrator who thinks that he or she is telling the story as it happened, but who is wrong.

Vehicle: in relation to a metaphor, the vehicle is the thing or object that the author is comparing the subject to.

Villanelle: a 19-line poem with two repeating rhymes and two refrains. The poem is made up of five three-line stanzas and a final quatrain, with the first and third lines of the first stanza repeating alternately in the following stanzas. These two refrain lines form the final couplet in the quatrain.

Index

Acknowledgements

The Publishers would like to thank the following for permission to reproduce copyright material. Every effort has been made to trace all copyright holders, but if any have been inadvertently overlooked, the Publishers will be pleased to make the necessary arrangements at the first opportunity.

p.6 © **International Baccalaureate Organization; p.9** Regina Burreca, 'Nighttime Fires'. *Minnesota Review*, Vol. 27, 1986 pp.5–5; **p.14** Billy Collins, 'Introduction to Poetry' from *The Apple That Astonished Paris*. Copyright © 1988, 1996 by Billy Collins. Reprinted with the permission of The Permissions Company, LLC on behalf of University of Arkansas Press, www.uapress.com; **p.15** 'Eating Poetry' from *Selected Poems* by Mark Strand, copyright © 1979, 1980 by Mark Strand. Used by permission of Alfred A. Knopf, an imprint of the Knopf Doubleday Publishing Group, a division of Penguin Random House LLC. All rights reserved; **p.15** Quote by Rita Dove. Reproduced with the permission; **p.15** Quote by Paul Engle. Reproduced with the permission from Hualing Engle; **p.16** Amy Lowell, 'Bath' from *The Complete Poetical Works of Amy Lowell*. Copyright © 1955 by Houghton Mifflin Company. Copyright © renewed 1983 by Houghton Mifflin Company, Brinton P. Roberts, and G. D'Andelot, Esquire. Reprinted with the permission of Houghton Mifflin Company. All rights reserved; **pp.16–17** © Rodney Gomez; **p.17** '60 words from an article from 'Write Tight' by Damion Searls from *The Paris Review* April 21, 2015 https://www.theparisreview.org/blog/2015/04/21/write-tight/; **p.20** 'We Real Cool', Selected Poems by Gwendolyn. Harper Collins Publishers, 2006. Reprinted by Consent of Brooks Permissions; **p.21** London By William Blake; **p.21** Extract (102 words) from Williams, Miller. Patterns of Poetry. Baton Rouge: Louisiana State University Press. Reprinted from Patterns of Poetry, LSU Press, 1986, by permission of the publisher; **p.23** 'America' by Claude McKay. Poets.org, Academy of American Poets, 8 Aug. 2017, www.poets.org/poetsorg/poem/america-2; **p.24** Poem: 'We Wear the Mask' by Paul Laurence Dunbar. *The Complete Poems of Paul Laurence Dunbar*. CreateSpace Independent Publishing Platform, 2015; **pp.24–25** 'Anne Hathaway' from *The World's Wife* by Carol Ann Duffy. Published by Picador, 2010. Copyright © Carol Ann Duffy. Reproduced by permission of the author c/o Rogers, Coleridge & White Ltd., 20 Powis Mews, London W11 1JN; **p.25** From *The Poems of Dylan Thomas*, published by New Directions. Copyright © 1952, 1953 Dylan Thomas. Copyright © 1937, 1945, 1955, 1962, 1966, 1967 The Dylan Thomas Trust. Copyright © 1938, 1939, 1943, 1946, 1971 New Directions Publishing Corp. Used with permission of David Higham Associates (World excluding US rights); From *The Poems of Dylan Thomas*, published by New Directions. Copyright © 1952, 1953 Dylan Thomas. Copyright © 1937, 1945, 1955, 1962, 1966, 1967 The Dylan Thomas Trust. Copyright © 1938, 1939, 1943, 1946, 1971 New Directions Publishing Corp. Used with permission (US rights); **pp.25–26** 'Incident' from *Native Guard*: Poems by Natasha Trethewey. Copyright © 2006 by Natasha Trethewey. Reprinted by permission of Houghton Mifflin Harcourt Publishing Company. All rights reserved; **p.26** 'O Captain! My Captain!' Leaves of Grass by Walt Whitman published by Createspace Independent Publishing Platform, 2009; **p.27** 'From 'The Painter' by John Ashbery (The Mooring of Starting Out, 1997) is reprinted here by kind permission of Carcanet Press Limited, Manchester, UK; **p.28** Poem 'To Autumn by John Keats' by John Keats. Poetry Foundation. www.poetryfoundation.org/poems/44484/to-autumn; **pp.29–31** 'Daddy' *Ariel: The Restored Edition* by Sylvia Plath, copyright 2018 Estate of Sylvia Plath. Reproduced with the permission from Faber and Faber Ltd; **pp.31–32** 'I Go Back to May 1937' from *The Gold Cell* by Sharon Olds, copyright © 1987 by Sharon Olds. Used by permission of Alfred A. Knopf, an imprint of the Knopf Doubleday Publishing Group, a division of Penguin Random House LLC. All rights reserved; **pp.33–34** 12th November: Winter Honey' from *Bee Journal* by Sean Borodale. Published by Random House, 2001. Copyright Vintage © Sean Borodale. Reproduced by permission of the author c/o Rogers, Coleridge & White Ltd., 20 Powis Mews, London W11 1JN; **pp.35–36** 'Death of a Naturalist' by Seamus Heaney. Copyright 2006. Reproduced with the permission from Faber and Faber Ltd (World excluding US rights); Excerpts from 'Death of a Naturalist' from *Opened Ground: Selected Poems 1966-1996* by Seamus Heaney. Copyright © 1998 by Seamus Heaney. Reprinted by permission of Farrar, Straus and Giroux (US rights and World excluding United Kingdom, British Commonwealth and Canada); **pp.37–38** Excerpt from 'The Fish'; from *Poems* by Elizabeth Bishop. Copyright © 2011 by The Alice H. Methfessel Trust. Publisher's Note and compilation copyright © 2011 by Farrar, Straus and Giroux (US, Canada and World rights excluding UK, British Commonwealth); Excerpt from 'The Fish' from *Poems* by Elizabeth Bishop. Copyright © 2011 by The Alice H. Methfessel Trust. Publisher's Note and compilation copyright © 2011 by Farrar, Straus and Giroux. Reproduced with the permission from Chatto & Windus (UK and British Commonwealth rights); **p.38** B. H. Fairchild, excerpt from 'The Machinist, Teaching His Daughter to Play the Piano' from *The Art of the Lathe*. Copyright © 1998 by B. H. Fairchild. Used with the permission of The Permissions Company, Inc., on behalf of Alice James Books, www.alicejamesbooks.org; **p.38** Extract from 'The Water Carrier' by John Montague from *New Collected Poems* reproduced by kind permission of the author's Estate c/o The Gallery Press. www.gallerypress.com; **p.38** Excerpts from 'Blackberry-Picking' from *Opened Ground: Selected Poems 1966-1996* by Seamus Heaney. Copyright © 1998 by Seamus Heaney. Reprinted by permission of Farrar, Straus and Giroux (US and World rights excluding UK, British Commonwealth and Canada); Poem 'Blackberry Picking' by Seamus Heaney. Reproduced with the permission of Faber and Faber Ltd (World excluding US rights); **pp.39–40** 'Double Dutch' from *Totem* by Gregory Pardlo. *The American Poetry Review*, 2007. Reproduced with permission; **p.40** 'Cold Knap Lake' from *Letting in the Rumour* by Gillian Clarke. Published by Fyfield Books, 1989. Reproduced by permission of the author c/o Rogers, Coleridge & White, 20 Powis Mews, London W11 1JN; **p.41** Extract from poem Dickinson, Emily. 'Because I Could Not Stop for Death' (479) by Emily Dickinson. Poetry Foundation, www.poetryfoundation.org/poems/47652/because-i-could-not-stop-for-death-479; **p.41** Extract from poem Wordsworth, William. 'Composed Upon Westminster Bridge.' Poetry Foundation. https://www.poetryfoundation.org/poems/45514/composed-upon-westminster-bridge-september-3-1802; **p.42** Coleridge, Samuel Taylor. 'The Rime of the Ancient Mariner' (Text of 1834) by Samuel Taylor Coleridge. Poetry Foundation, www.poetryfoundation.org/poems/43997/the-rime-of-the-ancient-mariner-text-of-1834; **pp.42–43** Patricia Smith, '5 p.m., Tuesday, August 23, 2005' from *Blood Dazzler*. Copyright © 2008 by Patricia Smith. Reprinted with the permission of The Permissions Company LLC on behalf of Coffee House Press, www.coffeehousepress.org; **pp.43–44** Imtiaz Dharker *Postcards from god* (Bloodaxe Books, 1997). Reproduced with permission of Bloodaxe Books www.bloodaxebooks.com; **p.44** Extract from poem: Adcock, Betty. 'No Encore'. *Rough Fugue*. Louisiana State University Press, 2017. Reprinted from *Rouge Fugue*, LSU Press, 1988, by permission of the publisher; **p.45** Extract from poem: Yeats, W.B. 'The Lake Isle of Innisfree'. *The Collected Poems of W. B. Yeats*. Wordsworth Poetry Library, 2000; **pp.46–47** Lochhead, Liz. 'Men Talk (Rap)'. *A Choosing: Selected Poems*. Polygon, 2011. Reproduced with